P. H. MOUNTAIN

THE WORLD IS MY ASHTRAY VOL.2

NUNS WITH SHOTGUNS

P. H. MOUNTAIN

To Jim Morrison, human sacrifice.
Thanks for going all the way, man.

Nuns with Shotguns

Oh, I know about war

But I just wanna fuck!

I know about pain and suffering and being cold

But I just wanna *fuck*!

– Jane's Addiction, *Pigs in Zen*

1.

Poop Coiling Into a Tight Spiral Biscuit

E L D O R A ,   C O L O R A D O

1 9 9 0

Rummy panted heavily, his tongue hanging out his mouth like a half-eaten salmon filet.

"You need a drink, boy?" I asked him.

He wagged his tail excitedly. Little guy didn't understand a word I was saying – he could barely form a full sentence himself – but he loved it when I talked to him in *that tone*. *That tone* meant treats, car rides with open windows, long walks in the woods.

I stood up from the large rock I'd sat on, snubbed out my smoke on the dirt path, and stuffed the butt back in my half-empty pack of Marbs. I didn't litter as a rule, but I especially wouldn't clutter up this pristine piece of planet. Stretching, I gazed out at the immense valley a few thousand feet below. The top of the mountain directly behind my cabin provided a breathtaking view – the Continental Divide's snowcaps to my left, Barker Reservoir's shimmering waters to my right – and if I stretched my eyeballs to full eyeballity, I could just make out Boulder, twenty miles down the canyon. This was *my* mountain, mine alone. I discovered the path buried on the other side of Middle Boulder Creek, and in the many times Rummy and I hiked to the top of my mountain, we'd never passed a single soul.

"Well, don't just stand there," I said, then flicked my hand forward, "go get yourself a drink, dude."

He waited until I took one step down the path, then bolted off, leading the way. He knew the routine. The path wound around the mountain's summit, rolling through the woods and crossing over to the other side before looping back. A few hundred yards away was a freshwater pond, created each spring by winter runoff from even higher mountains. By the time I reached it, Rummy was already submerged up to his neck, the freezing water cooling his little Benji body as he gulped in huge mouthfuls. After he drank what seemed like a third of the pond, I found a good stick, and for the next ten minutes, I hurled it into the water. Rummy splashed after it, brought it back, and begged for another launch. I threw it further and further, and Rummy went after it with the idiotic enthusiasm of an aging businessman chasing a stripper from stage to stage, convinced she wants more than just his money.

"Alright, alright, that's enough, boy," I said after the fiftieth toss.

Rummy cocked his head, wondering why the hell I was stopping the game right when it was getting so awesome. Who the fuck stops playing fetch when they could play *more* fetch? To punish me for ending the party, he sidled up to me and shook his little body as hard as he could, showering me with freezing mountaintop water.

"Thanks, dick."

He tore off before I could react further, guiding us further along the path. He knew it would loop back around the mountain and bring us right back to the summit on our side of the mountaintop. He also knew I liked taking the full tour, catching the backside scenery, as well. There was something back there that made me look forward to winter for the first time in my life.

Following my dog around a final bend on the path, the Eldora ski area floated into view. How cool. Until I'd climbed this mountain the first time, I didn't even know Eldora had a ski area. But there it was, in all its summertime stillness. A ski resort feels completely different in summer than in winter, long swaths of soft green fields cutting lightly through the deeper green of summer pines. Mountain flowers bloomed on the slopes, dotting the ski runs with whites and blues, purple columbines, yellow dandelions. Everything seemed so soft, feminine even, when contrasted against the banzai warfare skiers and boarders waged against the mountain in winter. Eldora was particularly deserted in summertime, probably quieter than any other Colorado resort. There was no town to sustain the ski area, no hotels or condos, no reason for anyone to be at the resort if they weren't skiing. It was one of Colorado's smaller ski areas, but to my Minnesota eyes, it still looked enormous. I couldn't believe I had an actual Rocky Mountain ski resort practically in my back yard.

To keep Rummy happy, I kept moving until we eventually looped back around to "my" rock on "my" mountain. It was Paul Mountain's Mountain, Mount Mountain. A little redundant, but screw it, I dominated this part of the world. I'd call it whatever the fuck I pleased. I sat on my rock and watched the wind roll across the distant mountainsides, the aspens bowing in unison to the superior force of Wind. I could have stayed there all day, smoking, wandering, studying my wonderfully deserted planet, but Lonnie was cooking up a late breakfast back at the cabin. And once we finished eating, she and I had a huge decision to make.

After an easy hour of downhill hiking and a ten-minute stroll through the woods along the creek, I pushed open our cabin's screen door. Lonnie stood at the stove, her back to me. She'd tied an apron decorated with log cabins around her waist, presumably to keep her gigantic knockers from escaping into the frying pan. Lonnie looked perfectly in place in our little mountain cabin, almost part of the landscape itself. Her pretty blonde hair had grown longer since our Boulder days, now flowing halfway down her back in wandering, wavy curls. I liked it better that way. She was gorgeous when I'd met her almost a year before, but the two of us falling in love seemed to bring her beauty to fruition.

"Jesus, I thought you guys got lost up there," Lonnie said as Rummy blasted over to her.

The house smelled fantastic. It was August, way too soon to fire up the wood stove, so Lonnie simmered my trout catch from the previous morning on our gas stovetop. She'd prepped the fish in my favorite lemon and cornmeal batter, the scent scurrying up my nostrils to wake my appetite.

"Just taking my time," I said, "too beautiful a day to hurry."

"I know. I wish classes weren't starting up again so soon. I want to stay up here all day every day."

Our fish was ready before long. Lonnie brought it out to our deck and served it with basted eggs, a hash brown scramble, orange juice and coffee. Damn, the girl could cook, which was wildly attractive. It wasn't as hot as watching her do my laundry, of course, but it was still pretty sexy. We ate slowly on our deck, the summer breeze gently pressing the pines, loosening their scent. Neither of us spoke while we ate, but I knew we were both thinking the same thing.

I finished up my breakfast, stretched out in my ridiculously comfortable reading/smoking/drinking/napping hammock, and lit up my dessert.

"So," I said.

"So," Lonnie repeated, smiling at me.

"You ready to add to this little slice of perfection we've created?"

Her smile grew into a laugh, and she nodded quickly. "I'm so excited!"

"Me too."

"Then let's get going!"

Fifteen minutes later, Rummy, Lonnie and I were in her Skyhawk, rolling through Eldora. We passed one person walking her dog. We waved. The woman waved back. Rummy barked once at her dog. Her dog barked once at Rummy. Just another frenzied day on the bustling streets of Eldora, Colorado.

"Are you sure you're ready for such a big commitment?" Lonnie asked when we exited the canyon and drove into Boulder.

"I think I can handle it. I've already been doing it for almost a year."

"True, but it's a little different when it's your own."

I smiled at her. "Let's be honest, Lon, Rummy's mine."

"He is not!" She punched me lightly in the arm. "He's my little man."

I shrugged. "Try telling him that. Dude adores me."

"He loves me, too." She rolled down her window for fresh air, Boulder's summertime temp at least fifteen degrees warmer than our 8,700-foot-high home in Eldora. "Do you have a name in mind yet?" she asked.

"Nah, gotta meet the little guy or girl first."

"I want a girl."

"It's not your decision to make."

"Yeah, but I still want a girl." Lonnie stared out her window for a few seconds, then asked, "Do you think you'll be ready for human babies after this?"

"Nope."

"I was hoping this was practice for bigger things."

"Nope."

She pouted. "I only want two."

"Two kids to ruin one life: mine." I glanced over at her hopeful face. "Let's just stick to the plan, Lon."

Sticking to the plan, I pulled into the Boulder Humane Society parking lot and found a place in the shade so Rummy wouldn't overheat. We cracked the windows for our little guy and headed toward the building to find him a friend.

The Humane Society is the happiest and saddest place in the world. The instant we pushed open the door, the roar of animal life filled my soul. Squawking birds, yowling cats, and barking dogs fought to be heard, like a band tuning up before a big concert. The reality that only one of them would be leaving with me, however, soon dampened that initial blast of positivity. Walking away from a hundred animals, leaving it up to someone else to free them from their cages, is heart wrenching. I wanted to take them all, set them loose in a field, then wait for them to overpopulate and dominate the planet. A world of puppies and kittens was a world I could handle, a furry world of unlimited play, long afternoon naps, and big piles of poop.

I'd wanted a dog of my own for as long as I could remember. Some people with horrible fathers want children, hoping to prove to themselves, their dad, or God that there's a better way to raise kids. In the same way, I wanted a dog. My dad loved our family dog way more than he loved any of his children, but he was still cruel and militant and physically abusive with her. Several times, I watched him kick her in the stomach and throw her down our stairs, drag her through the house by her neck and hurl her out the back door. Even those my dad loved best took it on the chin from time to time, which I kind of had to respect. At least his violence was universal, if not always equally distributed.

"Let's go find the puppies!" Lonnie said loudly, raising her voice over the symphony of two hundred caged animals. She grabbed my hand and tried to yank me past the kennels, but I resisted.

"Maybe we should get an older guy." I stopped in front of a cage. Back in the corner of the kennel, a quiet, graying dog lay curled up near his bowl. Without lifting his head, he stared at me, his eyes resigned, knowing I wouldn't save him. Someone had raised him and then abandoned him when he got older, left him out on display like an old whore in a brothel filled with cheerleaders, no chance of being chosen. It was the saddest thing in a universe overflowing with sad things. I wanted to crawl into his cage, let him cry in my lap, then slip him a few hundred bucks and tell him he could and should spend it all on booze.

"Don't stop," Lonnie said, pulling me away from the old dog. "If you stop, you'll want to take every dog in this place. I know you, Paul. You're a softie when it comes to animals. We're here to get you a puppy."

She was right, of course, so I pressed on and tried to forget, doing my best to avoid further eye contact with any of the other dogs. It was hard, though. I could feel their desperation, heard the urgency in their barks. *Get me outta here, man! They MURDER us in here! Putting us "to sleep" is a fucking euphemism, dude!*

At the end of the cages – they make you walk through the kennels to get to the puppies, counting on hearts as pliable as mine – we finally reached the puppy rooms. All sadness immediately fled. The Humane Society had three current litters: one group of boxers, a maniac batch of yellow labs, and a pack of German shepherd / black lab mixed pups. I walked right over to the mixed dogs, knowing a couple different bloodlines calmed the wilder side of puppies. We'd raised Rummy through his madness year, kept my shoes and socks locked in closets, no clothes on the floor, no food on the counter. When I went for a middle-of-the-night whiz, I had to keep my eyes peeled for the land mines Rummy occasionally scattered in the early days. Nothing worse than dog shit between the toes at 3:00 a.m. I didn't want to go through another puppy year like that, so a calmer mixed breed suited me.

Lonnie and I stood outside the German Shepherd / black lab room – Shepradors – and watched seven furry clumps roll all over each other. Some crawled on top of the pile of bodies before falling off, while others pushed each other playfully with their soft paws, all of them struggling against puppy narcolepsy to keep their eyes open.

"Oh my god, that is the cutest thing I've ever seen!" Lonnie said, her hands over her mouth. I glanced at her, and sure enough, she was crying. Good lord, Lonnie could cry at Mardi Gras in New Orleans, finding the beads just so…so…*beady*.

"Your face is leaking, Lon."

"I know," she said, sniffling, wiping her eyes. "I can't help it. Those little guys are just too adorable. Let's take them in the yard and find you a new best friend."

Ten minutes later, Lonnie and I were out in the Humane Society's play yard with seven little maniacs. Actually, there were only six maniacs. The seventh was extremely calm, strangely so for a pup, and that particular one came right over to me when I stretched out on the ground. The tiny dog sat a foot away and stared at me, its mostly black face beautiful and inquisitive.

"I think she likes you," Lonnie said.

"How do you know it's a she?"

"A woman knows." Lonnie reached out, picked up the little pup, and checked the undercarriage. "Yep, it's a she."

She set the puppy back on the ground, and the little girl didn't run back to her brothers and sisters. Instead, she wobbled even closer to me, made her way right up to where I lay stretched out in the grass, and gave my face a good long smellin'. After several seconds, I must have passed the sniff test, because she sat down six inches away and stared into my eyes. I reached out and rubbed her puppy-soft black head, tickled the tan swath down her nose, and smoothed the little splatters of tan above her eyebrows. I scratched her right behind her floppy, color-flecked ears, and she rolled her head playfully under my fingers. When I pulled my hand away, she didn't demand more attention. She simply stayed seated and watched me. Other puppies from the pack came over, crawled over her, crawled over me, played with each other, and tried to pull my patient pup away. She'd play along as much as necessary, but when her siblings bounced away, she remained.

I tilted my head to the right and the little puppy tilted hers to the left, mirroring me. I reversed the tilt, and the puppy played along.

Lonnie laughed and clapped her hands. "I don't think you get to make the decision, Pablo. I think this little girl picked *you*."

"Is that right?" I asked the pup. "You want to come home with me?"

"Yes!" Lonnie answered for her.

I laughed. "You sure this is the one, Lon?"

"Yes!"

I nodded. "Me, too."

After a half-hour of filling out a strangely personal adoption form that asked about everything from my income to my smoking habits to whether I took my LSD intravenously or anally, I carried the new family addition out to Lonnie's car.

"I'll sit in back with the dogs," I told Lonnie, "see how they do together."

Rummy was always thrilled to see us, whether we'd been gone ten minutes or ten hours, but when I slipped into the back seat with the carrier, he knew something was off. Mom and Dad rode up front together, no one in back. A second after seeing the carrier, Rummy's nose caught the puppy's scent, and he grew agitated. I opened the lid, Rummy stuffed his head in, then stepped back in shock. His tail sprang into action, whapping the seats, and he moaned and groaned with concern. I checked in on our pup, and for the first time, she looked uncomfortable.

"She'll get used to Rummy, it'll just take a little time," Lonnie said. "Besides, she'll probably outgrow him in about two months." Lonnie reached into the backseat, grabbed Rummy's collar, and gave it a soft yank. "Come on up here, buddy, sit with your mom."

He did, but he turned around in the front seat and stared at the new puppy the entire drive through Boulder. I lifted her out of the carrier and held her close, letting her know she was safe, and before long, puppy yawns turned into puppy slumber.

"So now that you've met her, what's her name?" Lonnie asked as we drove out of Boulder and headed up the canyon.

"I'm toying with Brutus."

"Right."

"How 'bout Thunder?"

"She's a girl, Paul."

"That's true." I rubbed my chin. "Fallopian?"

"Be serious."

I laughed and scratched my new little girl behind her color spattered ears. She rolled her head, pawed the air, but didn't open her eyes.

"I think I'll name her Eve, actually."

"Eve?"

"Yep, as in Adam-and."

Lonnie studied me in the rearview mirror, scanning for sarcasm. "Why Eve?"

I shrugged. "I don't know, pretty name, first female, innocence and all that."

"What about the whole apple thing, going against God's will and cursing the world with original sin?"

I laughed. "All the better! Eve it is." I reached down and pet my pup's head, still not waking her. "What do you think, little girl? You want to go against God's will and curse the world?"

She groaned, pressed her small paw into my palm, and licked her nose. I took that as a yes.

Lonnie stretched her hand into the back seat and scratched our new puppy. "I kind of like it, too, now that I think about it. Suits her. She can be my little Evie-girl. I can teach her how to cook and do her makeup, make her some cute little dresses."

A half hour later, I carried little Evie – she'd already had her name elongated – down our walkway. Rummy bounced up and down, dying to wrestle with his new playmate, but I thought it best to go slow with the introduction. I walked Evie into the yard for her very first poop and pee at her new home. She did a great job at both, her poop coiling into a tight spiral biscuit, her pee flowing like Middle Boulder Creek. I was so proud.

The four of us spent the night on our living room floor, drinking, rolling around, hurrying Evie onto the newspaper we'd spread out in the kitchen whenever she started to leak. Rummy learned quickly that he wasn't allowed to roughhouse with her too much, and when he mellowed out, little Evie-girl started approaching him cautiously, sniffing his face, introducing herself. It was the cutest damn thing I'd ever seen. Lonnie cried many, many times, a tear here, tear there, sob here, blubbering there. The beer didn't help her emotional rollercoaster, either. I did not and never would understand such depth of feeling. Women have an experiential advantage over men, *feeling* this life invade them, torment them, uplift them, clean them out and resurrect them. As if that wasn't enough, the lucky bastards could have multiple orgasms, too.

Night fell, and shortly after, a crescent moon rose slowly over the Eldora valley mountains. The forest symphony warmed up their instruments, the crickets tuning their wings, the night insects vibrating their organs. Squirrels slipped cautiously through the woods and delicately shuffled leaves, fearing night predators. A soft summer breeze oozed through our open windows, quickly growing chilly at 8,700 feet. We latched the windows closed long before midnight and switched from forest songs to rock 'n' roll records. Eventually, we had to fuck, because no nineteen and twenty-two-year-old can drink that much beer without reverting to sex, so we arranged our couch cushions on the floor, turned out the lights, and fucked slow and passionate in the moonlight. The dogs snored while Lonnie came, and I studied her as she straddled me, her back arched, hips thrust forward, palms flat on my chest. The moonlight grazed her body with thin strokes of lunar paint, accentuating her beautiful breasts, her neck, her thighs. After she came a second time, we fell asleep folded together like origami animals, and in the night, our dogs snuck onto our makeshift bed. The four of us slept soundly under the heavy influence of contentment, the most effective sleeping pill the world has ever known.

2.

A Good Chance of Dying Aggressively

ELDORA, COLORADO

1990

I knew it was bad after a hundred pages. There was no other way to spin it. It was better than the stories I hacked my way through a year ago while working graveyard shifts at the Amoco gas station, but it was far from a mature piece of writing.

"But it's a novel, dammit, for better or worse," I muttered, staring at the growing stack of pages on my desk. I finished my Budweiser in one long swallow. "That's the important thing, Pablo; you're finally writing a novel."

I stood up and walked to the fridge for some more thinkin' juice. Unfortunately, the thinkin' juice only made me think about how weak my book was, how unimaginative and forced. It was a revenge story, nothing more. Dude gets wronged, dude seeks vengeance. Basic stuff. It was a story I should have told in thirty pages, max, but I was determined to push it out to three hundred. I needed to get a full book under my belt, but trying to pad the pages meant I'd filled it with unnecessary characters, superfluous scenes, and long dialogue sequences where no one said anything of any real value.

Evie waddled up to me as I stood at the sink, staring into the night. We'd only had her a couple weeks, but every time I looked at her adorable face, I felt better about everything.

"What do you think, little girl? You think I should keep going on this?"

She wagged her tail. She was very supportive of my writing. She was very supportive of everything *me*. I was the most awesome dude in the world, because I was the guy who put the food in the bowl.

"Yeah, I think I should keep going, too."

Forcing myself back to the small desk I bought at a garage sale shortly after moving to Eldora, I knew I had to finish this book. This was a test, a long, sustained workout that would prove invaluable in time. It didn't matter that the finished product would go right in the filing cabinet, never to see the light of day. The process of writing it, the commitment, the endurance, the focus, was the reward. I grew up playing sports; I understood the value of training. And there *was* steady improvement; I could feel it as I wrote.

I didn't last much longer that night, two more beers – without a watch, I told time in beer – because I had a morning work shift, a rarity for me. I powered down my huge electric typewriter, the powerful hum of its innards fading fast, leaving the room suddenly silent, and then the dogs and I crawled into bed with Lonnie. Rummy curled up alongside my body, the best spot on the bed, asserting his firstborn status. Evie-girl hopped up on the stepstool we left at the end of the bed, then crawled onto the mattress and stretched out on my feet, her little body warm on my toes.

It was strange to wake to an alarm clock, even stranger to see Lonnie in the morning. Usually, she was off to work her summer job at a Boulder bookstore long before I woke, and I was on my way to Pizza Place before she returned. Most days, we passed each other on the canyon, flashing our lights, honking our horns, and waving out our windows. Until I crawled into bed at 4:00 a.m. and gave her a beer-soaked smooch goodnight, our canyon drive-by was all we saw of each other four or five days a week.

"Morning," I mumbled as I scooted past her in the bathroom. I pushed down my underwear and unleashed a forever morning whiz. "Jesus, how do you day people do this shit?"

She stopped in mid-mascara and turned to me. "What shit?"

"Mornings. Alarm clocks. Early to bed, early to rise, all that shit."

Lonnie laughed. "Poor baby. It's tough facing the real world, isn't it?"

"It's the fake world, created by millions of people with no imagination. It's a bunch of leftover bullshit from pre-electric times when there were no lightbulbs, no reason to stay up when the sun went down. We should have a twenty-four-hour world by now, three blocks of eight hours, everyone picks the shift that feels best for them. I bet almost no one under sixty would pick the morning shift."

She rolled her eyes, then went right back to her mascara. "I like getting up early."

I grunted out my disagreement and walked past her, aiming for the coffee pot.

An hour later, I sped my motorcycle along the Peak-to-Peak Highway, feeling a thousand times better. Amazing what a big cup of coffee can do, and outside of the clinically depressed, no one can blast a motorcycle along the Peak-to-Peak Highway from Nederland to Estes Park in late August without feeling their spirits rise. The deserted highway rose and fell through the mountains, twisted, turned, the snowcapped hood of Mt. Evans popping in and out of view. High on the hills, the first traces of autumn appeared, yellow splashes squirming through the deep green pines. I rolled past Brainerd Lake and the weird little town of Ward, Colorado, the morning mountain air cold on my cheeks, then dipped down to where St. Vrain Creek straddled the highway, the rushing water urging me on toward Estes. All along the route, the distant towers of Rocky Mountain National Park loomed above all else, tempting a tourist invasion from around the world.

I wasn't a tourist, but those seasonal invaders were the reason I was on my way to Estes Park, the town that bordered the national park's eastern edge. Joel, the owner of Pizza Place, also owned a waterslide in Estes. The pizza business slowed considerably in summer, the vast majority of CU's students heading home to demand more free room, board, and beer money from their parents. Without the students, Joel closed the store a few hours earlier each night, making it a little harder to make decent money. But he always needed help at the waterslide. He only kept the slide open four months a year – too cold for tourists the other eight months in Estes – so he didn't hire a regular staff. Instead, he counted on his Pizza Place employees to man the controls. Since we all liked Joel and could use the extra money in summer, we took turns keeping the waterslide rolling.

"Dude!" Joel called out as I walked through the front door of Peak Plunge Waterslide.

I laughed. Joel liked calling all of us "dude," fully aware that he was about as un-dudey as a dude could dude. He was in his early forties – ancient, to my nineteen-year-old eyes – and stereotypically fat, just as a pizza store owner should be. He wore thick glasses, constantly listened to talk radio, and was born and raised Mormon in a small town in Utah. Joel never talked about his religion – I had no idea what Mormonism entailed – but he didn't drink, didn't smoke, didn't swear. He had five kids, all boys, all under the age of twelve, and keeping his businesses afloat while attempting to tame his lunatic pack of wolf-boys dominated his time. The only place Joel fit in perfectly with the rest of the Pizza Place crowd was when he occasionally joined us on the softball diamond. There, he was every bit as awful as the majority of my co-workers.

"What's going on?" I asked.

"Everything. If you're looking for action, dude, you found it." He waved me back behind the counter. "Come on back and stock the shelves. Kids will be pouring through the door in about a half hour."

"Cool. Where's Phil?"

"He's up scrubbing the paw prints off the slide's opening. It was long overdue."

I scooted past the Galaga and Centipede video games, wound my way between the pool table, foosball table, and air hockey table, before joining Joel behind the counter. I grabbed a box and started arranging sugar bombs right where maniac children could best drool over them. Skittles, Milk Duds,

Snickers, everything a kid craved in the morning went on display under high-powered lighting.

"Hey, Paul," Joel said from behind me, "any chance you want to buy a waterslide?"

I laughed and turned to look at him. He sat at the folding table he used for a desk, his big belly keeping him awkwardly far from the tabletop. A stack of the previous day's receipts sat in front of him, half of their numbers already plugged into his old adding machine. A long roll of tape flowed out the machine's top, and I assumed it told a story of thin margins and barely breaking even.

"Probably not this week," I said, "finances are a little tight."

"How about next week?"

"Possibly. Check back with me."

Joel tapped the receipts with his pen. "You really should think about it, you know," he said more seriously. He took a long sip off his Big Gulp of morning Coke, then bit into a doughnut the size of his head, jelly squirting onto his hand. Keeping that belly bulging took real commitment. "Not my waterslide, of course, but some type of small business. Running a business can be a lot of fun, actually, even when it barely pays. Sure beats working for someone else."

"I know. Working for you totally sucks."

"You're hilarious, Mountain," he said. "Seriously, though, you should consider it someday. I think you'd make a good businessman. You've got a decent head on you, you're good with numbers, and you have a pretty bad work ethic, which is key to keeping a small business going. Most small businessmen are primarily motivated by laziness and fear, scared to death they'll have to do real work for someone else someday, become part of the grind."

"Thanks, I think." I chuckled a little. "I'll pretend that was a compliment."

"It's not a compliment, just a statement of fact," Joel said. "Look, I'm the same way. I never wanted to wake up every day and grind it out for someone else at some 8:00 to 5:00 job. Took me a couple years after college to realize

I'd just wasted four years and a ton of money on a degree I'd never use. Don't want you to make the same mistake. I mean, why do you think I own a pizza store and a waterslide?"

"I don't know, the babes?"

He pushed back slightly from the table, spread his arms wide, and shoved his huge gut forward. "The chicks totally dig my physique, dude."

I laughed. "I actually had a neighborhood snow shoveling service from the time I was ten, then added a lawn mowing service onto it when I was thirteen. Had a little trailer affixed to my BMX bike, dragged my mower all over the neighborhood until I could drive. I even kept some of my older customers, people who couldn't physically shovel or mow anymore, all the way up until I left Minnesota. They were pretty bummed when I finally split."

"See? I thought you had it in you. Did you keep books, pay taxes?"

"Hell, no."

"Good man." Joel pointed a serious finger at me. "Hide your money from the government whenever you can. They're just going to waste it, and you can do that on your own. Nobody needs a middleman to help them throw money away."

Phil exited the stairwell that led to the top of the waterslide, ducking down so that his tall body didn't connect with the doorframe. His size and strength were an advantage when we were on the ski slopes, but not in the tight corridors and stairwells of Peak Plunge Waterslide. Surprisingly, Phil wore only flip flops and his swimsuit – I would have thought he'd thrown away such warm-weather wear during his ski bum years up in frigid Steamboat – and he carried a half-full water bucket into the lobby. He was drenched in sweat. It was only 8:30 in the morning, but the dude who first taught me how to ski the Colorado mountains – making it look effortless – appeared totally burned out already.

"That was awful," Phil said. "Those little shits are slobs."

I laughed. "You look horrible, man."

Phil furrowed his brow. "And good morning to you, too."

"Our friend Phil is badly hungover this morning," Joel informed me.

Phil turned to Joel. "What makes you say that?"

"I may not drink, big guy, but I know a hangover when I smell it. I had to smell you in the car all the way up from Boulder."

"That bad?" Phil asked.

"Worse. You know, you're never going to land a girlfriend smelling like that."

Phil rolled his eyes, but he shuffled his feet and looked a little uncomfortable, which seemed weird to me. No one could figure out why Phil wasn't dating anyone. He was a big, strong dude, great all-around athlete, unbelievable skier. On top of that, he was finishing up his business degree, destined for financial stability, and all the women I knew said Phil was a very good-looking guy. Some girl should have scooped him up by now.

"No time for women when I'm always slaving away for you," Phil told Joel.

"Or drinking with the dudes all night," Joel replied, laughing.

I turned to Joel. "Let's punish him with the pool, man. He can take first shift down there, nice and long."

"God, no," Phil said. "Please. Come on, you bastards, have mercy."

The pool was a form of torture, the worst of the three jobs at the slide. Some sadistic lawyer wrote the job description, filled it with litigation mitigation operation procedure-ation, and gave no thought whatsoever to the sanity of the person performing the duties. The pool attendant couldn't sit down, couldn't read, couldn't even listen to headphones. If he was found under the influence of AC/DC, headphones blasting to drown out the happiness of children, *BAM!* lawsuit. Oddly, the pool attendant was not legally required to be a certified lifeguard – the water was only three feet deep – but he performed similar duties. He watched the water as crazed children infected with chlorine euphoria raced by, their screams like electroshock therapy.

The thought of a bitter, hungover pool attendant enduring screaming children suddenly struck me as a great opening to a short story: *The unlicensed pool attendant strolls the water's edge, struggling with his hangover.* Damn screaming kids, *he thinks,* only time you bastards shut the fuck up is when you stand still in the water, gaze into the distance, and whiz in the pool. I'm not fooled, you little pricks; I know what a pool piss looks like. *He's supposed to tell the little maniacs to stop racing around on the wet tile, but he doesn't, because kids are lunatics who regularly hurt themselves or others no matter what anyone tells them. The pool attendant's mind slowly drifts into dark, dangerous territory, and he envisions a single toaster that could end all their happy screeching once and for all. ZZZZTTT! Problem solved.*

"We'll flip for it, just like always," Joel said.

Phil came back behind the counter to join us, and Joel tossed us each a quarter. At the count of three, our quarters twirled in the air. Two came down heads, one tails. Mine was tails.

"Fuck," I said.

Phil laughed. "That's what you get, dick!"

Joel rubbed his chin thoughtfully. "The universe does have its own strange version of justice, doesn't it, Paul?"

"Screw you guys."

Joel picked up his quarter and flipped it a second time. Phil called heads and it landed tails.

"What did I tell you?" Joel asked, glancing back and forth between me and Phil. "Justice. The man who writes the checks gets the reward. Enjoy the top, Phil. Paul, have fun at the pool. I'll be right here working on my foosball game." He checked his watch and glanced at the front door. The invaders were already lining up in agitated fashion while their parents waited in the car, smoking cigarettes. "Looks like we have about fifteen minutes before the floodgates open," Joel said. He extended his arm, hand in the air between me and Phil, palm down. "Alright, dudes, Peak Plunge on three."

Phil and I stared at Joel's lonely hand hovering in space.

"No?" Joel asked.

"No chance, old man," I said.

Phil shook his head and sighed. "Pretty lame, Joel."

Joel laughed, turned, and went back to his receipts. After finishing stocking shelves, Phil and I split off to our designated stations – Phil dragging his hangover up to the highest point of Peak Plunge, me strolling dejectedly down to the pool. In minutes, the hordes would invade, I knew, their bodies shivering, lips blue, arms crossed to retain the last shred of heat trapped inside their bony bodies. Those little Peak Plunge waterslide warriors could splash around for days it seemed. And no matter how long their parents left them in our care, these aqua-addicts screamed like torture victims the instant their folks showed up to haul their shriveled asses away. *Just one more ride! PLLEEAASSE!* That crucial moment separated the married from the divorced. Divorcees let their kids go down the slide one more time; married parents told their kids to knock that shit off and get in the fuckin' car.

It's only an hour, I told myself as I strolled down to the pool, but the instant I exited the stairs, I was already bored senseless. Five minutes later, I heard the initial voices tumble down the tube. Seconds after, the first kid pooped out the shoot like a hot turd on a Sunday morning, all fresh and glistening. The tube dropped even more kids off at the pool, one after another, plop plop plop, the smaller ones twirling through the air chaotically before splashing into the water. There was no way to flush the pool, so these little shits floated to the rim, scrambled out, then ran to the stairs leading back to the top. All of them babbled at once, explaining their ride, none of them listening to each other. *And then I totally spun around and then I swallowed some water and then I was like screw it I'm going headfirst but I flipped back to feet first just before I hit the pool so that stupid lifeguard wouldn't yell at me, but he's so stupid and lame – my dad says he's a loser, that's why he works here – and I like totally fooled his dumb butt, that dummy.* They were the child version of adult golfers, everyone explaining the intricacies of their last shot in detail, no one giving two shits about anything other than their *own* divot, their *own* wicked slice, and possibly when the smoking hot beer cart girl would deliver another round.

During my hour at the pool, I didn't admonish a single kid a single time. Screw 'em. I was there to handle the big shit. If one of those kids cracked their skulls open, I'd be right there to…to…I don't know what. I'd never taken a CPR course in my life, had no idea what to do in any medical situation. It was a great time to be alive in America, an era when everyone was qualified for every job without any credentials or specialized training.

Phil finally tapped me out after my hour, switching things up. We had a good system at the Plunge, a punishment-reward arrangement. Counter man went to the top of the slide; top of the slide went to the pool. After being stuck at the pool, the worst job, the pool attendant got to take over the counter, the best job. After the initial morning rush, new customers were scattered throughout the day, leaving plenty of time for the counter man to hone up on his foosball and Galaga skills.

During my second stint at the counter after lunch, I decided to spend my time fine-tuning my pool game, the long green shots in particular. Just as I lined up my cue in search of a practical application for all the geometry classes I'd taken, a woman's delicate voice slipped into my ears, light and lilting. The accent was southern, soft like cotton, pure like moonshine, the prettiest twang in the USA.

"That there's a load'a green, pahdner," she said. "I got me five dahla' say you miss it left."

Jesus Christ, what a voice. What a sweet-tea, fuck-me-all-night and fry-me-up-some-chicken voice. How did those southern boys handle hearing that gorgeous lilt all day every day? It was enough to make a man's cock as hard as Mississippi race relations.

I turned to her. She wasn't as hot as she sounded, but she was moderately attractive for an older woman. "Older" meant over thirty, and she was probably that, but not by much. She was tall, at least 5' 9", slender, with dark brown hair that gently curled in a single slow wave over her bony shoulders. Her face was a little too angular, her nose a little too pointy, but her eyes were dark and sharp. Dressed in a white, sleeveless top and tight summer short-shorts, she was obviously displaying her wares, so I felt well within the boundaries of southern etiquette to pan over her tits. Her cleavage was ample, if a bit overly tanned and freckled, and her breasts pressed against her tight top, threatening the shirt's official capacity. But I liked her hat best of all. She wore a large, white, floppy sunhat, something that belonged on a Georgia porch. I could almost see that white hat next to a pitcher of lemonade, a well-maintained Victorian house behind, a lazy old hound dog on the porch's top step, a couple of wicker rocking chairs creaking in the soft, humid breeze.

"Sorry, that's too rich for my blood," I told her. "And my pool game's spotty, at best."

She smiled sweetly, studying me. "Well, I bet you're good at other things." *Wail, ah bet you good at otha' thaings.*

Wow, that almost sounded like flirting. But I was from Minnesota, what did I know about southern flirtation? In Minnesota, chicks just whipped a walleye at you, and next thing you knew, the two of you were pumping out the next generation of Vikings fans.

"Yes, ma'am, I sure am."

"Really?" She tilted her head coyly, her sweet smile remaining in place on her sort-of-pretty face. "What other things are you good at?"

I puffed out my cheeks and exhaled loudly. "Wow, that's a long list. I'd hate to keep you here all day."

She laughed lightly. "Then just tell me what you're *best* at."

"Humility," I answered immediately. "Of my million awesome traits, I'd have to say I'm best at remaining humble."

This time, she lifted her hand in surprise to cover the laughter that escaped her mouth. "You're funny," she said.

"That's my second-best quality." I let her laughter subside before asking, "So what can I do for you today here at the Peak Plunge Waterslide?"

"Can you babysit my sister's kids for the next three hours or so?" She paused long enough to bat her eyelashes at me. "Pretty please?"

"Babysitting is our primary job here at the Plunge."

"No, I mean take 'em outta here and actually sit 'em for me."

I shook my head. "No can do. Sorry, ma'am, but you can't pay me enough to *literally* babysit children."

"Tell me about it," she said, rolling her eyes. "If I wanted to sit kids, I'd have me my own. But this is the only way I could get a night to myself."

"Yeah? How's that?"

"Family trip." She waved a dismissive hand in the air. "Daddy still likes to take a family trip each year, get everyone out of the heat. I'm from down south."

"Really? I had you pegged for Alaska."

She brought her hand to her mouth shyly. "Oh my, is my accent that noticeable?"

"It's gorgeous. I could listen to you talk all day."

She stared at me for several long seconds, smiling, and then she reached out and touched my arm. "You're so nice."

"And so funny."

"And so funny," she repeated, smiling. "And humble, and handsome, and lord only knows what all else."

"Not even sure the lord knows." I caught that "handsome" word and squirreled it away like a box of bullets. I'd break it out later when I moved in for the kill. I reached into my swimsuit pocket and pulled out my ciggies. "You mind?" I asked her.

"Not at all. You have an extra one in there for me?"

Shaking a Marlboro out of the pack, I handed it to her, then flicked my lighter. As I brought the flame to the end of her smoke, she reached out and held my hand in place with both of hers as she puffed the ciggie to life. Once it was lit, she pulled her head back but only slowly released my hand, her red fingernails tickling my skin.

Okay, *that* was flirting. That was flirting everywhere, whether in the great white north of Minnesota or the deep down swamps of Louisiana, whether in German beer halls or Moroccan mosques. I casually lit my own cigarette, trying to play it cool, so cool, when all I wanted to do was dive headfirst into this woman's cleavage and make juvenile motorboat sounds.

"I'm Madeline." She reached her hand out limply, palm down. I didn't know the southern custom, so I took her fingers gently and shook them softly, as if ringing a dinner bell.

"Paul."

"Charmed." She smiled at me. "Well, as I was saying, Paul, I told everyone I wanted a night to myself, and Sissy – that's what I call my little sister – she said she could use some time, as well. She said she'd keep our parents entertained in the national park today if I'd take her little monsters to the waterslide and watch them for a couple hours afterward until she got home. Then our parents promised to take the kiddies tonight so that Sissy and her hubby could have their evening, and I could have the whole night all to my lonesome."

I nodded. "Right on. Any big plans?"

"Well, you see, that's just it, Paul." She took a long, thoughtful drag off her cowboy killer and exhaled upwards without coughing. "I just don't know what to do with myself. I don't know the first thing about this here cute little mountain town. What I need is someone to tour me around, show me a real good time." She paused long enough to let the implication settle in, and then she moved slightly closer to me. "Do you live here in Estes Park?"

I shook my head sadly, suddenly wishing I did. "Afraid not. I live in the mountains about an hour south of here. I'm just in town to help my boss run his waterslide this week."

"Shame." She pouted a little but moved in even closer, reached out, and placed her palm flat on my chest. She gazed up into my eyes, and her voice grew sultry. "Still, I do believe you and I could have a good ol' time together, don't you?"

I nodded slowly. "Yes, ma'am, I do believe we could."

Her cute pout evolved into a knowing smile. "I do believe we could find *some* way to entertain ourselves, don't you agree?"

"I wholeheartedly agree," I wholeheartedly agreed, and then I made a snap decision. *Fuck it,* I told myself, *go for it. Women are like basketball: if you want to succeed, you have to take it hard to the hole.* "How 'bout I swing over to wherever you're staying when I get off work and we'll figure it out from there?"

Madeline's smile widened. "Ooo, I do like a man who knows what he wants." She studied me intently while she made her final decision. "I'm just up the road a bit at The Lazy Ranch Inn." She paused for a lingering second. "Room 305."

"So I should probably stop by, eh?"

She giggled lightly, then took a step back from me. "Eh? You northerners have such funny mannerisms." She pointed toward the stairway that led down to the pool. "I better go collect the youngins before they turn into little ol' raisins. But yes, I would like it very much if you stopped on by."

She turned and walked away, smiling over her shoulder beneath that floppy southern sun hat, twirling her fingers in a flirtatious wave. I saw the outline of her right breast pressed against her low-cut top, and as she disappeared down the steps, her ass swayed back and forth inside her tight-tight shorts like a hypnotist's watch. Damn. If I didn't do something quick, I was going to lose a load in my swimsuit, and Joel's puritanical Mormon rules strictly forbid noticeably giant cum stains on his employees' swimwear. I dashed into the bathroom, took matters into my own hands – so to speak – and unloaded the poison in under thirty seconds. Not a personal record, but definitely on the leaderboard.

The rest of the day, the clock ticked like a stalactite drip. I got one more whack in so that I didn't show up at The Lazy Ranch with a loaded pistol ready to fire, because that's no way to brand a steer, corral a cow, or perform any other ranch-related sexual euphemisms. I wished we could close the slide early, herd the maniac children into the parking lot, and leave them shivering in the high-altitude chill of Colorado. *Your parents will be here before sunset, you sissies, huddle up for warmth!* But Joel would never go for shutting down. He had standards. Ethics. Morals. Not me. When closing time finally came, I raced through my chores. I hosed down the showers as if suppressing a hippie protest, then mopped around the pool like a janitor trying to get promoted to custodian.

"Wow, Paul, I've never seen you work so hard and fast," Joel said as we wrapped up the cleaning. "You and Lonnie got a hot date tonight or something?"

"Something like that."

"I wish you had hot dates more often."

I tried to keep a straight face. "Me too, Joel, believe me."

"Alright, get out of here. See you tomorrow, dude."

"You know it, dude."

"Okay. Go easy on the beer tonight because you should—"

But I was out the door and on my motorcycle before he could finish giving me his well-intentioned advice. I zoomed over to The Lazy Ranch, my heart pounding. I told myself to focus on driving, focus on driving, and not on the porno playing on my brain's giant movie screen. I parked away from the stairway that led to room 305. I didn't want Madeline to see me pull up on my little 350 bike. I wanted her to imagine I'd arrived at The Lazy Ranch on a stallion, simultaneously smoking a Marlboro and chewing Red Man plug tobacco, dragging some outlaws behind me on a rope. I took the stairs two at a time and was breathing hard when I knocked on her door.

"Well, well, aren't you an eager little soldier?" she said as she opened the door. She pushed her head forward and looked side to side, giggling. "Get on in here before Daddy sees you." She grabbed me by my Peak Plunge t-shirt and pulled me inside, then quickly closed the door behind me.

"Uh-oh, where's your dad staying?"

"He's all the way down on the first level, 'cause Momma doesn't like heights, but I never know when he may be strollin' 'round." Her southern drawl was so slow, so sexy. "I know it's silly, but I think I'll always be afraid of Daddy catching me with boys, especially such a young little thing like you." She stared at me for a second, her head tilted quizzically. "How old are you, anyway?"

"Twenty-two," I lied. "How about you?"

"Twenty-eight," she lied. "But you're never supposed to ask a lady such a thing."

"Sorry. Where are my manners?"

She shrugged. "Same place as mine, I guess. I haven't even offered you a cold drink yet. Do you like whiskey, Paul?"

"Madeline, I like the entire alcohol family, even the creepy uncles."

She smiled at me. "Oh my, me too. Have you ever had yourself some of our fine southern whiskey?"

"Doubt it. I usually go the cheapest route, whatever bourbon's on sale."

"In that case, you are going to *love* this."

Madeline swayed her ass over to where she'd set up a little bar near a TV that was pointlessly bolted to a dresser. I followed behind, watching her ass flip back and forth, her tight white shorts hugging her bony butt. She reached for a large bottle of whiskey, half-empty, and showed me the label.

"You ever drink Pikesville Rye?"

Based on the artsy label and shape of the bottle, I knew I hadn't. My booze came in uniform, mass-produced, low-cost cylinders. Anything more triangular than a tube was outside my price range.

"I don't think so."

"This is an old southern rye," Madeline told me, tapping the label with one fire red fingernail. "It costs a penny or two, but it's worth it. You ever had yourself a mint julep, Paul?"

"Nope, but I know that was Faulkner's drink."

She smiled in surprise. "Oh, so you're familiar with some of our southern writers?"

"I am, actually."

"That's impressive. I have to admit, I do find a well-read man very attractive."

Madeline turned and whipped up two drinks like an old pro, and I had to believe she *was* an old pro, what with the bottle of whiskey already half-guzzled. When she turned around, she stepped in very close and handed me my first ever mint julep. I raised it to my lips, partly to better understand

Faulkner, but mainly because I fuckin' loved booze. I tipped it back, and good lord, I tasted both the sound *and* the fury in that concoction. What a fantastic drink. Right then, I hoped that as I lay dying, a mint julep would decorate my nightstand.

"Damn," I said, "I see why Faulkner drank these."

She ran her finger around the rim of her julep. "Maybe if you drink enough mint juleps, you could be a writer someday, too."

I laughed. "God, no. I love to read, but let's be honest, writers are annoying."

She smiled, turned around, and set her drink near the bottle. Gently removing my own julep from my clutches, she placed it next to hers. Then, without any further flirtation, she stepped right up to me and pressed her full breasts against my chest. She languidly stretched out her skinny arms and linked her hands behind my neck.

"Can I tell you my dirty little secret, Paul?"

"The dirtier, the better."

"I love to fuck," she stated flatly. "Not sex, mind you, not making love, but straight up *fucking*. I just *looooove* it, I truly do, everything about it. Honestly, if I had my way, I'd fuck all day and all night long." She pressed her crotch against mine, rolled those tight little shorts around my instantly stiff prick. "Is that too forward of me, too un-ladylike?"

"Not at all. I love fucking, too."

"That's a good boy. I sensed as much."

Madeline gently pulled me forward by the back of my neck, guided my head down to hers, and pressed her lips onto mine. She was slow and saucy to start, her tongue barely tasting me.

"Mmm, that's so very nice," she said, our whiskey breath comingling. "But I don't like it too nice for too long. After all, I'm a southern girl; I like things a little hotter than most."

And that was the end of Little Miss Ladylike. So long Miss Sweet Southern, Madeline released the Kraken. She tore into me, jammed her lips onto mine, her breath sweet with mint and sugar. Her fingers clutched my hair, tugged it painfully, and her tongue shot into my mouth, showing great range, finding every erotic taste bud. She kissed me like she'd been starving and was finally feasting. Her desire was whiskey-laden and immediate, an addict's want, and after exploring my mouth for a full minute, she shoved me harshly backwards onto the bed. She stepped over to our drinks, took a giant pull off her own, and walked mine over to me.

"I should probably tell you that I love drinking, too," she said. "In fact, if I could fuck and drink all day every day, I think I'd be the happiest woman alive."

I laughed, staring up at her. "Madeline, are you my soulmate?"

She handed me my drink. "Drink up, young Paul. This party's just getting started."

I took a sip.

"Oh, no." Madeline shook her head from side to side. "You finish that drink, ya' hear? I'm not drinking heavy all by my lonesome."

I turned the glass up further, downing the booze, envisioning drunk driving wrecks involving motorcyclists without helmets or any other bodily protection. Oh well, fuck it, if this turned out to be my last day on earth, there were worse ways to go. Floating through the air and smashing my skull into a boulder wouldn't be such a bad way to die, a real whiskey way to go. It would be way better than Faulkner's slow-creeping alcoholic demise, anyway. I'd rather fly off a motorcycle than fall off a horse like that old sauce, and thrombosis always sounded more like a cool jazz instrument than some life-threatening illness. Only an old alkie like Faulkner could die so passively, whereas a young alkie like me still had a good chance of dying aggressively.

"You're such a good boy," Madeline said after I loudly slurped the last drops of her expensive rye through all the crushed ice. She took my glass away, walked it back to the bottle, then crawled on top of me, straddling my hips. "And now, young Paul, it's time for you to give me a damn fine fuckin'."

Madeline descended like an Oklahoma thunderstorm, coming out of nowhere, pounding the fields. When Madeline said she *loooved* to fuck,

Madeline meant she *loooved* to fuck. She ripped off my shirt as if she were pissed at cotton, flung it across her hotel room with real hatred. She fell on my nipples, devoured those two pepperonis. Madeline bit me, the little bitch, bit me all over, and I fuckin' loved it. She chewed my shoulders, bit my neck, gnawed my stomach, my sides. This was going to be aggressive fucking, I realized, bordering on violent, so I lifted her skinny body off me, flung her on her back, and pinned her hands above her head.

"You're a rough little bitch, eh?"

Biting her lower lip, she nodded her head up and down, her long brown hair splayed out on the pillow.

"Then let's get these fucking clothes off, you little slut."

I reached down with my right hand and tried to push her shorts down, but they were on too tight. I had to let her hands go, but she kept them in place above her head, staying submissive. Lifting her legs and peeling off her shorts, I was not surprised she didn't wear panties. I flung open her sleeveless top so I could view those enticing breasts, but I didn't remove her shirt. A little bit of clothing was always hotter than full nudity for some reason, stockings or boots, bra or shirt, something to remind me of all the societal taboos I was breaking. I stepped off the bed and dropped my shorts to the ground. My dick threatened to poke straight through my Fruit of the Looms – the grape cluster, to be precise – so I wiggled out of my tighty whities. Crawling back on the bed, I slithered along Madeline's side and again pinned her hands over her head with my left hand. I tickled her thighs with my right hand, dragged my fingers up and down her flesh until she spread her legs for me.

"Oh my god, put something in me," she whispered.

I stuffed my index finger inside her and she moaned in pleasure, her hips immediately grinding it in deeper. I slid my middle finger into her, as well, and her eyes slipped close.

"God, yes," she groaned, "more."

I got my ring finger and pinky up in there, and then Madeline went to town, fucking my fingers like they were four skinny cocks. I clamped her hands in place above her head, but it was a difficult maneuver with most of my other hand buried inside her. I didn't have to keep it up long, though. She rode my fingers hard, twisted and writhed on them, and when I pressed my thumb onto her clit, that was all it took.

"*Oh fucking god yes!*" Madeline exploded with orgasm, her back arched, all my fingers buried in her pussy, her hands locked above her head. "Oh fuck oh fuck oh fuck!"

Damn, I thought, *this girl really DOES love to fuck.*

Her arched back collapsed on the bed, and her eyes popped open immediately. "Tie me up!" she demanded. "Quick! And grab a condom from the top drawer!"

"Huh?"

"Tie me *up*," she almost growled. "Tie me up, put on a condom, and fuck the shit out of me. *Now!*"

I nodded, looking around for something to strap her down.

"Use the sheets," she said. "Hurry up, I need to cum again!"

I never joined the Boy Scouts – the whole uniform was a little too "Hitler Youth" for me – so I didn't know much about tying knots, and I knew even less about strapping a woman to a hotel room bed. *Can't be that tough*, I thought, *all kinds of dangerous idiots do it all the time*. I ripped the bedsheet out from under Madeline's ass, and after a few seconds of consideration, I strapped her into a pretty good bondage trap. It wouldn't hold up in any kind of *real* sex crime, but this was only a "just for fun" sex crime. Madeline groaned as I tightened the sheets on her wrists. She slithered her long skinny body around on the bed like a restless snake, thrashed her legs a little to pretend she was resisting.

"Quit fighting, bitch," I said, playing along with her fantasy.

She moaned seductively and licked her lips.

"You're going to lay there, and you're going to fuckin' love it, slut."

She closed her eyes, inhaled sharply, and pushed her hips up, calling for my cock.

I strapped on a condom to protect Lonnie from all my assholery, and then I fell on Madeline with a vengeance. I stuffed it in aggressively, one sharp thrust past the labia, and she turned her head away from me, the perfect victim. I mauled her, squeezed her ass, bit her, spanked her, choked her a little, enjoying the aggressor role. She couldn't keep up the illusion, though, her need was too overwhelming. In short order, she jammed her hips into mine, caught my rhythm, and then her lips demanded my attention, her tongue in my mouth, searching. She broke away and chanted, "*Fuck me harder, fuck me harder, fuck me harder!*" in time with each thrust, and a minute later, she came again, biting my lower lip. I unloaded seconds after, giving her every last inch God gave me – all twelve of them, if I measured from my knees – my teeth buried in her flesh. After the last drop dripped into my condom, I looked up and saw most of my hasty knots had given way, and although Madeline kept her arms spread wide, there was no actual bondage restricting her movement anymore.

"Oh my sweet Jesus," she breathed, "that was *soooo* god damn good, exactly what I needed. I haven't had a good, dirty fuck in over a week."

I rolled off her. "Jesus, a whole week? How'd you survive?"

She giggled. "Well, it hasn't been easy for this little gal, I tell ya'." She pulled her hands down to her chest and easily unwound my remaining half-ass knots.

"What, you have a boyfriend back home, all kinds of regular sex?"

She glanced over at me, reached out her hand, and lightly pet my face. "That's so old fashioned and sweet, honey, but no. I don't want just one man, darlin'. I have a regular ol' boy stable back in Birmingham, rotate through 'em. I add a new one from time to time, let others out to pasture. I'm usually much more careful pickin' than I was with you, but I really did need some masculine attention. And you seemed so very nice." She smiled at me. "And so *very* willing. I do have an excellent eye for easy prey."

I laughed a little uneasily. "Oh yeah? I'm easy prey?"

"You *ooze* easy, darlin', practically have 'willing' tattooed on your forehead." She patted my leg. "But enough about all my dalliances. How 'bout you? There a special little lady waiting for you somewhere?"

"I suppose you could say that." I stood up, found my shorts, and pulled out my smokes. "Guess you wouldn't know it by my actions, eh?"

Madeline shrugged. "Love and fucking are two different things, hon. Love satisfies the soul, fulfills us, but fucking satisfies the animal within, fills us up with that old instinctual pleasure. It's almost impossible to truly fuck what you truly love. I mean, fulfillment and pleasure are related, but they are not always one in the same, darlin', and they are certainly not *inseparable*." She pushed herself off the bed, stepped past me toward the makeshift bar, and began mixing up a couple fresh juleps. "A lot of people don't know that, Paul, but a lot of people don't know much about much, I'm afraid. People mainly go along to get along, don't give much thought to much of anything. Sometimes, I do think we're all just actors and actresses, playing along with the parts we're given, kinda' like that ol' Shakespeare fellow said. Not sure why we feel we have to live that way, but I don't worry myself too much about it. I play my part when I have to, but when no one's looking, I do exactly as I please."

I lit up and dragged on my Marlboro. "I try not to play a part, don't want to live like some Shakespearean actor on a stage."

Madeline laughed knowingly. "God, you're so young, darlin'. Good luck with that approach. Don't you know that the world needs you to pick a part and play it so that everyone can easily define, categorize, and judge you? This world does not suffer improvisation too kindly."

I drank two more of her strong mint juleps, fucked her hard from behind against her bathroom sink where we could watch ourselves bash it out in the mirror, then took a quick shower for Lonnie's benefit. I got dressed and sincerely wished Madeline the very best of luck in this long, weird, twisted life. She thanked me for fucking her so recklessly and told me I better be extra sweet to my girl, since I could not and would not ever be faithful or trustworthy.

I opened up the throttle on the Peak to Peak Highway, trying to get through the Rockies before full dark. I knew that once night fell, the mountain air grew colder than societal judgment on habitual cheaters, and dusk deer often dashed across the highway, slapping high hooves on the other side whenever they killed a motorcyclist. I ripped through the mountains and made it home just as true dark arrived. Evie and Rummy sprinted down the elevated walkway to drown me in happiness.

"Hey, you two!" I called out. They jumped all over me, licked the last lingering scent of Madeline from my skin. "Let's go say hi to your mom."

I walked into our cabin and saw Lonnie curled up with a blanket and a book on our couch. She was dressed in her favorite flannel pajamas, looking so peaceful, so happy, so *fulfilled*. Lonnie was perfectly suited to the mountain life we were living.

"You made it home alive," she said, smiling up at me. "I was getting worried."

I shrugged. "Phil and I sucked back a few beers after work."

"Phil's a bad influence on you," she joked, knowing my bad habits didn't require outside encouragement. "Drinking before getting on your motorcycle is dangerous."

"I'm a dangerous man, Lon." I walked over and kissed her, kissed her with real depth of feeling. "I love you, Lonnie. I really do."

And I did, I really did. Something about fucking another woman made me love Lonnie even more, appreciate her anew, because sometimes love and sex and motorcycles and rye whiskey and waterslides and Faulkner and cabins and mountains and youth get all mixed up and dumped into a weird and uncontrollable blender. The final concoction often makes no sense at all, like playing Shakespearean parts or enjoying sex crime fantasies or believing that love is limiting or exclusive or forever.

3.

Draining His Fluid Does Not Make It Gay

ELDORA, COLORADO

1990

Autumn in the Rocky Mountains is an event. Summer stretches, autumn yawns, and exhausted nature strips naked before slipping under winter's wide white blanket for a good long nap. I was essentially a city boy, had never been too aware of the planet around me. To be a part of the cycle, immersed in nature in my tiny mountain valley, was a real awakening. For the first time, I had a front row seat to the full force, immense power, and startling beauty of my planet. It was a religious experience of sorts, all the better because it came without pamphlets or prophets, and I couldn't help shedding shifts at Pizza Place to stay home and watch the process unfold.

"Let's go for a walk," I suggested to Lonnie as we lay reading in bed. I kept my voice low so the dogs wouldn't hear the "W" word.

"Ah, come on, it's the weekend, I don't have any pressing homework, and I'm *soooooo* cozy," she whined, looking over at me. "Besides, it's cold out there."

"It's probably in the forties."

"That's *cooooold.*"

Fuckin' Denver girl. That wasn't cold. Minnesota was cold. In Minnesota, the sweat on a man's balls froze, sealing him to his own underwear. In

Minnesota, Vikings fans dripped hot coffee onto their eyeballs at halftime to keep their pupils from freezing.

"Come on, you baby," I said. "It's my twentieth birthday, you have to do whatever I say."

She raised her eyebrows above the rims of her glasses. "It was your twentieth birthday three weeks ago, Paul."

"It was?"

"Yes, we had a party up here. You took acid with Erik and Eddie and all of you drank too much whiskey. Eddie threw up in our sink."

"Weird. I don't remember any of that."

"Exactly." She glanced at the clock, then turned back to me. "Okay, I'll go for a walk, but let me finish this chapter first."

"No problem. I'll get ready."

I closed my book, *The River Why*, by David James Duncan, a writer I'd never read before. Great stuff. Now that Lonnie worked for Golden Age Books, she constantly brought home new writers for me. The bookstore had a solid employee discount program, but even better, Lonnie could take home all the damaged books for free. She regularly came back to the cabin with five new writers at a time – new to me, anyway – stuffing the novels onto our already overloaded bookshelves. For a heavy reader, it was like fresh confessions at an AA meeting, so new and interesting compared to all the old, tired tales of childhood abuse and abandonment.

I flipped off the bed covers, and at the end of the bed, both dogs lifted their heads expectantly. Little Evie was growing fast, the Labrador fighting the Shepherd for dominance in her coloring, both bloodlines quickly pushing her out of puppyhood.

"Go outside?" I asked them.

Boom, dash! Off the bed and through the cabin in a half-second flat. My dogs stood at the front door, their tails whipping into each other's sides. I let them out, then threw on a heavy flannel shirt before stepping onto my deck to join them.

Wow, what a day. The aspens were in full autumn bloom, bright yellow swaths splashed across the mountainsides. The sky above was as blue as an old guitar picker whose baby done left him, and the chilly October air slapped the sleep right out of my skull. Far off down the valley, snow dusted the mountaintops of the Continental Divide, threatening the nation with winter. Middle Boulder Creek rolled through bulging aspen groves, the leaves dropping softly onto the water's surface before drifting off to Barker Reservoir and beyond, down the canyon into Boulder, meeting St. Vrain Creek, onto the Platte River, and finally entering the mighty Mississippi where an Evinrude's propeller would chew those peaceful leaves to paste. Ah, that mystical moment when the soft cycle of nature encounters the raw horsepower of man.

Twenty minutes later, Lonnie and I strolled the path along the creek, listening to cold autumn water splash over rocks. Rummy dashed ahead, ripping through the undergrowth. Not Evie, though. She walked right on our heels, stopped when we stopped, went when we went, and she did it without a leash or any verbal instruction from me. She was the most instinctively well-behaved puppy on the planet, almost laughably so.

"So are you going to apply?" Lonnie asked. She pointed up high to our left where I could barely see a couple of the ski runs at Eldora Resort, still untouched by snow.

I nodded slowly. "I'm debating."

"I think you should. You should stay up here in the mountains, get away from all the partying in Boulder. It'll help you focus on your writing."

"We'll see. I don't even know what to apply for."

"They'd probably start you pushing chairs."

"Why do you say that?"

She shrugged. "Lowest job on the totem pole, gotta start somewhere."

I decided to at least interview, which I did later that day, and the very next day, Eldora offered me a graveyard shift job making snow. Two weeks later, still considering the offer, I lay alongside Sabrina's beautiful body, her black skin sparkling with sex sweat. She'd suggested I come down a little before our Pizza Place shifts that night to "take the edge off," as she now referred to our sporadic romps. Even now, after nearly six months, I had a hard time believing I had an ongoing affair with a woman as gorgeous as Sabrina. I certainly wasn't going to end it, and for her part, she still seemed to enjoy our semi-regular romps.

She reached for my Marlboros on her nightstand, lit one for me, and guided it to my lips. Pulling out a Camel for herself, she puffed it to life. We silently smoked our cigarettes on our backs for a minute or two, staring at her ceiling, catching our breath.

"So what do you think I should do?" I asked, turning my head toward her. "Should I work at Eldora, cruise around in a snowcat, move the snow cannons around the mountain?"

Sabrina dragged long and thoughtfully on her ciggie. "Well, that would make it a little harder for me and you to take the edge off, of course. And I can't figure out why the hell you'd want to spend an entire winter freezing your skinny ass off outside for half the pay of slinging pizza out of your nice, warm car."

"It would be a good experience."

"A good experience for what?"

I shrugged. "I don't know."

But I knew, of course. Rolling around all night in a snowcat under the frozen Rocky Mountain stars, positioning snow cannons at long, empty hillsides, and using my free season pass to swoosh away my afternoons on the slopes would provide ample fodder for future writing. I didn't talk to many people about writing, though, and I definitely wouldn't discuss it with Sabrina. She was too practical for any artistic bullshit. Her military father had her marching in formation through life's proper channels, trudging down well-worn roads to make her way in the world. Besides, Sabrina would laugh her ass off at the idea of me writing a letter, no less a novel, and then she'd spend the next six months needling me about it. I already had enough self-doubt on my plate; I didn't need a second helping from Sabrina.

"Honestly, Paulie, it sounds kind of stupid to me."

I blew out a long stream of Marlboro smoke. "Maybe you're right."

She stayed silent for several more seconds, smoking, appearing to give the idea real thought before pushing herself up on an elbow and gazing down at me. She lowered her head and kissed me gorgeously, as Sabrina always kissed me. Sabrina's kiss was better than full-on sex with most girls. She kissed like Janis Joplin sang ballads, longingly, suggestively, always with an underlying hint of maddening desperation.

"But I don't think you'll do it," she said, breaking our kiss. "You need money, Pablo, and you're practical. Face it, you're poor, just like me, and neither one of us has the kind of parents that send checks. There's no way you'll take that big of a pay cut. You may think it's all tough and shit to work all night on top of a mountain, but once you start crunching numbers, you'll never let yourself do it."

I sighed, having thought that very thing many times as I debated the question. Sabrina and I stopped discussing it, and minutes later, we resumed the fucking. After all, that's what we were there for. We didn't put in the time and effort to get all naked so that we could discuss employment opportunities.

I considered the dilemma for a few more days, talked to Lonnie, talked to Joel, talked to Franzen. Lonnie promised more blow jobs if I took the Eldora job, swore a full season in the mountains would add a whole new layer of experience to my writing. Joel offered me a raise and whatever shifts I wanted if I stayed at Pizza Place. *Please don't leave, dude! You're one of my main dudes, dude!* Erik Franzen, my original Pizza Place trainer and best friend at the store, replied in exactly the way I would have expected a great friend to reply: *Do whatever the fuck you want, man, I'm not your fuckin' dad. But hey, if you can get me a free pass, I'll come ski every weekend!* I had to laugh. Guys can always be counted on to openly not give a shit about each other unless there's something in it for them.

I listened to everyone's advice, but in the end, Sabrina had it right. After six months of secretive boning, the girl understood me on a fundamental level. It came down to money, raw numbers. I loved having Pizza Place cash. I didn't want to live on a budget again like those dark days at Amoco, didn't want to revert back to single-ply toilet paper. I'd acquired double-ply tastes, a far more refined asshole. I ate Big Macs instead of cheeseburgers now, drank Budweiser instead of Busch. I couldn't turn the clock back on such a grandiose lifestyle.

Lonnie pouted when I told her, but I thought Joel might actually kiss me on the lips when he heard I was staying at Pizza Place. He was Mormon, though, so we couldn't smooch. That man-on-man shit was for Unitarians and Catholic priests. Latter Day Saints mated for procreation, dude.

I knew I'd missed out on something, knew that making snow for a season on a frozen mountaintop would have been a deep well to draw from when the stories dried up. But poverty does that to a person; it rips opportunities away, replaces possibilities with practicalities. Lonnie thought I'd find inspiration working the mountain, and she was probably right, but every time Lonnie ran short of money, she didn't call up inspiration and ask for cash. Nope, she called Daddy, and her dad dutifully topped off Lonnie's bank account whenever it dipped slightly below spoiled.

I could have taken the job anyway, suffered the financial blow in exchange for the experience. Hell, there were people all over the world who starved for their art. But I had a sneaking suspicion most starving artists either had a debilitating mental illness or a substantial financial safety net. I had neither. Even van Gogh had Theo, and although Vincent lived like a sewer rat most of his life, when push came to shove, Theo swooped in and bought his brother's brushes, purchased his paints, and peddled his canvasses. Vincent wouldn't have painted a fucking thing if he'd had to work graveyard shifts making snow on the mountain to pay the goddam rent. Bye-bye, *Starry Night*. So long, *Café Terrace*.

Fuck that. Fuck poverty right in the food stamps. Struggling was for suckers, at least in America. I kept my job at Pizza Place, then paid for a season pass like every other normal person in the world's most prosperous nation. I tuned up my skis and waited for winter. I didn't have to wait long.

* * *

Winter comes early and often in the Rockies, a seasonal pubescent with no cock control, spewing his seed in every direction. November and December crushed my tiny town, buried it in snow. The wind roared through the valley like a wounded lion screaming for an animal ambulance that would never arrive because animals suck at driving, especially in the snow. I was used to Minnesota winter, the cold, cold, forever cold, the depressing gray, the torturous longevity and tenacity of winter. Rocky Mountain winter was violent by comparison, a blitzkrieg as opposed to trench warfare. I measured the snow in feet, not inches, and I hunkered down for days in the living room with books and beer while the onslaught ripped past my cabin's windows.

"We need more wood," Lonnie said. She was reading on her end of our old sectional couch, her blanket pulled up over her gigantic breasts. Evie covered her feet, a Sheprador foot warmer.

I glanced at Lonnie over the top of my own book. "No way. I went out for the last batch."

She pouted. "You're the man of the house."

"I'm an overgrown boy. I was still a teenager four months ago."

"You're more of a man than I'll ever be. You have testicles."

Damn, got me with the ol' testicles argument.

"Fine," I said, "but after this story. I'm almost done with my book."

I was working my way through some of Hemmingway's short stuff, *The Snows of Kilimanjaro and Other Stories*. I loved *The Snows of Kilimanjaro*, loved the language, the mood, but I couldn't really get a feel for the time and place. The Europe Hemmingway spoke of did not exist anymore, literally was not there, so many borders and nations rearranged after two world wars. And World War I felt a million years in the past, a complicated mess of a conflict that even historians had trouble explaining. To me, WWI was a war of grainy photographs and ancient film coverage where all the troops moved unnaturally fast, like middle-aged moms speed-walking through the suburbs. *Just fucking jog already!* World War II was much more comprehensible – big, bold villains and easily identifiable heroes. Still, the way Hemmingway's Harry spoke of death while awaiting it, the way he pondered all the beautiful and horrible things he'd left unsaid and unwritten throughout his life, struck me as particularly profound.

I finished the story fifteen minutes later, forced Rummy off my legs, and emerged from under my blanket. Our old iron stove was roaring a couple hours before, but those coals had cooled, and the temp in the living room was steadily falling.

"I don't want to do it," I said.

"You have to."

"It's ridiculous out there."

"Toughen up; you're from Minnesota."

Damn, got me with the ol' Minnesota argument. Testicles + Minnesota = Go Gather Wood, Pussy. I bundled up as best I could, opened the door, and entered the mayhem.

The wind and snow *screamed* past the cabin, slamming down from the Continental Divide at 30 miles per hour. The trees in our yard danced like meth-crazed bikers at a Motorhead concert, banging their heads to ass-crackin' rock 'n' roll. Glancing down our walkway to the left, I saw wild walls of snow gusting down Eldorado Avenue, shoved on by the merciless hand of Wind. The roar was everywhere, an actual threat from nature: *Get off my fucking mountain before I* REALLY *get pissed!*

"Jesus Christ!" I yelled, but I couldn't hear my own blasphemy. The wind grabbed the lord's name, lifted it above the trees, and hurled it all the way to Arkansas, where it belonged.

Hustling down the steps, I ducked underneath our deck. I piled up as large an armload of mixed hardwood as I could carry, dumped it at the door, then went back for a second load.

"Yeah, don't get up," I told the dogs as I pushed open the door. Usually, they dashed outside at every opportunity, but with winter roaring, they hardly raised their heads off the couch.

"Hurry up!" Lonnie said from under the warm safety of her blanket. "You're letting out all the heat!"

I picked up the pace, brought in the rest of the wood, and stacked it next to the woodstove. I thought it was enough to last Lonnie until she went to bed, but if not, she'd have to brave the outdoors herself or switch to the cabin's primary propane heater. After adjusting the flue, I arranged the wood in a log cabin formation in the stove's woodbox, then swung the iron door shut, letting the coals work their magic.

"There you go, female. That should get it roasting in here soon."

Lonnie set her book on her lap and smiled sweetly at me. "I really love you."

"Yeah, when I build fires for you."

"And when you shovel out my car."

I nodded. "Speaking of that, I better start getting ready for work. I'll probably have to dig the Bird out of a drift."

"Have fun." Lonnie reached for her pipe and grabbed her lighter. It was Saturday afternoon, no work or school for Lonnie, which meant a long night of books, dogs, and dope.

After showering up, I piled on heavy clothing for the trek to my car. I trudged down my walkway through the blasting wind, and sure enough, the Bird was a round mound of snow. Damn, the things I made my old battleax of a car endure. The Bird had carried White and I all across the American West as we scoped out our initial escape from Minnesota, a cross-county trek far too demanding for my old wheels. Now, I depended on the Bird for my livelihood, and I repaid his indispensable efforts with long shifts of stop-and-go delivery driving, the worst kind of wear and tear a person could inflict upon an old car. To top it off, I forced the Bird up and down a steep mountain canyon every work night, then left him buried outside under a few feet of snow without so much as a blanket. No wonder I thought so highly of the Bird; the ol' boy was a fucking tank, tough as nails.

It took a full twenty minutes to shovel him out while the engine idled and the defrost warmed the windshield enough for me to scrape off a thick layer of ice. With rear-wheel drive and questionable tires, I drove very carefully through my snowbound town. In rare moments of honesty and practicality, I knew the Bird was a Rocky Mountain death trap, exactly what a person *shouldn't* drive up and down a mountain canyon three to five nights a week throughout winter. But I loved the Bird on a very deep level, could never part with him. It wasn't homosexual or anything, just a platonic love between a boy and his Bird. Just because I worked his stick every night didn't make it gay. Just because I drained his fluid once in a while didn't make it gay. And just because we cranked Elton John together and both knew all the words to "Tiny Dancer" definitely did *not* make it gay.

Or did it?

I drove down Boulder Canyon, the climate changing with every mile of descent. That was the best part of going to work, gradually moving away from full winter madness towards a mildly chilly December night. A howling 30 mile per hour wind in Eldora dropped to an almost imperceptible 10 mile per hour breeze in Boulder. Eighteen inches of snow could bury our Eldora cabin at the same time Boulder only got a light dusting. I couldn't get over how bizarre it was to have two completely different climates separated by a mere twenty miles of road.

I turned up 9th Street as early winter dusk settled on the town. Saturday night was ramping up, the young students and mid-twenties hangers-on wandering past as I drove through The Hill neighborhood, everyone heading to bars or parties, ready to start drinking beer and ordering pizza. I turned left onto Baseline, and just as I was about to throw in *Appetite For Destruction* to get fired up for work, one of Boulder's finest lit me up. Blue and red rolling lights bounced off the Bird's mirrors, blinding me, and one loud siren blast ensued.

"*God dammit!*" I yelled before flipping on my blinker and pulling over to the side of the road.

I placed my hands at 10:00 and 2:00 on the steering wheel like a good little citizen and waited patiently for my constitutionally guaranteed hassle. There was no good reason to pull me over. I'd come to a full stop at the last stop sign, hadn't been speeding, and I'd even used my turn signal. My tags were up to date, had no outstanding tickets or warrants. But the Bird was old, beat to shit, and I was young, in need of a haircut. By Boulder's standards, that made me a target, one of the few po' folk in town. I'd always heard black men got pulled over regularly and randomly, and although I'd never been a black man – not even for a single day – I knew the authorities relentlessly targeted poverty, regardless of skin color. In fact, if I was behind the wheel of the Bird and a black man was behind the wheel of Lonnie's nearly new Skyhawk, I'd bet a dozen doughnuts the cops would pull me over first. Sure, they'd pull over the black dude right after that, just to round out the profiling, but they'd get to me first.

"License, insurance, and registration," the female cop said as she stepped up to my window. She didn't bother with anything resembling, "How are you this evening, sir?" The police only called poor twenty-year-olds "sir" when the cameras were rolling for an episode of *Cops*.

I tried looking up at the officer, but her flashlight was in my face. A flashlight in the face is almost as annoying to the human eye as disco is to the human ear…almost.

"Sure," I said, then reached for my glovebox. "Can I ask why you pulled me over?"

"License, insurance, and registration," she repeated.

I rummaged around my glovebox. "I'll take that as a no," I mumbled under my breath.

She carried my documents back to her car without another word, leaving me to wallow in the slow, intimidating roll of red and blue lights, such cold, cold colors, so accusatory and unforgiving. Those lights should switch to green when the driver pulls over without a chase, a little reward for playing by the rules. And then, if the driver is ultimately deemed no threat to society, the police could fire up some festive orange rollers, just to reassure the passing Boulderites that there was still nothing to fear on their perfect little island of wealth and homogeny.

Nearly ten minutes passed, making me annoyingly late for work, before the cop returned to my window. This time, she held off on the flashlight. When she handed me back my documents, she included a ticket.

"What's this?" I asked. "Look, I don't want to be a jerk, but I know for a fact I wasn't doing anything wrong."

"That's an emissions ticket," she stated flatly.

"A what?"

"An emissions ticket."

"A what?"

"Your vehicle is emitting far too much exhaust," she explained with noticeable irritation. "You have thirty days to address the issue, after which, you will need to pass an emissions compliance test or destroy the vehicle. If you don't provide proof of emissions compliance or vehicle destruction, you'll be fined $200 dollars, and that fine rises exponentially if you continue operating the unrepaired vehicle beyond the allotted thirty days."

Did she actually just suggest I destroy the Bird?

I turned my head up to see what kind of a monster would propose such a thing. The officer's face was cold and humorless, past its prime. I suddenly saw her, not as a cop, but as a poorly aging bartender at the opening of a gritty sci-fi story: *Jenny Keating languidly wipes down the whiskey bottles and sighs, still bartending all these years after promising herself she'd quit slinging drinks, follow her dreams, and enroll at the Police Academy. She pushes an Old Gold cigarette into the corner of her mouth and waits for the small town regulars to arrive. They'll wander through the door soon, just as they do every Tuesday night. As they do every Wednesday night, for that matter, not to mention Thursday night and all the other squares on the calendar that blur together in a long, pointless parade of old bills paid and new ones acquired. The regulars will bring their tired laughter to the bar, their stupid jokes, all the same old cocktail double entendres: "I'll take a long slow screw up against the wall, Jenny." HAHAHAHA! "I want a martini, Jenny, and you know I like it dirty, the dirtier the better." HAHAHAHA! So hilarious.* Good lord, *Jenny thinks,* if only there was an escape from all those idiotic voices. *And then, as if answering her silent prayer, a strange green light slips through the dirty bar's only window, growing brighter, brighter, enveloping Jenny in its cold, emerald embrace...*

"Seriously?" I asked.

"Seriously," the cop/bartender answered.

"I've never heard of anything like this. Are you saying there's a legal amount of exhaust I can have?"

"There is. Boulder County is very committed to its air quality."

"Apparently."

"Just do the repairs, pass the test, and you won't have any problems. It's for the good of the entire community. You have thirty days." With that, she turned and marched away, off to sling drinks and suffer sexism until the green light arrived to save her or destroy her, no one knew which.

I sat in my car, stunned. *Destroy the Bird.* Who would ever think such a thing, let alone say it out loud? And she said it right in front of him, too, like *that* wasn't going to totally freak him out. I mean, sure, the Bird spewed big, black clouds of exhaust, but I didn't choose to drive an old beater. Poor people drove old beaters because that's what poor people could afford to drive.

I waited a full week to address the problem, giving me plenty of time to rant and rave about America's suckshit laws. The Man was coming down on me like an overly involved Woman, a mom, a nagging wife, ordering me to clean up my fucking act for the good of the planet. What a crock of shit.

"Dammit, Paul!" Lonnie said, exasperated after one of my hour-long, beer-fueled rants against society in general. "The environment is *extremely* important! We're destroying the earth! I agree with the city on this one, you should fix the Bird."

"Don't give me your political garbage, Lon. This goes way beyond environmentalism. We're talking about potentially killing the Bird, the legalized murder of a family member. If you think we should start murdering family members in the name of nature, you're one sick puppy, darlin'."

She rolled her eyes. "You *are* aware there's a giant hole in the ozone layer, right? You want to widen it by driving the Bird a million miles a night to deliver pizza?"

"How much is the Bird widening the ozone hole?"

"Paul," she said tiredly, then shook her head, "don't be so simplistic and literal."

"No, come on, by *exactly* how much am I widening the ozone hole? One trillionth of one trillionth of one trillionth of one millimeter?"

"God, I can't talk to you about these things!" She threw up her hands. "If you want to stay politically ignorant the rest of your life, be my guest!" She stormed out of our living room and closed the bedroom door hard. She didn't quite slam it, but I still thought it best to sleep on the couch that night and preserve what remained of domestic harmony.

This was not our first semi-political argument. It was becoming a growing nuisance in our relationship, actually. Lonnie had always been a hippie chick, inclined toward all the standard left-leaning stances of young stoners. She hated littering, despised war, openly advocated for all seven black people in Boulder, and she believed strongly in the legalization and forced inhalation of marijuana. It was boilerplate stuff, positions anyone could reach after listening to the entire Woodstock album, all six sides. Hell, I casually agreed with most of it, but I didn't give anything political too much thought. Lonnie, conversely, was diving deeper and deeper into politics. Several of her new friends/coworkers at Golden Age Books were activists on the political left, and they regularly invited Lonnie to BYOB gatherings – Bring Your Own Bong – where everyone got nicely toasted and giggled their way through various political problems. Lonnie was joining some after-class feminist campus groups, as well, where they bandied about some lunatic notions concerning equal pay for equal work, and even crazier, the elimination of domestic violence, as if men could use words and reason to properly express their displeasure. Whatever the topic, I noticed a subtle coldness evolving in Lonnie as she shed the bliss of ignorance. Conversely, I was perfectly content to remain blissfully ignorant of the world's problems, and this opposite approach made things steadily less pleasant at home.

I drove the Bird down to my favorite mechanic in Boulder the following day. The entire trip down the canyon, I couldn't shake the feeling that I was taking an elderly relative to the hospital, anticipating a bleak diagnosis.

"So you got one of those fuckin' emissions tickets?" Steve, my favorite mechanic, asked me.

"Yep. You've heard of them?"

"Seeing more and more of those stupid things all the time." He took a puff off his perma-cig and miraculously managed not to light his oil-soaked uniform on fire. "I guess this fuckin' rich-boy town decided to crack down on the underclasses some more. You know who doesn't have to worry about this shit? Those fucking brats at CU. Mommy and Daddy make sure their precious little shits have brand new cars every other year." He extended his filthy hand for my keys. "I'll give it a look and try to keep it as reasonable as possible, but honestly, Paul, the shit the city's requiring to pass these new emissions tests is usually pretty expensive for older cars."

"Bummer. Well, keep me posted. I'll be at the store." Pizza Place was only a block away, my waiting room whenever the Bird was in surgery.

An hour and a half later, I answered the store's ringing phone.

"Hey Paul, Steve here." I heard the ominous crackle of burning tobacco, followed by a deep, pronounced inhale into a region of the lungs only hardened smokers could reach. "I got bad news for you, buddy. It's the entire shit, the whole kit and kaboodle. We're talking pipes, muffler, catalytic converter, front to back. If you want to pass that stupid fucking emissions test, you'll need to replace everything."

"Jesus." I shook my head and stared out Pizza Place's plate glass windows, bracing myself for more bad news. "What's that going to set me back?"

"Parts and labor, $700 low-end, maybe $850 high-end if we run into some snags."

"Wow, that's more than the Bird's worth." I let a long pause ride the line. "What about doing it myself, pulling parts from the junkyard?"

"I wouldn't, Paul. You never know what you're getting off those junked cars. Say you pull a catalytic converter that's not up to snuff, you'll have done all that work for nothin'. The chances of all the parts you pull being compliant is pretty low, especially with Boulder's high emissions standards."

"Fuck."

"You said it."

"*Fuck.*"

"You said it again."

"What do you think I should do, man?"

He sighed. "Honestly, I think you're going to have to let him go, buddy. Scrap him for parts. I'm guessing the junkyard will give you $100 bucks or so."

"That's it? No compensation for sentimental value?"

Steve laughed. "Afraid not, pal. Not a real sentimental bunch over there at the junkyard."

"Cold bastards." I shook my head. "Okay, well, I guess I'll be down in a few minutes to pick him up. What do I owe you?"

"Nothin'. I can't charge you for telling you to scrap your car. Just throw me a free pizza one of these days." I heard the bells jangle on his shop's door, a new customer arriving, before Steve said, "Let me guess, the Bird's the first car you ever bought?"

"Yep."

"That's a big deal. Dudes get as unreasonably attached to their first car as they do to their first girlfriend."

"Yeah, I have that other issue, too. I won't have to scrap her for parts, will I?"

"Nah, I don't think so." Steve laughed knowingly. "Actually, a dude's first girl usually gets stolen right out from under him before he's ready to scrap her. Grand theft female, buddy." And then Steve laughed harder.

Driving the Bird back to Eldora was like bringing an old, loved pet home from the vet after scheduling a euthanasia appointment. The Bird even drove like he knew what was coming, shifting halfheartedly, burping exhaust, his stereo stuck on depressing Pink Floyd music: *All in all, it's just a-nother brick in the balls.*

"What's the verdict?" Lonnie asked when I walked through our door.

"I have to put him down. You happy?"

She stuck out her lower lip, feigning sympathy. "There are other beaters in the sea, Pablo."

"Not funny," I said. "Maybe I should just ask your dad to buy me a new car?"

"If you marry me and get me pregnant, I'm sure he would."

"Pass. I'd rather buy my own, less expensive in the long run." I lit a cigarette and flopped down in my blue, papasan chair, one of the last remaining pieces of my past. "Unfortunately, I think this might screw up our plans to head back to Minnesota for Frannie's wedding."

"No!" Lonnie said immediately. "We *have* to go to that!"

My third-oldest sister, Frannie, was getting married in a month, a January wedding in Minnesota. I could never figure out why Minnesotans did anything other than drink and screw and sleep their way through January. But there were maniacs all over that state that *loved* winter, did polar plunges, sat in frozen fish houses, roared across lakes on snowmobiles when it was twenty below a witch's tit outside. My sister Frannie was one of those ice-veined lunatics, kept her deck furniture out year-round so that she could sit outside on a wicker rocker and watch the sunset on a ten-below evening. Frannie always wanted a winter wedding, was probably praying for a huge snowstorm on her actual wedding day.

"Lonnie, that's a lot of money," I explained slowly, knowing Lonnie wasn't overly familiar with the concept of *I can't afford it*. "I should probably buy a car with four-wheel drive to get up and down the canyon, so I'm sure

I'm looking at a thousand bucks, minimum. And I was already planning on another five hundred or so for the trip back. If I had a little more time to pick up shifts, I could probably swing it, but Frannie's getting married in three weeks."

"I'll loan you the money," Lonnie offered without a thought.

"You don't have an extra thousand bucks lying around."

She paused for several seconds, then shrugged. "I can get it."

"No," I stated. "I am not taking money from your dad. No fucking way."

"It would be coming from me, technically. I wouldn't tell him what it was for."

"No, Lonnie, not up for debate. Thanks, but no thanks. Case closed, conversation over."

"Fine," she said. "But I really, really, *really* want to go to that wedding. I had so much fun with your family last summer."

That was an understatement. Over one long weekend, Lonnie endeared herself to the entire Mountain clan. I'd taken her back the previous summer to our big annual family gathering at my parents' lake trailer in northern Minnesota. She was the first girl I ever introduced to the tribe, and my family celebrated like I'd swiped a Lombardi trophy from the Packers and delivered it to the Vikes. They ooh'd and aah'd over Lonnie, my sisters adopting her as a brand-new sibling. Mainly, I think everyone was pleasantly surprised I didn't bring home some blue-haired lunatic, bull ring through her nose, needle sticking out a vein, illegitimate child hanging off her hip.

"I love her!" my sister Debbie confided to me. "She's so…so…*normal!*"

I laughed. "What's that supposed to mean?"

"Oh, I don't mean it *that* way."

"What way?"

"You know what I mean, Paul."

I didn't know what Debbie meant, but I let everyone fawn over Lonnie because it kept the pressure off me. Lonnie validated me. *If that wonderful woman could live with him, hell, maybe he's not so weird after all?* My mom was particularly happy. Although Catholicism forbid her from letting Lonnie and I share a bed in the lake's single-wide trailer, I had to think my mom was secretly proud of all the pussy I was getting. *Let 'er have it, son, you deserve it! Just not on my property, praise Jesus!* My dad treated Lonnie like royalty, charmed her, showed her all the sides of his personality he reserved for people fortunate enough to be someone else's child. For the most part, my brothers managed to keep their eyes off her tits, even if my brothers-in-law weren't quite so restrained. But I couldn't blame my sisters' husbands; there was no blood relation there. If I wasn't related to Lonnie, I'd be totally into her tits, too, which I wasn't, so I was.

"Sorry, Lon, I know you want to go back to Minnesota. And I should definitely be there for my sister's wedding, but if I can't swing it, I can't swing it." I shrugged. "That's the price of poverty, eh?"

"You're hardly poor. You always have more cash on hand than any twenty-year-old I know."

"*Relatively* poor," I clarified. "I have drinking money, rent money, play money, all that good crap. But I don't have new-car-on-a-moment's-notice money."

"Maybe you'd have new car money if you didn't blow so much on beer, acid, and playing around?"

"Now you're talking crazy, Lonnie." I pushed myself out of my chair and stood up. "And I'm not going to sit around and listen to that lunacy."

I loaded up on as many shifts as I could get over the next week, trying to build the bank accounts. Night after night, I rolled the Bird through the streets of Boulder, same as always, idling next to the police, pulling away from them at stoplights on The Hill. Not one of them pulled me over, no matter how black or thick the clouds pouring out my tailpipe. It was so wrong on so many levels. If the state insisted I commit vehicular homicide, then there should be an objective standard for the violation. It wasn't like drinking and driving, something I could easily hide from the authorities. Emissions were out in the open for every cop on the street to see. And yet, none of them cared, except for one, that bitch. She should have stuck to bartending. One damn cop's subjective opinion was forcing me to put down my old pal like some kind of mechanical Ol' Yeller.

After buying the Daily Camera newspaper every day and pawing through the classifieds for cars, Frannie's wedding began to look more and more unrealistic. Four-wheel drive cars were expensive, and I wasn't going to settle for anything less now that I lived in Eldora. Ten days before her wedding, I decided to give Frannie a call and break the bad news.

"Paul?" Frannie's voice sounded apprehensive and curious at the same time. "Uh-oh, this can't be good."

"Why would you say that?"

"Because you haven't called me a single time since you moved to Colorado."

"I've been busy."

"For eighteen months?"

I laughed. "Put it this way, Frannie, I've called you exactly as many times as you've called me."

She paused. "Touché."

Our lack of communication wasn't anything personal, of course, but Frannie and I were over ten years apart in age and one crucial chromosome in sex. Twenty-year-old men and thirty-two-year-old women have very little in common, even when they're siblings. I was six years old when Frannie headed off to college, still collecting baseball cards and watching Saturday morning Warner Brothers cartoons. Frannie had zero interest in baseball cards, wouldn't even chew the free gum, and she never watched Saturday morning cartoons. She watched Saturday Night Live with the big kids. Essentially, Frannie and I rooted for the same sports teams and had all the same relatives, but that was about the extent of it.

"So why are you calling, then?" she asked.

"Well, sis," I started, then took a long, thoughtful drag on my Marlboro, "it looks like I won't be able to make your wedding."

"No," she said. "No way. You're coming."

I sighed. "It's not looking good, Frannie. Long story, but I have to get rid of the Bird and—"

"The what?"

"The Bird."

"What's the Bird?"

Wow, we really didn't know each other at all. Everyone who knew me knew the Bird. The Bird was a fucking legend.

"You know, my car?" I explained.

"Oh, Jesus, that old piece of shit Sunbird? You're still driving around in that hunk of junk?"

I held my tongue. Frannie was getting married in just over a week – no need to start a sibling squabble. Besides, it was a long-distance call, and the phone company charged double for arguing.

"Well, not for much longer," I said, then explained the whole situation, including the need to buy an expensive, four-wheel drive vehicle. "In other words, sis, I'm strapped," I finished.

When Frannie spoke again after a long pause, she sounded excited. "You know what, Paul? I think I've got exactly what you need. Let me call my friend Emily and get right back to you."

"Um, I'm not following."

"Just let me give her a call. I'll give you the details once I confirm with her. What's your number?"

I rattled off my phone number and hung up. Thirty minutes later, Frannie called me back.

"Hello?"

"God, finally!" Frannie said, exasperated. "Why'd you lock up your phone for so long when you knew I was calling you right back? Your line's been busy for twenty minutes!"

"Oh, right, sorry 'bout that. I should've warned you, we're on a party line up here."

"What's a party line?"

"It's like a community phone. Four different cabins in the valley use the same line but with different phone numbers. So if one of my neighbors is on their phone, I can't use mine until they're done."

A long pause rode the line. "God, you're so weird. What, do you live at the North Pole or something?"

"Close. Santa's a couple miles further up the road."

She scoffed. "Yeah, Mom mentioned you were living in some little cabin in the middle of nowhere or something. Do you, like, have cable and stuff?"

I laughed. "God no, not even regular TV. No TV, no cable, can hardly get a radio station except late at night. I gotta read books like a goddamn cave man. Pretty primitive up here."

I swore I actually heard her eyes roll. Frannie had started working for an accounting firm straight out of college – the only Mountain child to actually complete a degree, as yet – and was now very comfortable in her career. She drove a sporty new car, owned her own home, and took elaborate vacations. Frannie, to say the least, was not a cabin-in-the-woods type of gal.

"Whatever floats your boat, I guess," she said, then quickly changed the subject. "Anyway, I've got great news! I just talked to my friend Emily, and she's got just the car for you, Paul. It's an older Subaru wagon, almost two hundred thousand miles, but those Subarus last forever. *And* it's a four-wheel drive, *and* it has studded snow tires. I mean, it's not the prettiest thing to look at, kind of rusted out, but your old Sunbird isn't that pretty, either, if I remember right."

Once again, I chose not to defend the Bird.

"I talked her down to five hundred as a huge favor to me," she continued. "She was originally asking twelve, so you're getting a *smokin'* deal." Frannie paused for several seconds, let me do the math, then asked, "So does that work for you or what?"

"Um…"

"You and Lonnie can fly one way into Minneapolis," she quickly added before I could answer, "and then you guys can drive the car back. Sound like a plan?"

Her voice was so hopeful. Sure, she'd openly disrespected the Bird right in front of me, but I obviously meant enough to her that she'd called in a big favor to get me to her wedding.

"Okay, Frannie, I'll be there," I said, accepting the Subaru sight unseen. "Tell your friend to bring the car and title to the wedding, and we'll take care of all the paperwork at the reception or whatever."

"Perfect! I knew we could work something out. I mean, come on, you can't miss your *favorite* sister's wedding, right?"

I laughed. "Weird, Frannie, that's the exact adjective I was going to use."

"That's what I thought! See you in a couple weeks!"

4.

The Pope's Peeps Hit the Sauce

I strolled down a jetway, psyched for only my second trip on an airplane, the first since I was fourteen years old.

"The beer is free on flights, you know," Lonnie said as we settled into our assigned seats.

I turned to stare at her. "Did you just say what I thought you said?"

She nodded her head up and down, gravely.

"Will you say it again, please?"

"The beer is free on flights."

"Jesus Christ, why didn't someone tell me this? All this time, I've been driving back and forth across the country like a sucker, paying for booze. I could have saved a fortune."

Lonnie laughed. "The flight's only a couple hours long, big guy, better hit it hard."

They served us drinks before we taxied away from the terminal, and by the time the wheels left the ground, I was finishing my second Bud. I claimed the window seat because flying was still spectacular to me, damn near miraculous. Staring out the window as we rose sharply into the sky, I popped an excitement boner as strong and straight as the skyscrapers below. There I was, a comparatively small creature, zipping through the sky at roughly a million miles per hour. I watched the lights of Denver disappear, and then there was nothing but the vast black empty of the American plains, the windblown fields swirled by January snows. In the sky to my left was the moon, the fucking *moon*. It sat on an even plane with me, almost full, illuminating the night as I glided along like some kind of male Luna, dragging the moon aside my metal chariot.

"This is so fucking cool," I told Lonnie, pointing at the moon.

She smiled at me. "You're such a little boy."

I grabbed her hand and placed it on my bulging boner. "Does that feel like a little boy to you?"

"Hard to say, I've never felt a little boy's penis."

"Well, I have, and this ain't no baby dick, Lon."

"That's gross."

"I was referring to my own when I was a kid."

"That's still gross. I don't want to think about your little boy penis."

I laughed and turned back to the window. Took a slam of beer. I felt like God on high, felt like God if He drank free Budweiser in the sky. Way up in the air, beer between my legs, I gazed down on all the little country towns, small splashes of light in an endless sea of black. All those pockets of human life, tiny people leading tiny lives, just like me, their heads filled with loves and hates and beliefs, jobs, journeys, histories, ambitions. From way up next to the moon, I could see the immensity of human civilization, and the larger it was, the more meaningless I seemed, but I was perfectly at ease with my relative insignificance. I knew I could vanish that instant, plucked from the sky by aliens, and those Nebraska lights below would still shimmer, two million television sets would still illuminate Denver, and the staggering majority of the world would not give one single shit that I had come, gone, and delivered a whole mess of pizza in between, most of it in under thirty minutes.

Wow. Cosmic.

"Would you like another beer?" my stewardess asked. She was hot and young, dressed in a skirt so tight it made me proud to call myself an air traveler.

"Of course. Might as well bring two, save yourself a trip."

She winked at me. "That's exactly what I'll do."

Everything kicked ass in the sky. My stewardess never asked for ID. Lonnie guessed it was because alcohol laws changed over different states, but I knew that wasn't the reason. The stewardess didn't ask because The Law did not apply in The Sky. Laws were for land mammals; in the sky, laws were ludicrous. We were gliding next to the moon, for fuck's sake, who's worried about identification? That's the fucking *moon* out there – Mars, Jupiter, the Big Dipper, all those other constellations that inspired centuries and centuries of astrological nonsense and semi-religious prophesizing. Aquarius, Taurus, the Conjoined Twins Separated at Birth, all the star clusters that supposedly dictate a person's fate from birth to death. All I knew about astrology was that I was a Virgo, and as far as I could tell, Virgos popped big boners on airplanes and drank free Budweiser as hot stewardesses winked at them. From an astrological point of view, that seemed ridiculously lucky.

* * *

Catholic weddings are grueling, especially on a hangover, but especially on a *hangover*. I stood and sat and kneeled in one of my brother Dane's old suit jackets, circa 1979, and wondered how much of my sweat was whiskey and how much was beer. It was Minnesota, four below outside, a chilly sixty-five inside St. Mary's, but I still poured sweat like a wayward priest facing his altar boy accuser. Maybe it was being back in the pews of St. Mary's, my old childhood school/church, that made me so uncomfortable. I hated that church, the boredom, the depressing ridiculousness of religion's impossible dream, like voting for communists or counting on a member of the opposite sex to somehow set you free. I wasn't a believer or an atheist, wasn't even agnostic. I was an ambivalent, simply did not give a shit if God existed or not – wasn't sure what difference it made either way – but organized religion always struck me as fantastically complex wishful thinking, a concocted reality ruled by good vibes and everyone's most benevolent imaginings of a cosmic patriarchy. Growing up with my own father in the house, I had few illusions about the benevolence of the patriarch, whether human or divine.

"How long does this go on?" Lonnie whispered to me during the homily. Her family was loosely Lutheran, and "loosely" was almost too binding a term. She thought she'd been to a full church service twice in her life, both times on Christmas. Conversely, I'd already been to church forty times in utero, after which my mom bottle fed me baptismal water until I could stomach solid food, like the Eucharist.

"Not much longer," I whispered back. "The homily is like halftime. The priest gives us a little locker room pep talk, psyches us up to get back on the field and tackle Protestants."

"We're only halfway through? How long have we been here?"

"Almost three days. Jesus should rise from the dead any minute now."

"I thought that was on Easter?"

"Shows what you know, heathen."

I glanced up at Jesus on the massive wooden cross that hovered above St. Mary's altar, his near-naked body almost floating in air. As an altar boy, I'd robotically genuflected in front of that damn cross a thousand times. I remembered walking the stage dressed in my black and white gown, an outfit most likely designed by the odder ducks of the clergy to feminize their fantasies. Made the sex more palatable that way, more molesty, less faggy. Staring at crucified Jesus as an adult, I thought He actually looked like He was stretching, yawning. In fact, with His eyes closed and mouth slightly open, it looked like He was catching a quick nap. I could relate; Catholic mass put me right to sleep, too.

My mom gave me a disapproving glance when I leaned back to let everyone pass on their way to communion. *What, no cannibalism for you, son?*

You too good to munch your savior? My hypocrisy only went so far, and I'd already hit max capacity as I sat and endured that marathon of tedium without laughing out loud at the more lunatic assertions. I didn't need to top it off with a Jesus biscuit. I'd eat at the reception; fuck the warm-up wafer.

"Thank god that shit's over!" my brother Barry said as we piled into his frozen car and he twisted the key. "I didn't think I'd ever wind up in those pews again."

"That makes two of us," I said. "I was hoping St. Mary's was in my rearview mirror forever."

"I thought it was interesting," Lonnie said, "but it was so *long.*"

"They're preparing you for eternity; gets pretty dull in heaven," I told her. "Once you master the harp, there's not much else to do."

Lonnie laughed. "And what was with all the standing and kneeling and sitting and all that? I never did that the other times I went to church."

"Catholic calisthenics," Barry answered. "Never know when you might have to outrun Satan."

Nearly two hundred Catholics fled St. Mary's and raced across town to the reception, where the celebration began in earnest. All Catholic piety disappears the instant the Pope's peeps hit the sauce. We Catholics attacked the open bar with real enthusiasm, disregarding most of the promises we'd so recently made to God, knowing the Big Guy would give our indulgence an approving wink this time. After all, He gave His ringing endorsement to boozing it up at wedding receptions long ago. For His very first trick – and arguably His best – God's only son turned water into wine at a wedding, transforming a pleasant party into a real rager.

"There you are!" my sister Frannie said as I came around a corner in the hotel's hallway after abandoning everyone to go feed my nicotine addiction in Minnesota's frozen outdoors. "We've been looking all over for you!"

"Sorry, I had to escape for a bit to choke down a ciggie."

We were two hours into the reception, everyone's red face radiating warmth, romance, and free alcohol. The woman standing next to Frannie had clearly taken full advantage of the generous open bar provided by my sister and her freshly minted husband, Evan. The woman swayed in place, struggling against a steady wind only she could feel. Even her lips looked crookedly drunk when she smiled at me.

"Frannie, you never told me your little brother was so cute!" she said too excitedly, tugging on Frannie's arm. "He's adorable!"

Frannie laughed. "I think you're drunk, Emily."

"Woo-hoo!" Emily agreed, raising a glass of red wine high in the air. "That's what weddings are for, bitch!"

Rolling her eyes, Frannie turned to me. "Paul, this is my friend Emily, in case you haven't guessed already."

"Hey," I said, waving. "So I guess I'm buying your car?"

"Oh, I'm gonna need more than a wave, sweetie." She stepped toward me and wrapped me up in a warm, wobbly, too-long hug.

"Um, nice to meet you, too."

"Woo-hoo!" Emily said again. "We're having some fucking fun now!"

"Alright, my job's done here," Frannie said. "You two can work out the car's paperwork on your own. I've got two hundred people waiting in the reception hall, and I'm the star of the show!" Frannie caught my eye, then pointed a serious finger at Emily. "Watch out for her, Paul, she's a wild woman. I love her, but she's a nut, especially when she drinks too much."

"Damn straight!" Emily said. "I'm a crazy little saucy bitch!"

I laughed. "I'll be careful, sis."

"And get back to the party quick," Frannie added. "It's my big day; I want my whole family around!"

Frannie turned, her long white dress trailing behind her. She walked toward the ballroom, toward a long life of marital ups and downs, toward children, toward suburban struggles, toward a diverse financial portfolio and a potential pack of grandkids.

"I guess it's just you and me now, sweetie," Emily said in a lowered voice. She sipped her red wine suggestively, her eyes leering at me over her glass. "All alone."

"Looks that way."

"You really are cute, you know."

I laughed. Emily was dee-run-kay, *drunk*. She was also sort of hot in a bleary-eyed, dressed up, primped out sort of way. She had brown-gold hair, and she'd curled it in teenage girl ringlets, bouncy on her shoulders. She wore her makeup effectively, although she didn't really need it. She had clear, smooth skin and a naturally pretty face, angular features. Her dress was a silver, shimmery number, off her shoulders, and it hugged surprisingly generous curves for such a slender woman. But all women looked their best at weddings. It was almost a competition amongst them – the dresses, the hairstyles, the makeup, and, of course, their weight. All their dieting, all their self-restraint, all their suffering was well worth it, in my opinion. Their starvation was a small price to pay for my visual pleasure.

"Thanks," I eventually replied. "You're pretty attractive yourself."

She stepped in close, too close for a typical used car transaction, even if it was four-wheel-drive. Her breasts lightly brushed my chest. "Attractive?" she slurred-asked. Slursked. "Cutie, that's something you say to some old bitch. I may be older than you, but I'm no old bitch. I'm only twenty-nine. I don't want to be *attractive*, Paul, I want to be fucking *hot*."

"Fair enough."

"So am I fucking hot or what?" She tilted her head to the side, bit her lower lip seductively, and spread her arms wide to give me a full view of her body.

"Yes, you're fucking hot, Emily."

"Woo-hoo!" she yelled for what felt like the tenth time, then raised her glass in the air again. Some of the wine sloshed out, but Emily didn't seem to notice. "You're so sweet. Come on, let me show you your new car. All the paperwork's in the glovebox."

She reached out and grabbed my hand. Holding hands, we trudged off down the hallway. I kept my eyes peeled for family members, knowing this would not go over well, considering how much everyone loved Lonnie.

Strolling hand-in-hand away from the party with some attractive, drunk friend of Frannie's would require some serious 'splaining, even if it was currently innocent. With each step I moved away from the reception, however, it felt less innocent.

"Aren't you going to freeze your ass off?" I asked Emily as we reached the hotel exit.

"I'll be fine. I'm tough."

I scoffed. "Here, take this." Pulling off Dane's suit jacket, I wrapped it around her shoulders.

"Ooo, you're so chivalrous!" She held the jacket closed at her neck with one hand, hooked her other hand through my arm, and hugged her body tight to me. "Come on, let's go!"

We pushed open the door and Minnesota January attacked. The temp had dipped down as night fell, now closing in on ten below, and snow fell softly but steadily. Emily laughed out loud, yelled, "*Ho-lee sheee-iittte!*" and yanked me hard and fast across the parking lot. I couldn't believe she could move so fast in high heels across a snow-swept parking lot. When we reached a silver-ish snow mound near the back of the lot, Emily whipped a set of keys out of her small wedding purse, opened the driver's door, then ran around to unlock the passenger side. I slid into the captain's chair as she piled into the passenger seat, both of us slamming our doors hard against the Minnesota monster outside.

"Jesus fuck!" I said.

"Start it up! It's freezing out there!"

She handed me the keys and I fired up the engine. I flipped off the heater's blower — no point cranking more freezing air into the interior — but I twisted the temperature dial to full hot.

"How's the heater in this beast?" I asked.

"Good, but it takes a few minutes to heat up." She turned to face me in her seat, then spread her arms wide and wiggled her fingers. "Keep me warm in the meantime."

Maneuvering around the steering wheel, stick shift, and emergency brake was awkward, but I managed to pull Emily's thin body against mine, my suitcoat acting as a blanket of sorts. She squeezed me tight, and it was soon obvious she wanted more than body heat. She pressed her cold tits against my chest, her hard nipples rubbing on me. Turning her face into my neck, Emily breathed lightly on my skin, her lips grazing my flesh. She even massaged me, the little bitch, squeezed my spine, her fingers crawling up the nape of my neck and toying with my shorthairs.

"Mmm, you feel so good," she whispered.

Shit, all that recent churchin' for nothin'. I was about to sin egregiously. Satan, I decided, is a hot chick in a cold car. *Damn you, Satan, when did you get so good looking?* I should not be fucking around at Frannie's wedding. Lonnie was right inside, partying it up with my relatives, growing closer to them, steadily becoming part of the family. Nevertheless, I *would* fuck around at Frannie's wedding, I knew. I couldn't turn down an attractive woman any more than I could turn down a free beer. Didn't matter where, didn't matter when. If I were offered a free Budweiser at an AA meeting, I'd gulp it down right beneath a twelve-step poster. If some hot babe offered herself up at a funeral, I'd bang her at the burial.

"Yeah, you feel good, too," I said, sighing out my resignation. And she did feel good. Emily felt great, in fact, her dress all silky, her body pressed tightly to mine, the smell of many, many alcoholic beverages wafting up from her lips.

"Mmm, kiss me, sweetie," she said, but she didn't wait for me to kiss her. She kissed me instead, and it was sloppy and drunk and dirty, and I fucking loved it. I kissed her right back in the freezing cold car, our breath creating alcohol clouds that engulfed our heads and fogged the windshield. The stick shift dug into my knee, her teenage-girl curls tickled my face, and her slow, drunk tongue wandered around my mouth like some old, crippled dog staggering toward his bowl. Nevertheless, my dick sprang to life against the emergency brake. Emily breathed buckets of red wine into my mouth, moved her hands onto my chest, and squeezed my pecs. She finally broke free of my lips long enough to flip the Subaru's blower on high, and suddenly, blazing hot air poured into the car.

"Oh my god, that feels awesome!" Emily said, throwing her head back and laughing. "Now it's really getting steamy in here!"

I stared at her pretty face, her curls, her thin body, as the warmth began to fill our small confines. "You really are hot, Emily."

"And you are a bad, bad boy." She smiled and wagged her finger at me. "I heard you brought a girlfriend with you all the way from Colorado?"

I could only shrug.

"But here you are, getting all hot and steamy with me."

I shrugged again.

"It's okay." She reached out and ran a finger down my cheek. "My boyfriend's inside, too. I don't give a shit." She giggled, then dropped her hand down to my dress pants and popped the button. "But we need to be quick. Frannie will get suspicious. She knows how I am."

"Trust me, I can be super quick."

"Most men can." She laughed. "Still, maybe I should just suck your cock and save some time?"

I arched my eyebrows. "Well, if you insist..."

She giggled again. "Oh, I insist. I love sucking cock, actually. I'm kind of a slut, in case you haven't figured that out. It's not exactly a secret." Emily slid my zipper down, her bloodshot eyes locked on mine the whole time. "You'll have to pull them down for me, sweetie, it's too tight in this car."

I leaned the seat all the way back and pushed my dress pants down to my ankles. Emily descended. She was enthusiastic, exactly what I would expect from a self-avowed slut. Emily *needed* that damn cock in her mouth, like a baby needs a pacifier or a grizzled old gambler needs a cigar. Some things just belong in some people's mouths. Being in a time crunch, I didn't try to impress her with my stamina. I closed my eyes, focused my entire mind on the unbelievable pleasure radiating up from my crotch, and before she even had to give the shaft a single hand stroke, I peeled Emily's head off my knob. I unloaded onto my stomach as she tickled my balls and giggled at my thumping penis.

"Oh my god," I said under the racket of the car's heater.

"You like?" She smiled up at me, nibbling her lower lip.

"I love."

"So I'm pretty good?"

"You could go pro," I told her. "Not that you want to, of course, but you know, if times got tough."

She laughed, scooted her body back onto the passenger seat, and reclined it all the way. Hiking up her dress, she pulled her panties down past her knees. "Gimme your hand, sweetie."

I gave her my hand. She placed it underneath her dress on her extremely wet pussy.

"Can you feel my clit?"

"Sure can," I answered, but from that awkward angle, I couldn't really tell what I was feeling.

"Good." She closed her eyes. "Just keep your hand right there."

She actually kept it there for me, controlling my hand. Emily gyrated against it, rolled her clitoris against my fingertips, and miraculously masturbated herself into a beautiful orgasm in under one minute. It was mesmerizing, a real talent at work. It was like watching Michael Jordan drain jumpers – so effortless. I was used to Lonnie and Sabrina, women who had to warm up their clits and immerse themselves in the moment, and even then, it still took quite a bit of craftmanship to bring them to full throttle. Not Emily. Emily came like a man, as if she were yanking out a quick one on the toilet after a satisfying dump.

She gave me my hand back, pulled up her panties, and smoothed out her shimmery dress. "Okay, no telling," she said, smiling over at me.

"Don't you worry."

"Frannie would kill me."

"And that would be her second murder of the night, right after killing me."

Adjusting her chair back to its upright position, Emily leaned over and kissed me quickly on the cheek. "You're sweet." She reached into the glove box and pulled out an envelope of paperwork. "Let's sign this up quick and get back to the party, okay?"

It was a bizarre twist back to normalcy, but the business of America is business, after all, and Emily and I had a monetary transaction to transact. She signed over the title, I cut her a check, and her 1983 Subaru wagon became my new pizza car. Emily had me drive her around to the hotel's entrance, told me she'd go in first, and instructed me to wait ten minutes before returning to the reception in order to thwart any suspicion. I drove her to the front door as she fixed her hair and makeup in the visor mirror, and before she got out, she licked a Kleenex and wiped lipstick off my mouth and chin. Emily was a consummate pro, a habitual cheater who had the routine down pat. I could learn a lot from her.

"It's been fun, cutie!" she said, winking at me as she got out of the car.

"Amen."

"Take good care of my little Subie!"

"I will."

She closed the door, and off went Frannie's friend Emily, back to the reception and the booze and her boyfriend and her hypersexual life. I felt confident I would never see her again after that night, but if I did, she probably wouldn't remember our little tryst. I assumed I was one of dozens, if not hundreds.

As planned, I returned to the reception ten minutes later, penis drained, my brain a little shocked by recent events. No one was the wiser, though. Lonnie was out on the dancefloor with my father, juking and jiving to Elvis, the '50s rock of my dad's generation. She smiled and laughed with him, everyone having a ball. I walked straight past the dancefloor toward the free beer. Lonnie saw me and waved, shot me a huge, happy grin, and I knew right then that she'd hardly noticed I was gone. Man, it was great having a huge family; they could swallow up my girlfriend within their ranks and provide cover for all my lechery.

"Oh my god, your dad is so much fun!" Lonnie said breathlessly when she returned to our table.

"Yeah, he's always been a real blast, just ask any of his kids."

Lonnie ignored my comment, leaned in, and kissed me warmly. "I'm having such a good time. I really love your family."

"They love you, too." I saw a quick tear form in her left eye, the famous Lonnie waterworks ramping up. "Uh-oh, are we about to have an emotional moment?" I asked.

"I just…" she started, and a little sob fell out. "I just wish you would have kids with me someday so this could be my second family."

And then she did start crying, because that's what Lonnie did. I pulled her in close and hugged her, but I didn't try to soothe her with lies. We were way past soothing lies. We'd had the talks and the arguments a million times, and neither one of us was budging on the kid question. Instead, I let her cry on my shoulder for a minute or so, then told her, "I got the car all squared away."

She finished her short outburst, sniffled a little, dabbed her eyes. "Oh yeah? How is it?"

"Feels solid. Little rusty, but seems to run well enough."

"Good. You really need four-wheel-drive in the mountains." Lonnie sighed, bringing her emotional moment to an end. "Will you dance with me, Pablo?"

"Sure, once a slow one comes on."

A slow one came on two songs later, something about if you leave me now, a love like ours, letting it slip away, all that sappy bullshit that works so well at weddings. We danced to the soft rock of the mid '70s in the low, sparse, dancefloor light and gazed romantically into each other's eyes. Lonnie looked spectacular, all gussied up, her hair perfect, her boobs high and plentiful. She told me she loved me, and I made stupid jokes to distract from how poorly I danced. Before long, getting a blow job in the parking lot faded from memory, as if the blowie happened to someone else's penis, just some random cock Emily found lying in the snow. The beer flowed freely and my girlfriend was the most beautiful woman in the reception hall. I wished I could see her the way my brother Barry saw his girlfriend Marilyn or Frannie saw her new husband Evan, something solid and lasting. But Lonnie and I did not have the luxury of forever. So we danced to our tragedy and laughed and enjoyed what time we had, and when we stumbled back to our hotel room that night, we made slow, messy love on sheets someone else would have to clean.

5.

Short Sentences and Fuck Words

ELDORA, COLORADO

1991

"Maybe we should get a hotel in Lincoln," Lonnie suggested.

"It's not that bad out."

"Paul, seriously?" She pointed out the window.

The snow started in earnest in Des Moines, and now, just past Omaha, it was blowing sideways across the highway. It was starting to stick, too, the pavement disappearing beneath a gradually thickening blanket of white. The semis, the professional drivers, had slowed to 50, forcing me to plow through left lane drifts in order to pass.

"I've got four-wheel-drive and studded snow tires, Lonnie. I'm damn near invincible."

She shook her head. "The radio says it's only going to get worse as we go west, probably won't let up until we hit Colorado."

"What do those idiots know? It's not like they have radar and satellites and shit."

"Yeah, I'm sure they're just poking their heads out the window and guessing."

"Okay, they may have scientific equipment, but I have balls. Balls beats technology every time." Lighting a cigarette, I cracked my new, electric window. A blast of winter leapt into the car, carrying sleet and snow alongside it. "Sorry, Lon, but I have a closing shift tomorrow night. We gotta get home."

"I'm sure Joel will understand."

"Right!" I laughed. "You know Joel doesn't let us skip shifts, not for any reason."

Joel's Mormon work ethic allowed for exactly zero bullshit when it came to missing work. If Brigham Young could lead a starving pack of fifty-five wives and other assorted believers over the Rocky Mountains into Utah, we sure as shit could show up for a pizza shift. Nevertheless, every driver had tried to call in sick at least once, only to have Joel patronize them: *Yes, yes, I totally understand, Paul. Yes, you sound very sick, dude. Dude, I totally feel your pain; it's going to be a tough shift for you. See you at 5:00. Don't be late, dude.*

"Besides, the dogs will be all alone," I said, appealing to Lonnie's motherly instinct. Franzen and his girlfriend Cassie were happy to get away from the city and spend the weekend in the mountains at our cabin, but they were leaving that evening, and the dogs would be left outside.

"Yeah, I know," Lonnie said, sighing. "I don't want to leave them overnight in the cold, but I also don't want to die on some Nebraska highway."

She reclined the passenger seat all the way back, much like Emily had done two nights before, but Lonnie did not place my hand on her wet vagina to help her masturbate. Instead, she curled up and closed her eyes against the raging blizzard outside.

Two hours later, I was in the meat of the storm. The sun had abandoned all us fools to our fate on the Nebraska highways, left us to struggle our way through Midwest madness. The snow hurled across my windshield in sheets, I-80 disappearing from view for several long seconds at a time. Highway speeds dropped as precipitously as the temperature, and I now crawled along the frozen interstate at 40 miles per hour, dangerously creeping past semis. Wild gusts of wind shoved those giant trucks in and out of the left lane, and their enormous tires splattered my windshield with gallons of road sludge. Jesus, what the fuck were those idiots still doing on the highway? That was trucker mania, overconfident dudes with big beards and bigger stomachs, plowing their way across America in the mistaken belief their payload was indispensable. *I ain't never missed a delivery, boss, and I ain't gonna start today!* Crazy bastards. The west coast could survive a day or two without Kellogg's Raisin Bran or Maybelline mascara. It wasn't like they had to deliver important shit, for fuck's sake, like getting pizza to spoiled college brats.

"This is totally insane," Lonnie said, waking up long enough to glance outside and offer some unconstructive criticism.

"Shh, no chat." I had a perma-cig locked between my teeth, my body hunched stiffly over the steering wheel. The Subaru's defrost was no match for the ice and snow and wind, so I had to reach out and clear the inside of the windshield every two minutes with a ski glove.

"You're honestly going to kill me out here, Paul."

"Only if you keep talking."

"Hey, that's not very nice!"

"Lonnie, seriously, stop. I need my full concentration on what I'm doing."

Trucks began appearing in the ditch, lying on their sides like exhausted mechanical monsters after the great war of Man vs. Machine. Their red flashers splashed slow and lonely light into the Nebraska darkness. Wiser truckers stopped their rigs under overpasses, hiding from the mayhem. After another hour, I was almost the only driver left on the highway, the last man dumb enough or brave enough or arrogant enough to plow across the American plains in the height of a January blizzard. The relentless snow buried all the tire tracks, forcing me to guess where the lanes might be, and without the headlights and taillights of other vehicles, Nebraska grew as dark as a murderer's mind. Worse, the snow hurtling across my sightline made me snowblind, and I regularly had to look away for dangerous seconds, shut my eyes tight, and shake my head to get my vision back in order.

By the time I reached Ogallala near the Colorado border, the storm mellowed, but I was completely frazzled. With four-plus hours still in front of me, I thought I better fuel up both the car and my brain. I pulled into a huge truck stop where at least fifty semis huddled together, their engines idling, plumes of diesel exhaust ripping a second hole through Lonnie's precious ozone layer. I was the only customer at the pumps, apparently the last American left in Nebraska with more balls than brains. After filling my tank, I went inside and poured myself an enormous cup of old, burnt coffee that smelled like it had spent the better part of the '90s on the burner plate. Grabbing a big sugar blast of candy, as well, I carried my two items up to the young kid manning the cash register.

"That coffee's been there for hours," he said, pointing at my cup. "I thought everyone was off the interstate, so I let it sit. You want me to make you a fresh pot?"

"Thanks, but I need to get rolling. Still got a long way to go."

He nodded slowly, considering, then reached for a pill bottle on the display rack next to the register. "You ever try these?" He shook the bottle before handing it to me.

Ephedrine, the bottle read. I glanced at the image on the label, several little white pills with two indented lines crisscrossing each one.

"Looks like those white cross speeders some kids used to sell when I was in high school," I said.

"That's exactly what they are. They work like a champ, man."

I whistled low. "Damn. Those things were hard to get back then, had to go through headshops or mail order them from the back of rock magazines. Are they legal now?"

"Yep. They sell 'em at most truck stops. Truckers eat the fuckin' things like candy."

I rubbed my chin. "Well, those guys are professional drivers. If it's good enough for them, I guess it's good enough for me."

The kid smiled. "You're going to love this shit. Keeps me going whenever I'm stuck on the graveyard shift. The rest of your ride's going to fly by, trust me."

Back in my car, I swallowed three of the little pills with my coffee, and an hour later, my brain was on fire. I found some loud stuff on the AM dial, Z-Rock, the heavy shit no one played until well past midnight. When I twisted the volume, Lonnie rolled over and wrapped her scarf tightly around her ears, hoping to protect her brain from Metallica and Motorhead and Anthrax. Nice try, little girl. You can't run, you can't hide. *Fall on your knees for the Phantom Lord!* My head tingled with pins and needles, every hair on end. With each new song, goose bumps crawled up and down my arms and spine, and I slapped the steering wheel in time with the strong, meaty, satisfying Metal. Out of nowhere, new story ideas exploded in my brain, *great* ideas, and I couldn't wait to get back to my typewriter to start banging them out... *They hurled down the desperate Nebraska highway and the young blonde cringed beneath the onslaught of blaring thrash metal, unaware that the speed in her boyfriend's veins could not, would not, allow him to turn down the volume. She curled herself into a tight ball on the passenger seat recently occupied by a wilder woman, a Minnesota nympho who came like Michael Jordan shot jumpers...* My heart hammered in my chest, and there was not one fatigued cell left in my body. The very concept of sleep seemed ridiculous. Exhaustion was for weaklings, for chickenshit travelers who couldn't power through a Nebraska blizzard like I could, 'cause I was a fucking *man.*

Turning off the interstate, I swallowed three more pills to intensify the final two-hour slog up to Eldora, but also to gain the necessary energy to see my dogs. Rummy and Evie had never been without us for so long, and I knew my little buddies would go nuts the second we showed up. I had to be up for it, and boy oh boy, was I up for it. I'd play with them until the sun came up, and then I'd make a big ass breakfast, and then I'd write down some of my new awesome story ideas, and then I'd go ski a few runs at Eldora, and then I'd, and then I'd, and then I'd...

The ephedrine years had begun.

* * *

Phil and I stood on our skis at the top of Eldora mountain, choosing our lines for one last power blast down the slopes. With nearly two weeks of budding addiction under my belt, I was flying high, the ephedrine coursing through my veins. Mixed with afternoon whiskey, I'd finally achieved the perfect buzz I'd chased all my life. With ephedrine, I could experience all the beauty of booze without any of the sloppiness. The entire course of each alcohol outing was now like the first three beers on a Friday night, a steady continuum of energetic, euphoric boozing. There was no late-stage grogginess, no exhaustion, no stumbling and stammering. Everything was up up up, the booze and speed working together to focus my world and make all existence more interesting.

"Let's make it a good one before we head home," Phil said.

"I don't want to head home; this is too much fun. Besides, Lonnie's pissed at me."

"Yeah? What'd you do this time?"

"Grew testicles, as far as I can tell." I shrugged. "Something about being a man, not caring enough about polar bears or world hunger or the American patriarchy or some shit. Honestly, I really don't know. I stopped listening after a while."

That wasn't exactly true. While I did stop listening, it was only because listening interrupted my talking. I debated mercilessly these days. And then I debated, and then I debated some more. I didn't even care about the topic; I'd take any side of any issue so long as it was the opposite of Lonnie's position. Ephedrine made me a world-class blabbermouth, gave me the kind of argumentative stamina generally reserved for know-it-all assholes sitting at the end of every bar in every town in America. I now took any topic late into the night, gnashed every point / counterpoint between my teeth until Lonnie begged me to drop it. I eventually would, of course, right after I kicked that dead horse in the kidneys a couple dozen times.

"Sounds like Boulder's political campus atmosphere is getting to Lonnie," Phil said.

"Definitely."

"CU does that to everyone, man, given enough time." He shrugged. "Oh well, fuck it. Take out your frustration on the snow, dude!" With that, he dropped in, and in perfect Phil fashion, he manhandled the mountain.

Pulling off our boots on the bumper of his car twenty minutes later, Phil surprised me by returning to our previous conversation. "So is Lonnie really diving into the feminism thing?" he asked.

I puffed out my cheeks and blew out a long breath. "She's getting into all kinds of political stuff, man. You name it, she's angry about it. I swear, fuckin' purring kittens and smiling babies would piss her off these days. She's been going to all these campus meetings, reading a bunch of political books. Lately, she's been on this big kick about how everyone needs to pay more taxes, broaden the welfare state, food stamps, homeless shelters, whatever. Honestly, dude, coming from someone who's never had to think twice about money, it's pretty annoying. Easy to say that shit when you have an endless fountain of funds flowing from Daddy's coffers, you know?"

"Sounds to me like you're just selfish," Phil said, a weird smile on his face.

"I don't know if I'm being–"

Phil laughed and waved his hand, cutting me off. "I'm just giving you shit, Paul," he said. "You're a big reader, right?"

"You could say that."

"Good. I have a book you need to read, sounds like you're ready for it. I'll loan it to you."

"Right on. What is it?"

"Too complicated to get into right now. I'll explain more when I give it to you. Besides, I gotta get to work, and you gotta get to a funeral."

I sighed. "Yeah, no kidding. Thanks for reminding me."

An hour and a half later, I pulled the Bird into the Boulder Municipal Junkyard's parking lot, the funeral home and burial site for the poor's abandoned vehicles. Lonnie rolled up next to me. I grabbed the Bird's title from the glovebox, slipped the keys out of the ignition, and stepped out of my old friend.

"This won't take long," I told Lonnie.

She stuck out her lower lip. "You going to be okay?"

"No."

"Poor Pablo."

"Poor Bird. He deserves better than this."

She reached out her window and gently squeezed my forearm. "This too shall pass."

"It's not fair."

"Life's not fair."

"Got any more clichés, Lon?"

"Nope, fresh out."

"Good." I turned and walked toward the junkyard's corrugated steel structure, opened the door, and entered the office area.

I hated the fucking junkyard – hated the cold, cruel, scrap metal faces, the judgmental eyes that sized me up and dressed me down as they prepared to barter. The junkyard had an organized crime feel to it, like a business not quite legal but reluctantly tolerated, and I swore all the employees were packing. The shelves were filthy, everything greasy, and the whole place smelled like rusty bolts and bloody knuckles. Just stepping inside, I felt like I needed a Band Aid and a big swig of WD-40. There was too much testosterone at the junkyard, full radiators of testosterone, old gas cans of testosterone, everything a fuckin' contest of manly-man knowledge. Whenever I needed to pull a junkyard part to save a little money, I had to endure endless questions that had nothing to do with the part I needed. The junkyard dogs weren't happy until they could trip me up with cam shaft specs, manifold intake questions, and other unrelated automotive grilling. Those pricks only felt good about themselves once they emasculated every other dude in the room, knowing the average man's knowledge of the internal combustion engine fell far short of their own.

"Yeah?" a very hairy dude said as I stepped through the door.

"Selling my wheels," I announced, keeping my statement brief, waiting for an opening to insert profanity. Short sentences and fuck words – that was the junkyard way.

"Running?" the man asked, scratching his stubble, his hairy knuckles caked with old motor oil.

"Yeah."

We both lit cigarettes and stared silently at each other through our first long drag. Part of the ritual.

"Why the fuck you sellin' a running vehicle?" Hairy asked. "Fix the fuckin' thing."

I shrugged. "Too fuckin' expensive to fix. Fuckin' city's stealing it from me. Emissions bullshit."

He scoffed and shook his head. "That *is* bullshit."

"Fuckin-A."

Hairy nodded, smoked, and gauged me for several seconds. "Whatcha got?"

"'80 Sunbird."

"Miles?"

"One eighty."

"Four banger?"

"Yep."

"Two-point-five liter?"

"Yep."

"Sport hatch?"

"Nah. Regular."

"Hmm." He shook his head a little, feigning disappointment. "You got the title?"

"Yep." I pulled the thick, green square of paper out of my back pocket and shook it.

He nodded some more, smoked some more. We both ashed on the floor. Fuck it, it was a junkyard.

"I'll give you fifty bucks," Hairy stated flatly.

I shook my head and whistled low. "Come on, man, he's still running. You'll make eighty off his tires alone, twenty-five apiece off the battery, starter, and alternator. Gimme at least a hundred."

He pursed his lips, lifted his eyebrows, and shrugged. "I'll give you seventy."

"Come on, a hundred is such a nice, round number, easily divisible by all kinds of shit."

Hairy shook his head firmly at the entire concept of mathematics. "I'll give you seventy-five and not one cent more. You don't like it, I don't give a shit. Take your piece of crap somewhere else."

I sighed irritably, but he had the hairy-knuckled upper hand, and we both knew it. I walked up to the counter and unfolded the Bird's title. "Got a pen?"

He smiled smugly and slid a Bic across the counter. I scribbled my name and dated the title like a defeated general signing an unfavorable treaty. It was an awful feeling, a real gut punch to my self-confidence. I felt like I was turning my child over to social services, too broke, drunk, and lazy to feed the little fucker.

"Keys?" Hairy said.

I slid the keys across the counter. He flipped them up in the air, caught them on his palm, and they disappeared into his pocket. Ejecting the cash register drawer, he tucked the Bird's title under the money tray, then pulled out three twenties, a ten, and a five. All the bills were oil stained.

"Thanks," I said.

"Good doin' business." Hairy pulled out a ledger and dismissively began recording his most recent score. I stuffed my meager seventy-five bucks into my wallet and slunk away.

The Bird sat silently outside, no clue that I'd just betrayed him. I walked over to the old guy, stood at his driver's door, and stroked his roof reassuringly. "I gotta give you up, big guy," I told him, and right then, the memories poured in. I remembered the long weekends during my University of Minnesota days, just me and the Bird and some huge novel weighing down the passenger seat. We'd drive down to Iowa and tool around farm country, not really looking for anything, just a teenage kid and his car, checking out the world. I'd find an empty field or some hidden dirt road where I could recline on the Bird's hood, smoke cigarettes, and pound a few cans of Busch while reading. When night crept over the fields, I'd fold down the back seat and set up my sleeping bag, read beneath my reading light, and stare up through the Bird's large hatch window at billions of Iowa stars. I roamed northern Minnesota in the Bird, South Dakota, North Dakota, wandered all over the Great American West before eventually landing in Colorado. The Bird was my only possession that had any real meaning for me. But that was all over now, per governmental decree. I had to dump the Bird off as if he were a metal hunk of valueless nothing, leave him to get picked apart by junkyard scavengers like some dead animal in the desert.

"We had a good ride, pal." I slapped the Bird's roof three final times. "Thanks for the memories, buddy."

I walked away, slipped into Lonnie's passenger seat, and tried not to focus on my poor old friend anymore. He looked so lonely. So abandoned. Instead, I turned to look at Lonnie, and oddly, I saw a few tears dribbling down her cheek. Damn, even for Lonnie, this scenario seemed pretty far outside the emotional landscape. I couldn't help laughing a little.

"Don't laugh at me."

"I'm laughing *with* you, Lon."

"I'm not laughing," she said, sniffling, "and I don't know how you can laugh right now. It's so sad."

"It's sad for me, but I don't see how it's sad for you."

She pointed at the Bird. "That piece of junk's always been such a part of you, part of us. Now he's gone, just like that." She snapped her fingers. "I guess it just reminds me how time moves on, how nothing lasts. Someday that will be us, you going one way, me the other. Everything changes, whether we like it or not."

I slid over and kissed her, wiped her wet cheeks. "That's sweet of you." Sitting back in my seat, I reached for my ciggies and cracked the window. "But that's the way it goes, Lon. Life's a dick and then you suck it." I lit my smoke, took a long drag, and blew a stream out the window. "Fuck it, though, let's get out of here and stop thinking about it. What do you say we go get super drunk? I mean, *super* fucking drunk. We can go see if the Sundowner will serve me, and if not, we can head up the canyon to the Pioneer Inn."

Lonnie smiled at me. "There's nothing you can't drink your way through, right?"

"Bingo," I said, pointing at her. "I've taught you well, Skywalker."

The Sundown Saloon in downtown Boulder served me plenty. But plenty wasn't enough on the day I lost my oldest friend, so we drove up to Nederland where the Pioneer Inn served me plentier. Lonnie and I toasted the Bird, told Bird travel tales. We laughed about me having to jump in and out the driver's window to deliver pizza for the last six months after the Bird's door hinge finally gave out and couldn't be trusted to open and close anymore. Lonnie revealed that she almost didn't date me after seeing my car, too embarrassed to ride around in that old rust bucket, so I made her apologize publicly and dedicate the next round of Jagermeister shots to the Bird's colorful personality. All the ephedrine pills I swallowed kept me whizzing along until closing time, but no amount of speed could overcome that much alcohol. The drive home to our cabin was hazy at best. Still, I managed to keep one eye on the road and both feet on the wheel. I never did find out how I got into bed, but I woke up feeling miserable and empty, one Bird less of a man.

* * *

"Jesus Christ," I said.

"I know," Phil replied, "it's a whole lotta novel."

The paperback was gigantic, *War and Peace* gigantic, *Les Misérables* gigantic. I didn't recognize the title: *Atlas Shrugged.*

I pointed at Ayn Rand's name on the cover. "Never heard of her."

"She's Russian, fled to America after the Bolshevik revolution in the early 20th century. This is the book I was telling you about when we were skiing. I think it's time you read it."

I flipped the book open robotically, but the print was too small to see in the 3:00 a.m. darkness. We stood at our idling cars, our Pizza Place closing shifts running late after a wildly busy night.

"This is going to take me a year to read, dude."

"You might be surprised," Phil said, shrugging. "Once you fall in, it's pretty addictive. I've read it twice. I read *The Fountainhead* twice, too. That's another one of hers that's almost as huge. When Ayn Rand gets rolling, she's hard to put down, man. I think I even read somewhere that *Atlas Shrugged* got voted, like, the second most influential book of all time by some big readers' club or something."

I looked at him, my eyebrows arched. "Wow. In that case, I'm surprised I've never heard of it. What was the first most influential book?"

Phil smiled. "The Bible."

"Huh, pretty heavy company." Although I was not on Good Terms with the Good Book, anything mentioned in the same conversation as *The Fate that Awaits* had to have some merit. I tapped the cover of the book. "So what's *Atlas Shrugged* about?"

Phil laughed. "It took her twelve-hundred pages of miniscule type to explain what it's about. Hard to summarize. I mean, technically, it's philosophy, but it's written out as a fictional story." He turned his eyes up to the sky and thought about it for several seconds. "I guess I'd say it's primarily about whether it's better to build a society around the individual or the group." He shook his head briskly. "Nah, that's not even it, really. Just read it, dude. You'll see what I mean once you get going. Trust me, you and I will be talking about it a lot over the coming months. If nothing else, *Atlas Shrugged* sparks conversation and debate." He pointed at the book in my hand. "That shit will change your life, Paul, one way or the other. Changed mine."

I cocked my head, my curiosity growing. Phil gave me a brief wave and slid into his Subaru. I slid into my Subaru. Subaru was the de facto Colorado State Car – *Colorado, brought to you by Subaru!* – but my new ride was no Bird, not even close. It had so little personality that I didn't even name it, didn't know if it was a he or a she. It was just "my car" or "the Subaru." The doors all worked, engine started every time, and I could barely see any exhaust puffing out the tailpipe. I blew more Marlboro smoke out the window than the Subaru blew out its tail. How lame. The Subaru was great in the snow, though, so I kept it around, like an uninspiring girlfriend I kept dating simply because she was great in the sack.

I got back to Eldora late that night, went straight to bed, but I started in on Phil's book the very next afternoon over a hot mug of coffee and a chalky ephedrine or two. I read the first page, then the first chapter, and I didn't stop reading until I had to go to work that night. The following day, I did the exact same thing.

"Jesus, you've been at that for six hours," Lonnie said on my third day of reading. She'd just returned to our cabin after a long walk with Rummy and Evie, only to find me sitting in the exact same spot on the couch. "What are you reading?"

I flipped the cover around so she could see it.

"Never heard of it."

"Me neither. Phil gave it to me."

She raised one eyebrow curiously. "Interesting. What's it about?"

"Everything."

"Everything?"

I glanced up at her and shrugged. "Yeah, pretty much. The entire dynamic of human society, the world, nature, human nature, God, organized religion, history, philosophy, human beings' place on the planet, who we are, what we are, how we can live individually and together."

"Sounds like something Phil might give you. He can be a little intense,"

Lonnie said, rolling her eyes.

I disregarded her, returned my attention to the task at hand, and continued the marathon.

Ayn Rand wrote stiffly, her characters wooden and unrealistic, almost robotic. The dialogue was often forced, inhuman, and redundantly superfluously repetitively excessive. Why say in ten words what you can say in ten months? But polished writing was not the point of her book. She only used fiction as a means of expressing an individualist worldview, a perspective that deeply appealed to a twenty-year-old man who started a snow shoveling business at age ten, a lawn mowing service at thirteen, then moved across the country at eighteen without a whiff of financial assistance. When Ayn Rand told me that I was not saddled at birth with some cosmic debt to others, I replied: *A-Fuckin'-Men, Ayn-Fuckin'-Rand!* I'd always wished everyone the best, but I had my hands full taking care of my own shit. When Ayn Rand explained how the great altruist experiment in her native Russia almost immediately morphed into a genocide, I reached for Lonnie's Popov vodka and drank several shots in honor of the millions of dead comrades in the Soviet Union's various gulags. Funny how quickly "Live for Others" in theory became "Die for Others" in practice.

"Alan says that's trash," Lonnie said, pointing at *Atlas Shrugged* as I sat reading on the couch for the seventh day in a row. "He says it's a bunch of libertarian poison, corporate capitalist nonsense."

I looked up from the book. "Is that what Alan says?"

"Yes."

I shrugged. "Oh well. Alan's a dweeb."

"He is *not!*"

Actually, he was. In fact, Alan was one of the biggest dweebs I'd ever met, maybe the dweebiest. If he could throw a football from his hand to his foot, I'd be surprised. The ol' pigskin would probably stop in mid-air at his knee, not enough thrust to make it all the way to his man-sandals. Alan was a manager at Golden Age Books, technically Lonnie's boss, but he also arranged several of the political gatherings she now attended. He wore round, John Lennon specs and sported a thin goatee, and on the few occasions I'd met him, he compulsively stroked that little goatee as if it were an unresponsive penis he was desperately trying to lengthen. He shook hands with his fingertips, and Alan never laughed – Alan tittered. To his credit, he certainly was well read, but like too many well-read individuals, he wrapped himself in intellectualism as if it were a magic cloak that could ward off the intimidating, less-literate world of Denver Broncos football, heavy metal music, and full-nude strip clubs.

"Has Alan actually read *Atlas Shrugged?*" I asked.

"He said he wouldn't waste his time on such simplistic thinking."

I rolled my eyes. "Tell him to read the fucking thing before he passes judgement. When he's done, I'll be happy to discuss it with him at your next work party. But I'm not going to debate this shit with someone who won't bother reading it."

Lonnie snickered. "I highly doubt Alan will read it, Paul."

"I highly doubt it too, Lon." I dropped my eyes back to my book and continued devouring pages, dismissing her manager's strong opinions on a novel he would never read.

For two solid months, whenever I wasn't working or skiing, I took handfuls of ephedrine and read at least five hours a day. I added more Ayn Rand books to my bender, and by the time I flipped the last page of *The Fountainhead*, I glanced out my window and saw winter had almost completely fled the Eldora valley. Little dabs of green now wrestled their way into the world on aspen limbs, signs of warmer temps to come, and the lashing winds fell below twenty miles an hour for a change. With the warming weather, I read Kurt Vonnegut instead of Ayn Rand in my hammock on the deck – my brain needed a break from her humorlessness and intensity – and I walked Evie and Rummy along the creek in the late afternoons, my winter mood brightening as the days grew longer.

I could never get on board with Ayn Rand's workaholism – I hoped life was more comprehensive than endless, grueling employment – but her characters' relentless work ethic now made me feel guilty whenever I wasn't doing *something* productive. When it came to doling out the guilt for laziness, Ayn Rand was every bit the equal of Catholicism. Egged on by those two motivating forces of shame, I forced myself to the typewriter even when I wasn't feeling the least bit inspired, and in the middle of April, I pulled the last sheet of paper off the roller. I grabbed a red pen, and below the final paragraph of my first novel, I scrawled:

THE FUCKING END, THANK FUCKING GOD

"Finished it, girl," I told Evie. She lay next to my desk, zonked out at 5:00 a.m. on the floor. She barely opened her eyes when I spoke. I placed the final sheet of paper on the 400-page stack, then grabbed the whole book and held it out for my dog to see. "First novel."

Her tail thumped a few times on the old red carpet, but she apparently didn't think enough of my achievement to actually get up. I couldn't blame her. It was awful stuff. I couldn't stand re-reading my book, tried not to go back through it except when I had to find a name or reclaim the thread of the story. I didn't even bother rewriting the thing to any serious degree. This exercise, I knew, was not about writing a good novel; it was about writing *a* novel. Commitment. Stick-to-it-iveness. Howard Roark, an Ayn Rand hero, would be proud of my endurance, but it was her most notable protagonist, John Galt, whose stoic voice I heard in my head: *Nice work, Pablo. Now stuff it in your filing cabinet and never think of it again. Don't gloat and don't wallow. Start writing something better tomorrow.*

"Will do," I replied out loud, "but can I at least have a few beers tonight to celebrate?"

Of course, John Galt answered. *In fact, you should drink a fuck-ton, slugger.*

John Galt was totally cool with my drinking. In fact, all the voices in my head were totally cool with my drinking. I didn't tell him I'd already pounded six Buds while finishing up the book, didn't want him to think I was one of those rare writers with an alcohol problem. I went to the fridge, pulled out a seventh Bud, and cracked myself a 5:00 a.m. beer at the kitchen sink. Yum. Tasted like victory.

Gazing out the window, I saw a tinge of light tracing the high ridgeline in the distance, the morning mountain silhouettes slowly emerging from beneath the blanket of night. I loved writing until sunrise after a closing shift at Pizza Place. It was such a beautiful time of day in the mountains, as peaceful as prayer without all the groveling. Usually, sunrise was my final "go to sleep" reminder. This time, though, I had the next day off and something to celebrate.

"You up for a sunrise walk?" I asked Evie.

The magic W-A-L-K word perked up my little girl. She lifted her cute black head off our deep red carpet and thwacked her tail.

You serious, dad?

"As serious as a socialist," I answered. "Let's get your brother, too."

I walked as quietly as I could down the squeaky hallway, Evie tiptoeing behind me, and gently pushed open the bedroom door. Rummy lay stretched out in my place on the bed, one furry arm wrapped around Lonnie's waist. Both Rummy and Lonnie lifted their heads when the door creaked open.

"Mmm, what time is it?" Lonnie whispered.

I moved quietly to her side of the bed and sat down by her legs, massaged her calves. "Just after 5:00," I said, keeping my voice low. "Sorry, didn't mean to wake you."

"You didn't wake me; I had a bad dream. Something about war, running around the mountains and hiding from bombs. Can't really remember now." She rolled over onto her back, rubbed her eyes open, and reached for her glasses on the nightstand. "I think I'm up for the day. Got a ton of studying to do for finals. Are you just wrapping up your writing for the night?"

"Yep." I tipped back the bottle of Budweiser I'd carried into the bedroom and took a long swallow. "I'm celebrating, actually. Finished the book."

Lonnie's face brightened, and she pushed herself up on her elbows. "Seriously?"

"Seriously."

Her lips spread into a huge smile, her face beaming. "That's awesome, hon! I'm so proud of you!"

I laughed. "You wouldn't be if you read it."

"*Can* I read it?"

"Absolutely not. I told you, this one's a practice book."

"Come on, it can't be that bad." She pouted a little. "I love your writing. I'm sure it's way better than you think."

"Lonnie, it's probably way worse than I think. I didn't even do a decent rewrite, not worth it." I lit a cigarette and filled our bedroom with the rich smell of morning Marlboro. "But hey, it's done, I finished. That's the important thing. Step one, write a novel. Step two, write a good novel. Step three, write a great one and drink myself to death on the proceeds, just like every other respectable writer."

She folded her arms across her huge breasts. "I better get to read the next one."

"You can, I promise." I pointed out our bedroom window at the steadily brightening sky. "Looks like a beautiful morning out there. I was just going to take the pups on a sunrise stroll down by the creek, drink a couple beers, celebrate finishing the book. You want to throw on some clothes and join us?"

She turned her head to the right and gazed out the window for a few seconds. "Is it freezing?"

"Nah, winter's over."

"Winter's never over up here."

"The worst of it's over, I mean. It'll be a little chilly, just dress warm. Come on, I'll even let you drink one of my beers."

"Thanks, but I don't do beer for breakfast." She flipped her legs over the side of the bed, yawned and stretched. "Make me some coffee and I'm in."

Thirty minutes later, Lonnie and I strolled through the woods hand-in-hand, Middle Boulder Creek bulging with winter runoff, its waters fast and loud as it pushed past. The sunrise now painted the upper half of the mountains yellow and orange, quickly melting the night's frost off the trees. The pines sparkled with sunshine. Evie walked directly behind us, occasionally running over to the river for a quick drink before racing right back to our heels. She was the best untrained dog I'd ever seen, never more than five feet away. Rummy, conversely, wore his lack of training proudly on his sleeve. He blasted off in every direction, never listening, stuffing as much of Planet Earth up his nostrils as possible.

"This is so unbelievably beautiful," Lonnie said, squeezing my hand.

"Yep, Eldora's quite the spot."

"No, I mean *everything*." She swept her arm out in front of her. "Me, you, the dogs, the creek, this coffee, the mountains, the sunrise, *everything*. I mean you writing all night is beautiful, finishing a novel in our little cabin is beautiful, me about to finish school is beautiful. I just love this, all of it. I love my life."

I stopped walking, gently turned her toward me, and planted an ephedrine, Budweiser, and Marlboro smooch on her. She kissed me back warmly, ignoring the taste of booze and tobacco. She probably dismissed the weirdly sour flavor of ephedrine, as well, but that one was harder to spot. I didn't exactly hide my relatively new pill popping habit from her – I insisted my late-night job and later-night writing efforts warranted the addiction addition – but I certainly didn't share the full extent to which I now depended on the little white cross speeders.

"You really love me, don't you?" Lonnie asked.

"Of course I do."

"Do you really, *really* love me?"

"Yes, Lonnie, I really, *really* love you. I love you more than anything in the world."

She smiled. "Will you stay up here with me for another year?"

I didn't have to think too hard about that one. How could I not? Lonnie was right, everything was beautiful in our lives, damn near perfect. And I had more writing to do, *good* writing this time. I could think of no better place to pump out good stories than in our little cabin in the mountains.

"I know we're not going to last forever," Lonnie continued before I could respond. "I get it. But I want at least one more year up here with you. Will you stay with me at least one more year?"

I shrugged. "If you give up the kid idea, I'll stay with you the rest of my life."

"You know I won't give that up." Predictably, a tear formed and dropped.

I moved in and kissed her cheek. "I'll stay with you, Lon. There's nowhere else in the world I'd rather be and no one else I'd rather be with. Let's talk to Billy this week and get another lease signed."

She smiled, wrapped her arms around my neck, and squeezed her body tightly against mine. "Goodie," she whispered in my ear. "I love you so much, Paul."

I loved her so much, too, but I didn't need to tell her again that morning. Better just to stand there at sunrise, feel Lonnie's body pressed against mine, and listen to fast-flowing water pour over river rocks in the Colorado Rocky Mountains.

INTERMISSION

Becoming a Mountain

I heard a car pull into our driveway. *Finally!* I thought. Pushing myself off my bed, I scrambled to the large picture window in my room. The struggling, rusty Oldsmobile sedan in the driveway belonged to Chris, my oldest brother and personal hero. He'd finally arrived to take me to his place for a sleepover to celebrate my fourteenth birthday. A week before, my twenty-four-year-old bro promised me it would be a night to remember, but he wouldn't elaborate. Still, "a night to remember" was enough to keep me nearly paralyzed with anticipation for seven days.

I pulled open the door in my bedroom that led out to the driveway. "Over here!"

Chris saw me, got out of his car, and jogged over. Well, "jogged" was a flattering description of Chris moving any faster than a walk. My brother was the smartest person I knew, but he was no athlete.

"So, is the birthday boy ready for an important night at his wiser brother's home?" Chris asked, stepping into my bedroom.

"It's about damn time, man! You're like twenty minutes late!"

Chris waved me off with a theatrical flourish of his hand, likely practiced on some small stage in the Minneapolis theater scene. "Time is irrelevant, young Pablo, especially as it pertains to me being on it, so to speak." He grinned at me. "Come on, grab your stuff. Let us venture into the great unknown!"

I hooked my hand under the loops of my Minnesota Twins duffle bag – packed and waiting impatiently for two full days by my bedroom door – and walked to his car.

"Did you fast, as I instructed?" he asked.

"Yep. And just so you know, fasting sucks ass."

Chris told me I couldn't eat a single bite after my birthday dinner the previous night, and I always followed my brother's orders. I did cram down eight tacos at my birthday dinner, however. In our home, the birthday boy or girl always got to pick the grub and stuff themselves. I chose tacos because tacos were messy, and my father *despised* messiness. With great satisfaction, I watched dear ol' Dad struggle through a couple hard shells before sighing angrily and disappearing from my birthday celebration. Fine by me. The less my dad was around, the better I felt. *More fuckin' tacos for me, dick.*

"Yes, fasting sucks," Chris said, backing out of our parents' driveway, "but trust me, it's necessary."

"Why?"

"I said *trust me*, Pablo." He glanced at me and laughed weirdly.

Chris pushed in the car's lighter and reached into his shirt pocket for a smoke. The lighter popped out like a piece of toast, and Chris pressed it to his cigarette tip. Minutes later, we turned toward downtown Minneapolis where the pillow-pad top of the Hubert H. Humphrey Metrodome peeked out from behind the skyscrapers. I didn't know who Hubert H. Humphrey was, but he had to be a dick. No one cool would ever let a city name a dome stadium after them. Even with the rainouts, mosquitoes, and blazing summer sun, the old Met Stadium was a thousand times better. When I went pro, I'd refuse to play indoors, wouldn't even play for my beloved Twins if they still played in the H.H.H. Dome.

Passing downtown, Chris rolled into Uptown, his eclectic neighborhood. Uptown was old and weathered, its inhabitants young and broke. The artists of

Minneapolis occupied Uptown – writers, musicians, actors like Chris. Wherever creative people planted their seeds, a bohemian culture blossomed. Uptown had drug dealers and prostitutes, head shops and hip record stores. Disturbed men stumbled around the Uptown streets, barking at God, presumably. It was a multi-racial neighborhood with a criminal vibe, subtle danger hanging in the air. Chris loved the old rundown area, loved crime and drugs and all things *not Dad*. Since Chris loved it, I tried to love it, too. But in the depths of my lower middle-class, suburban heart, Chris's neighborhood scared the shit out me.

"Alright, lock 'er up," my brother instructed after grabbing a parking spot a couple blocks from his house. A slender black man in a red leather jacket strolled toward us on the sidewalk, a boombox that likely outweighed him perched on his shoulder. The heavy rhythm of some "black music" I didn't recognize thumped so loudly it almost straightened the dude's Jheri Curl hair.

"Holy shit, was that Prince?" I asked once the guy was well out of earshot.

"It certainly wasn't Bob Dylan," Chris replied, smiling. "But no, Paul, I'm guessing Prince parks his little red corvette in a much nicer neighborhood."

I avoided eye contact with everyone on our way to Chris's place. The Uptown inhabitants were young, but I'd only been fourteen for one day, so those weirdos were plenty old enough to intimidate me. When we reached Chris's duplex, a wave of relief washed over me as I stepped inside the relative safety of his pad.

Chris's place was small and old, exactly as much home as a 24-year-old actor / parking lot attendant and his unemployed actress girlfriend could afford. Directly in front of the entranceway, a creaky, narrow staircase led to the upstairs bedroom Chris and Charlotte shared. A wood-floor hallway ran the length of the main floor, with a small living room, dining room, and downstairs bathroom off the hallway's right side. The hall ended at Chris's dirty kitchen, unwashed dishes always in the sink, unmopped spills always on the floor. At the back of the kitchen, a door opened onto a small yard where there was just enough space for a couple lawn chairs and a little table.

I tossed my baggie of toiletries in the bathroom, stuffed my duffle bag under Chris's couch in the living room, then took a seat on his round papasan chair that I loved. Chris joined a minute later, handing me something rectangular in a brown paper bag, the name *PAUL* written across it in his artistic, almost feminine cursive.

"Wow, you wrapped it and everything." I grinned and shook the brown paper bag.

"Only the best for my youngest brother. Happy birthday, Pablo."

I tore the paper apart hurriedly, already knowing what the present was. It was the best gift any young boy could ask for: a full carton of Marlboros.

I held up the Reds. "It's exactly what I wanted, Santa!"

Chris laughed. "Use them wisely, young man."

Six months earlier, at the tender age of thirteen – nothing near the maturity level I'd reached at fourteen – I got drunk for the first time, a historic theft from my dad's liquor cabinet. Once the puking and bleeding stopped, I bragged about my escapades to Chris. Chris congratulated me on my bravery, said my childhood was almost over, and therefore saw no reason to deny me the perks of adulthood. Within days, he jammed a pot pipe in my mouth, his personal drug of choice, and insisted I get laid, ASAP. He even gave me instruction manuals – *Playboy* and *Hustler* – and offered tips on how I might convince a girl to go all the way. He started loaning me more challenging books to read, too – Heinlein and Tolkien, Steinbeck and Twain, Philip K. Dick and Kurt Vonnegut.

Cigarettes followed soon after. Everyone cool smoked. Chris smoked, my second oldest brother Dane smoked, Jim Morrison – my favorite badass rock star – smoked copiously. Obviously, *I* should smoke, so Chris taught me how to smoke correctly. He laughed as I coughed my way through the inhale learning curve, but he refused to give me cigs if I only "mouth-smoked." I would inhale *properly*, dammit. I powered my way through a couple hundred practice smokes, coughed and hacked until I got it right, and now, I was an accomplished cigarette smoker.

Unwrapping the cellophane from a pack, I lit up and inhaled deeply. The buzz hit me immediately. God, I loved that feeling. It was like getting drunk for twenty seconds, not quite as euphoric but somehow more *satisfying*. I was already in the early stages of nicotine dependency, and that first drag always scratched the addict itch.

"Alright, fess up," I said, exhaling. "What's the big surprise? You said we were going to have a night to remember or something like that. There's gotta be more than a carton of smokes, right?"

Chris grinned at me, nodding. "Fair enough, I suppose we should dive right into it." He leaned forward on the couch and steepled his index fingers beneath his chin. "May I ask what you know about the American Indians, Paul?"

It was a weird question, totally out of the blue. "Not much, I guess," I eventually said. "I know Jim Morrison was a big fan of their culture, even thought of himself as, like, a shaman or some shit."

"Ah, yes, Jim Morrison, your rock star fascination."

I shrugged. "The dude was cool as hell."

"Indeed the dude was," Chris agreed. "And who knows, perhaps Jim Morrison *was* a shaman. Who are we to judge the universe's forces of holiness and the possible deific distribution of spiritual endowment?"

"Beats me," I said, which was true. My brother often said things I couldn't follow. *The possible deific distribution of spiritual…*huh? When I thought of Jim Morrison, I thought of "Roadhouse Blues" and "Love Me Two Times" and "Break On Through." I didn't really care about the shaman shit. At fourteen, I was already worn out on priests and church and anything that smelled religious.

"Well, there's a reason your rock star genius was such a devotee of the American Indians," Chris explained. "They are fascinating people. They believe in ritual as an intrinsic part of human development, consider ceremony the ultimate method of marking important milestones throughout an individual's life."

"You mean like a wedding or something?"

"Yes, exactly." Chris lit up his own smoke, considering further. "Actually, the wedding is one of the few rituals of consequence in our modern culture that we actually recognize as significant. We simply roll through other rituals as a matter of course: baptism, graduation, promotions, retirement, funerals. They're all remnants from a more tribal past. But the Indians – " he paused and pointed his cigarette at me for emphasis " – the Indians make ceremony a fundamental tenet of the tribe's existence, stepping stones that define one's progression through life. Ceremony marks a child's entry into the world, marriage is the transformation of two lives into one, death rituals escort the soul into the afterworld. And most critical to our particular conversation, American Indians believe strongly in a ceremonial transition from childhood to adulthood. You following?"

"I think so." I sucked smoke into my young lungs and tried to appear cool and brilliant, a real intellectual heavyweight like Chris Mountain and Jim Morrison.

"I thought you would," Chris said. "See, the Indians believe a boy can not properly become a man without performing an appropriate ritual, one that involves entering the spirit world. There are all kinds of variations between different tribes, but the fundamentals of the ceremony are mostly the same. There's always a period of fasting – which you've done – followed by some sort of nudge into the spirit world, whether through isolation, exposure to the elements, physical exhaustion, or often times, that nudge can occur through the careful administration of hallucinogens." A strange smile slipped over Chris's face. "May I ask what you know about LSD, Paul?"

I smiled back. I knew a shit-ton about LSD, had read all about it in *No One Here Gets Out Alive,* a biography on Jim Morrison. Morrison practically bathed in acid – *Break On Through, baby.* As far as I could tell, LSD seemed like a gateway into an entirely different reality, something out of a Stephen King book, like going to The Territories in *The Talisman.*

"I've read a lot about it," I answered excitedly, hoping I knew where this conversation was going. "I hate to keep bringing him up, but it was one of Jim Morrison's favorite drugs. I researched it pretty heavily at the library."

Chris's eyebrows went up, impressed. "Then LSD is not an entirely foreign concept to you?"

"Nope."

"Very good, then." My brother reached out, set his cigarette in the ashtray, and locked eyes with me for several long seconds. "LSD is a very serious endeavor, Paul, nothing at all like alcohol or marijuana. You can read all you like about it, but until you've actually taken an acid trip, you have no real idea what you're in for. It's a whole new world."

I nodded seriously.

"It will change your life."

I nodded more seriously, lips tight, brow furrowed, as seriously as I could nod.

"And it *should* change your life, Paul. That's the whole point: change, growth, *metamorphosis*. This is an important milestone, your transition from boyhood to manhood." A slow smile spread on his face. "So what do you say, little bro, ready to leave your childhood behind once and for all?"

I grinned. "I've been ready since I was ten."

"Good man! I'll go get the acid."

"Holy shit, right now?"

"Of course!" Chris stood up and pointed his finger in the air. "There's never been a better time than *right now!*"

My heart rate quadrupled as he left the living room. *Oh my god,* I thought, *I'm actually going to trip on acid, just like Jim Morrison. How badass is THAT?* I lit a second smoke off my first, grinning like an idiot.

Chris appeared a minute later carrying two beers and a porcelain saucer. He set the saucer on his coffee table and handed me one of the beers. "That, young man, is LSD." He pointed at what looked like two very small squares of green plastic on the porcelain.

I leaned forward on the papasan chair and squinted. "Wow, really? It's tiny."

"Sure is, but it packs a punch. Most acid is pretty small, but there are various kinds. This is a gel tab, probably the next best thing to liquid acid, but liquid is extremely hard to find. This particular gel is called Green Pyramid."

"Cool." I glanced up at my brother. "So how do we actually take it?"

"Best to place it under your tongue and let it dissolve, quickest absorption into the bloodstream. But be careful that you feel it resting there, and *definitely* don't speak. You don't want it to shoot out. After a couple minutes, I'll have you grab your beer to wash down any of the dose that might be left. You with me?"

"Got it."

"Very good, then." He clapped his hands sharply once and rubbed his palms together briskly. "Here we go."

Chris reached out and pressed one of the two little green flecks onto the tip of his index finger. Showing me, he placed the speck under his tongue and closed his mouth. Nodding at the saucer, he indicated it was my turn. I got the Green Pyramid on my fingertip and placed it under my tongue. Chris nodded approvingly, sat back on his couch, and closed his eyes. I assumed that was part of the ritual, so I leaned back on my own chair and closed my own eyes, mimicking my brother.

LSD tasted like nothing. I assumed it would be bitter or rough, like drinking whiskey or suffering the harsh stab of weed when Chris or Dane forced me to smoke pot. With no flavor, I focused instead on feeling the little gel tab under my tongue, making sure I wasn't losing any. After a couple minutes, Chris shook my leg and pointed at my beer. Swish-swish-swallow, just as my brother instructed.

"Is everybody in?" Chris asked. "The ceremony is about to begin."

I laughed at Chris's reference to the old Doors lyric. After a few seconds, I said, "I don't feel anything."

Chris looked at me curiously, then nodded. "Ah, right, I should have mentioned that. Acid takes a little while to hit. It's not like pot or alcohol. You don't feel it right away."

"Oh, okay." I took another big swallow of beer. Damn, I loved beer, loved beer as much as I hated pot. "How long does it take?"

Chris glanced up at the ceiling and tapped his chin. "Depends on your biochemistry on any given day. Generally speaking, I'd say anywhere from forty minutes to an hour."

"Oh wow, that long?"

"Yep."

"How will I know when it hits?"

Chris laughed. "You'll know, don't worry."

I tipped back my beer again. While I couldn't feel the acid, I was already starting to feel the alcohol after only a handful of swallows. I had no food in my stomach, and I hadn't had a single beer in almost two weeks. Beer was a bitch to come by. Chris and Dane would always buy for me, but my brothers weren't around enough to satisfy my growing thirst.

"Mind if I grab another brewski?" I asked.

"No need to ask. Help yourself all night. Grab me one, too. It's always good to start the trip with some alcohol. Softens the brain for the onslaught of LSD, gives you the necessary courage to accept the energy of the oncoming wave."

"Cool." I belched loudly. "I'll go grab a couple."

A minute later, I returned to the living room, handed Chris a beer, and cracked my own. "So what should we do while we wait?"

Chris smiled. "I have some *fantastic* new comics, real quality stuff."

"Sweet," I replied, feigning enthusiasm. Chris loved comic books. He had entire bookcases dedicated to his best, most exotic comics. Chris was likely the most well-read 24-year-old in Minnesota, his graveyard shift at a parking garage giving him ample time to indulge both his love of novels and comics. As much as I loved regular books, I did not share Chris's passion for comic books. When I chose to lower the literary bar, I reached for *Sports Illustrated*, or even better, *Baseball Digest*. I would never tell Chris that, of course. Admitting I preferred baseball to Batman would diminish my brother's opinion of me.

"You want to check out anything in particular?" Chris asked, stepping over to his best comic bookshelf.

"You have any new Elrics?"

Chris grinned over his shoulder. "Just got the new one." He reached onto the top shelf – Elric was definitely a top shelf comic – and retrieved my choice. Unsheathing it from its protective plastic sleeve, Chris turned and walked it over to me. "I haven't read this one yet, so don't smudge it. Wipe your hands after every sip of beer."

"Yes, sir."

I hit my beer, wiped my hands, then opened the newest Elric as Chris walked to his turntable and spun up The Beatles *Abbey Road*. Settling comfortably into my chair, I drifted back into Elric's kingdom of Melnibone, where I'd immersed myself off and on for the previous year. I lost track of time, and a half hour later, I was totally into the story. I mean...*totally*. Damn, WHAT a goddam story. I suddenly realized Elric was possibly the GREATEST story ever told. Elric's wildly long, flowing white hair wrapped around the comic strip panels like a blanket, warming the pages, almost toasting my palms. And those eyes, Elric's fire red BLAZING albino eyes leapt off the page like some weird 3-D animation. His eyes were staring at me, sizing up my soul.

Oh my god, I thought, *Elric wants to eat my fucking soul.*

Wow, heavy. That was an unnerving thought, made me shudder. But I would never let that happen, no way. Elric would have to summon Arioch, Lord of Chaos and Duke of Hell, if he wanted to eat *my* fucking soul. Good fucking luck with *that*, dick.

I shivered. The goosebumps *crrreeeeped* and *crrraaaaawled* down my arms like little insects, each with twenty legs. Maybe thirty. Maybe a hundred and thirty. Reaching for my beer, my hand looked...looked...looked *extended*. I stopped before grabbing the bottle, then pulled my hand back. Ten hands followed. It was a train of hands, a streak of flesh following my actual hand, my real hand – what, exactly, is a *real* hand? – and then the whole damn streak caught up and became a singular hand again. Whoa, bizarre. I waved my hand in front of my eyes and it happened again, a train of hands following the original hand, the *real* hand, the true blue red blood flesh bone hand of the actual Paul, the literal inner being of Paul that was Paul's true reality.

"Holy shit," I mumbled, then looked over at my brother.

"And so it begins." Chris grinned widely.

Man, Chris's face looked off. Too short. Wait, no, too long. It was moving, actually, changing. I cocked my head, watched his face shift and change and...*melt*. That was it, it was *melting*.

"Holy shit," I repeated.

"You are now experiencing LSD, Paul." Chris's voice came from somewhere behind the couch, echoing. He reached out and gently removed

Elric from my hand. "This is the beginning, and it will be like nothing you've ever experienced. Accept its energy, don't struggle. Go wherever it takes you."

I leaned back in my chair and suddenly heard the music, heard the music, heard the music like I'd never heard the music before. We were in the later stages of *Abbey Road*, the gentle piano intro of "Golden Slumbers." *Once there was a way…to get back home.* Who the hell would want to go home, ever, when a person could be right here, right now, right here and now of…now in…damn, time is so…oh wow, those strings are perfect in the song, *on* the fucking song, strings lying down softly upon the song like a mist, something visible, like a misty chorus of nature in the woods. It's all so

"Perfect," I said. "It's all so perfect."

Chris nodded. "Yes, it is."

Chris knew about perfect. He brought me to this place to show me perfect, to show me the world was perfect exactly as

Whoa. Hold on just one fucking second, mister man. "Carry That Weight" started, a big loud drum that was a…a warning, right? Jesus, it *was* a warning, telling me I better not fuck it up, not this moment. The Beatles were warning me that if I did, I'd carry that weight a long time, a long-long long-long time. Long. What a weird word. Loooooooong. Gong. Long gong dong. China. But the weight was guilt, right? and guilt only applies to what a person *knows* is wrong not what they're *told* is wrong, right? but everyone says everything's wrong but most shit's not wrong, like smoking Marlboros or jerking off to Playboy or drinking fucking booze or tripping fucking LSD.

Throwing Jimmy Stedman in the snowbank for nothing and holding the little sissy down in the frozen cold snow…now *that* was wrong. It was years ago, I was only eleven, but I shouldn't have done it, god dammit. His little fat face, lips quivering, tears forming, as I shoved handfuls of snow down his shirt and laughed. So fucking wrong. Jimmy was just a pussy, couldn't help it, born that way. Still is a pussy. Always be a pussy. Jimmy Stedman will be a pussy when he's dead, just a rotting pussy in a grave somewhere. Fuckin' Jimmy Stedman.

"How long is long enough for what's wrong?" I asked Chris.

Chris looked at me curiously, his wild, multi-color eyes carefully considering my question. Eventually, he leaned forward on the couch. "I'm not sure I fully understand where you are, Paul."

"True wrong," I explained, then stopped and tried to clarify such a complex thought in my head. "I mean *doing* wrong, *being* wrong. Knowing you've done wrong, you know? Like Jimmy Stedman. And guilt. All the guilt. How long is long enough to carry guilt for what's truly wrong in a person's own head?"

"Well," Chris said, rubbing his chin, "I don't know about this Stedman character, but St. Michael's is only a couple blocks from here. A quick confession and a few Hail Mary's oughta lighten your load. Wanna go?"

Chris exploded with laughter, *exploded*. It burst out of him in a rainbow shower of spectacular color. I exploded, too, felt my guts detonate inside me. Fucking St. Michael's? Fucking *church?* At a time like this? Oh my god, that was the funniest thing I ever heard! How absurd! How insane! Like I could go to church right then! Like I could go to church ever again! Fucking Jesus and the cross and those statues of saints and the altar and the ominous organ music and some mystical, judgmental deity pacing the rafters, threatening the parishioners with Eternal Hell if we didn't drop to our knees, chant the magic words, and eat the fucking wafer. *INSANE!*

I reached for my beer and took a gigantic hit, trying to stem the laughter. I glanced over at Chris, he glanced back, and we both burst out laughing again. I leaned back in my chair and laughed and laughed, laughed and laughed. Oh my god, the world was funny. Life was hilarious, like goggles on a donkey, nuns with shotguns, extraterrestrial beings lighting dry farts in their spaceship. Everything, everyone, fucking life, fucking living, just breathing and eating and shitting and blinking was funny. I now understood that everything, at its core, was hilarious. Comedy was the universe's foundational element, the canvas upon which reality was drawn.

"Oh Christ, I need another beer," Chris said, standing up. "I am tripping my *brains* out."

"Get me one, too, man," I said through my laughter. "Fuck, bring out a shitload."

"Good thinking, little bro." He passed by with a *swooooosh*, his whole body trailing him, outlined by a hundred dotted colors.

The Beatles album ended, and in its absence, the sounds of existence invaded. Existence itself, I realized, was audible. I heard the world, heard the word, heard the word of the world in the language of *being*. With each subtle movement I made, I listened to the air in the room expand and contract, a deep bass resonance that sharpened and faded, disappeared, then returned like a forest wind. Outside our acid cave in the world that wasn't real like our world was real, horns honked and voices yelled. Or screamed. Shit, was that a woman screaming? *Screams the Night, the voice of my disease, release.* I tried to focus on her, but it was impossible to pinpoint her agony through the city's thousand webbed echoes. Oh my god, what if a bunch of Uptown ghouls were murdering her? I could picture the crime clearly – thick, crimson blood flowing from her nose into her hair, coagulating, lower lip split open, clothes torn in a dozen

A dog barked. Just one bark. Whew. All was fine. Dogs bark more than once when there's a murder in progress; everyone knows that. I reached out with – my mind? my consciousness? my essence? – and I felt the dog's soul enter my being and soothe my fears. *No one's screaming,* the doggie promised, *no one's getting killed. It's okay, Paulie, shhhh, shhhh, shhhh, pet me, feel peace, BE peace.* I petted his soul with my mental hand and became peace incarnate and suddenly realized people outside were *laughing,* partying, that's all, just like every other Saturday Night on Planet Earth. But damn, laughter sure sounds like screaming, or it did anyway, same shit, just like crying and dying are the same, only a question of degree. Do people laugh or scream or cry when they die?

Where was my fucking beer? Damn, Chris, *come on!*

I needed more music badly, almost as badly as I needed another beer.

Silence invited an endless parade of chattering fools into my mind, a thousand competing thoughts demanding my attention.

I stood up. Whoa, Bessie, what a thing to stand, a totally different reality from sitting. I felt blood fall from my stomach, trickle down my legs, and work into my toes, giving those pudgy little guys red strength, bloody life. Bloody toe life. My toes led the way toward the stereo, and I felt my entire body displace the thick, smoky air, rearranging physical reality, repositioning molecules to create an entirely new random chaos in the universe. Was that even possible? As I stopped to consider this wild potential, the whole room melted. The walls drained down, pooled on the floor, spun left, swirled right, then crawled back up the sheetrock. Everything bulged, pulsed. Shadows rolled across the ceiling, became recognizable shapes – fingers, tentacles – then melted into gorgeous patterns. Dashed colors like railroad ties outlined every doorframe, every piece of furniture, creating a living room of spectacular light and color that transformed each mundane object into something exquisitely fascinating.

I flowed the rest of the way to the stereo, merging with the energy of all things animate and inanimate. Thumbing through Chris's familiar record collection, I was immediately overwhelmed, a thousand different moods promised by such varied LPs. However, when I made it to the back of the B's, all indecision evaporated. David Bowie practically leapt into my hands, insisted I pick him and only him. *I'm Ziggy Fucking Stardust, bitch, and I have the cure for all that ails you.*

I managed to place *Ziggy Stardust* onto the turntable, clean the vinyl – maybe, I don't know, my eyes could barely focus – and drop the needle. When the stuttering drum opening of "Five Years" began, I knew I'd chosen perfectly. In fact, it may have been the greatest musical choice anyone had ever made, the *exact* album for the *exact* moment, and had I chosen differently, I would have ruined everything. But I didn't ruin anything because I was obviously a fourteen-year-old musical super-genius, just like Mozart. Or maybe something external had directed my decision, some outside force that occasionally manipulated human behavior so as to inject the world with sharp slivers of perfection.

God?

Oh, fuck no. Wasn't going down that road – too heavy. Returning to my chair, I melted into it and went everywhere in my mind, back to the childhood of an hour ago, then into the manhood I'd now entered. I *was* a man now, understanding life like

"Here you go," Chris said, and I almost pissed myself.

"Fuckin-A, you scared the shit out of me."

"Sorry about that." He stood next to me offering a glistening, cold beer. "Thought you heard me coming."

I looked up at his face that wasn't his face anymore. "Chris, I forgot all about you, to be honest." I accepted the cold, cold beer, then drowned my face in its awesomeness. Oh my god, beer was the greatest thing ever invented. "I seriously forgot you were here. Might've forgot you even *are*, you know? Hard to explain, man, super complicated. Where have you been, anyway? You've been gone forever."

Chris laughed a little. "Acid time is elusive, my friend. I haven't even been gone fifteen minutes, just stepped outside to get a breath of air, smoke an outdoor ciggie." He returned to his seat on the couch. "How's everything going in here?"

I shook my head in awe. "This is the most incredible thing in all of ever."

"Yeah?"

"Yeah." A cigarette sounded really, really good now that I had a fresh beer. I lit one up and felt the blissful smoke expand throughout my entire body. "I never…I mean, I never thought…damn, I don't know how to–"

"Don't," Chris interrupted. "Don't describe, don't explain, simply experience the moment and grow. Let's just sit back and experience this ride together." He lit a cigarette of his own, exhaled a cloud that evolved into twelve imprisoned faces laughing in cages. "We're just about there, little bro, just about to the peak."

I understood, or I thought I did. Best to simply experience. And exist. And drink. Always best to drink and drink and drink and drink. I needed to drink everything in the world, drink the fucking planet dry.

An hour somehow passed, and in that time, we reached the peak. On that acid summit, I explored ten thousand thoughts and traveled to ten thousand places I never knew existed. Some locations were horrifying, some so beautiful I thought my soul would implode, but all were enlightening on a level that no one, not me, not Chris, not Dane, not Jim Morrison, could ever attain without the magic assistance of LSD. Acid *was* magic, like in the fantasy novels, where potions moved characters between worlds. Somewhere, there was a real-life Gandalf conjuring magical LSD in his bathtub.

"I'm exhausted," I told Chris, the first words either of us had spoken in a half hour. "I'm completely wiped out."

"Really? I don't think I'll sleep for days."

"Not physically, I mean mentally. My brain is tired as shit. I've never thought so hard, had so many ideas. I don't know if I can keep this up."

Chris nodded. "You're having a deeply internal trip, exploring the profound recesses of your mind." He sat forward on the couch. "Maybe we should switch things up, bring the outside world into our experience? You want to take a little walk around the neighborhood?"

I scoffed. The notion was outrageous. I could hardly imagine switching seats, no less leaving the perfection of Chris's living room. "You mean we should leave all this, this whole...*thing?*" I swept my arm out in front of me to indicate Planet Living Room.

My brother nodded gravely, vapor trails chasing his chin.

"Man, I have to think about that." I cracked a fresh beer, drank decisively. I lit up yet another thinkin' stick and exhaled little smoke animals that hissed and barked as they escaped my mouth.

Chris lifted his own beer and shook it lightly. "Tell you what, let's pound these first, take a little more edge off the acid. Alcohol does wonders for one's sense of adventure."

I nodded. "Sounds awesome. I love beer."

"I've noticed."

We drank at a faster clip. I felt the booze, but I didn't. It was all mashed up with the acid, a part of the trip but not nearly so pronounced as regular drinking. The more beer I pounded, though, the more manageable the experience became. Alcohol quieted the hundred competing voices in my head, merged them together until they became a single clear instructor. Acid, I decided, required alcohol. It was too much to handle on its own, but when regulated by the all-powerful bottle, it became a near-perfect life experience.

"So, you ready to attempt the outside world?" Chris asked when I swallowed the last drop of my seventh or eighth beer.

"Can we take a few bottles of suds with us?"

"That's probably unwise. Bottles tend to attract authority figures."

"Ah, right." I envisioned my dad, the worst authority figure of them all, chasing Chris and I through the streets of Uptown. "That would be a total bummer."

Chris rubbed his chin. "I do have a flask and some whiskey, though. Can you handle drinking straight Windsor?"

"'Course I can." I belched loudly. "Bring it on."

Chris pointed at me. "I like your attitude. Maybe we should do a quick shot before we head out?"

"Maybe's for dweebs. Let's *definitely* do a shot."

He laughed, left the room, and returned a minute later with a bottle of Windsor, a flask, and two shot glasses. He filled the flask and poured the shots. Grabbing one glass, Chris held it high. "To this incredible life and all its interesting experiences."

I clinked my glass against his. "Agreed."

The whiskey burned like a hundred exotic spices, but I loved its barbaric bite and the immediate aggression it brought to my brain. *Whiskey is courage,* I thought, *and courage is crucial when facing a hard ol' world.* I liked that, knowing that nothing cool happened without courage. Mr. Dahlquist, my baseball coach, always talked about courage, aggression, fighting fear. *Fear is failure's foundation, boys,* he often said. After a shot of whiskey, I no longer feared what lay beyond Chris's front door. I wanted to go outside and devour the night.

It took a long, long time to leave. There was weather to discuss, jackets to remember, keys, smokes, shoes, manners, morals, my old favorite Twins hat. I even pocketed my heavy Swiss Army knife. In case we ran into trouble, I could spork my way out. *Spork you, motherfucker!* Pacifist nations should not manufacture an army's weaponry.

The second we stepped out the door, I wished we'd left an hour earlier. Outside was *insane*. I stood on Chris's front step and breathed in deeply, sucked in all that brisk, refreshing, *outdoor* air. It filled my lungs like a blood transfusion, shoved aside the stale indoor air and replaced it with all the good stuff human beings were supposed to breathe, like car exhaust. City night had crept across the land while we tripped indoors, and city night was *spectacular*. The sounds, the sights, the lights lights lights, glowing eyes on buildings high.

"This is incredible," I said breathlessly. "The whole world is a miracle."

"Yes, it is," Chris agreed. "You ready to walk?"

"Can I hit that flask?"

"Of course."

I hit that flask. Swallowed a lot. Whiskey fire scorched my throat, raced straight to my brain. I'd never, ever, felt so good. I never imagined a human being *could* feel so good. I was blown away by my own happiness, in awe of life itself, all of life, animate and inanimate, and I found it miraculous that I was a functioning part of the universe. How amazing to be alive. How lucky to live. How mathematically ludicrous. Consciously existing, I realized, was preposterous and impossible were it not for the fact that I was currently doing it. I was alive, an individual, self-aware being, and that was *un-fucking-real*. Did monks feel this way on their islands, hermits in their hills, all of them consumed by an endless and unbridled sense of appreciation and wonder? Was that what it meant to find God – to experience absolute reverence for all existence?

"Ready?" Chris asked.

"Absolutely." I handed him back the flask. "But you gotta lead, man. I'm not sure I can cross a street without getting killed."

"That's what big brothers are for. Follow me."

We walked, wandered, and explored a world that felt like something out of Chris's comic books…but not Elric's Melnibone. No, this was a good world, soft and forgiving, no red-eyed albino kings swinging soul-munching swords. The Uptown houses looked like Candyland cutouts, all drippy and trippy. The stars were God's eyes. He was a living creature, a weird voyeur with a million billion cameras focused on humanity. I reminded myself to close my mouth, stop gaping, especially when we walked past all the gorgeous Uptown girls. Those babes were so much older and out of reach, twenty-something beauties with huge hair suspended by Aqua Net, short short skirts hugging tight tight asses, small jean jackets barely restraining their young, bulging breasts. Damn, I wanted one of those girls. Better yet, I'd take a baker's dozen.

"Jesus Christ, I want a girl," I said. "I want them all, actually."

Chris laughed. "Well, I think we can safely say you've entered manhood."

"Definitely. Is that normal?"

Chris shrugged. "At your age, sure, seems healthy."

"Do you want all the girls, like, all the time?"

He walked awhile, giving my question real consideration. "Not so much anymore. But that's just me being realistic. Given the opportunity, sure, I'd probably have sex with almost any woman on the planet, at least within a certain age range. But the fact that I'm having regular sex with *one* woman, let alone *all* women, is kind of miraculous. In case you haven't noticed, most women aren't really into the broke, unathletic, bookish types." He grinned at me, then shrugged. "So I don't waste a whole lot of mental energy craving all the sex I'll never have."

"I think about sex all the time. I dream about it almost every night, have wet dreams at least three times a week. I go through fucking underwear like

Kleenex these days. Can't wait until I can have real sex with a real girl."

Chris nodded. "You're at a tough age, Pablo. You're probably as horny as you'll ever be, but getting laid at fourteen is probably harder than it will ever be the rest of your life."

"That sucks dick."

"Actually, that's precisely what it *doesn't* do, eh?" Chris clapped me on the back and laughed. "Well, just keep beating off like your life depends on it; that way, you'll be ready when lightning finally strikes."

We wandered and wandered, studied the neighborhoods, strolled through little parks where weird Uptownians participated in obvious illegal drug activity. At every intersection busy enough to warrant a stoplight, I felt like a duck at a dog park, small but noticeable, dangerously out of place. I obsessed over the red "Don't Walk" warning, so harsh, so authoritarian. The green "Walk" sign seemed equally tyrannical. What if I was happy right the fuck where I was?

It was hours or days or lifetimes before we made it back to Chris's. I felt as if I'd need twenty years of contemplation to properly process all my recent mental journeys. All I wanted to do was plop back down in Chris's papasan chair, crack another brewski or twelve, and ponder all my beautiful ponderings until I passed out. But when we stepped into the living room, Charlotte was in my chair. *My* chair.

"Oh, hey," Chris said to his long-time girlfriend. "Fancy seeing you here."

She turned to us and smiled. Charlotte was attractively plain, not pretty, not homely, just…*Charlotte*. She was Nebraska, the middle road of all things America, not mountains or deserts or oceans, just….*Nebraska*. Everything about her was medium. Charlotte was medium height, medium weight, medium length brown hair. She was medium weird – had to be somewhat weird to live with Chris. She was always extremely nice to me, so I liked her, but most of my family didn't. Like Chris, Charlotte craved the stage, and my family considered theatrical pursuits unbecoming of a Minnesota gal. *Leave that artsy-fartsy shit to New Yorkers!* Also, Charlotte smoked approximately three pounds of weed per day, giving my family ample ammo to unjustifiably blame her for my brother's identical vices.

"Sorry, just having a quick hit," Charlotte said to Chris, lifting up a three-foot water bong – a permanent piece of furniture in their living room – and shaking it a bit. "I know you said you wanted the downstairs to yourself tonight for your brother's big adventure."

Charlotte smiled at me and I shifted nervously on my feet. *She knows,* I thought, and suddenly, I didn't know how to act. Tripping around someone who knew I was tripping but was not tripping themselves felt wrong, like there was a spy in the castle.

"Don't worry, Paul," she said, sensing my unease. "I've dropped acid dozens of times. Nothing to be nervous about, no judgment here. I'll get high real quick and get out of your way." With that, she dropped her face onto the bong and sucked in an enormous hit.

"Wow, that smells delicious," Chris said as Charlotte stood up from the bong.

Her voice was tight while she held in her hit. "It is, lover." Stepping over to Chris, she laced her hands around the back of his neck and exhaled a thin stream of pot smoke into his mouth. When it was all blown out, she kissed him seductively, trapping the smoke in his lungs.

"Mmm, you taste wonderful," Chris said.

She cocked her head coyly. "And you taste like whiskey, mister."

Chris grinned. "I've been drinking quite heavily, my dear."

"Uh-oh, I better stay up for a while; I know how you get when you drink too much." She ran a slow finger down my brother's cheek, then pushed herself away from him. "But I'll leave you brothers alone, don't want to be in the way. Besides, I need to go upstairs and go over my lines. Big audition on Tuesday."

Charlotte walked toward me and caressed my shoulder affectionately as she passed, her fingers lingering. Charlotte was a toucher, and as always, her touch felt awesome, bordering on sensual. God damn, I needed a girl.

I took off my jacket and tossed it in the general direction of the world. "You mind if I grab some more beer?" I asked Chris. "I could really use a few cold ones to wash down the whiskey."

"Absolutely. I'll load the bong. I'm ready to move my mind in that direction."

I walked down the long hallway to the kitchen. Now that I was inside, warm, and less active, I noticed I was good and drunk. But I could get gooder and drunker. I pulled four beers from the fridge and carried them back to the living room. Just as I returned, Chris exhaled a huge blast of weed in my direction and held the bong out to me.

"Really?" I asked.

"Really."

"I don't know, man, I'm pretty fucked up." That was the lower-case truth. The TRUTH was that I hated pot. It made me paranoid, self-conscious, exhausted, got me too messed up to even talk. I never wanted to let Chris down, but I also never wanted the goddamn pot he was always pushing. Right then, I *especially* didn't want the demon weed. Might ruin my near-perfect buzz.

"I understand, Paul, but this is an entirely different kind of fucked up. Marijuana reinvigorates the LSD, guides you gracefully into the late stages of the trip."

I rubbed my chin. "I don't know, bro."

Chris shook the bong, raised his eyebrows, and held my eyes. "But I insist."

I sighed. My personal hero insisted. He knew so much more about life and drugs and girls and when I should take LSD and when I should drink Windsor. He was twenty-four and I was only fourteen; I had to trust his judgment. I reached out and accepted the huge bong, then returned to my round chair.

"I'll spark you," Chris said.

This is a bad idea, I thought, but my teenage misgivings were no match for sibling pressure. I dropped my mouth onto the bong, covered the carb with my thumb, and while the weed slow-roasted, I sucked in very slowly, performing every action exactly as Chris had meticulously taught me. When I'd pulled seventy percent of the smoke into the tube, I released the carb and power-sucked the whole chamber deep into my lungs.

"Hold it!" Chris called out, smiling.

I held it.

"Hold it!"

I held it.

"Hold—"

I couldn't. The smoke exploded out my mouth. Chris laughed loudly at my pain as I hacked and coughed until my throat felt attacked by dental instruments.

"Jesus fucking Christ." I reached for my beer and drained half of it to cool my throat. "You trying to kill me?"

"You just need more practice. Let's do another."

"You *are* trying to kill me."

"Trust me, Pablo."

"I don't think I should anymore."

"Come on, I'm your big brother; would I ever lead you astray?"

"I…I don't…" I was suddenly having a very hard time concentrating. Shadows crawled into my mind and darkened my soul.

"One more hit," Chris said, pressing the bong back in my hands.

I moved robotically and repeated the whole procedure: suck slow, release carb, aaaaannnnnd *INHALE!* I held it as long as I could, and this time, I released without coughing, my throat still numb.

"Your turn," I muttered, handing the bong back to Chris.

I leaned back unsteadily, and the chair swallowed me. The goddam chair was a mouth, hungry, gumming my flesh with its padded lips. That fucking chair didn't love me at all, probably didn't even like me. It had been luring me in all night, waiting to devour me once I was stoned and vulnerable. Suddenly, all the fading LSD hallucinations returned with a vengeance, only now they were sinister. Shadows reached out with long, spindly fingers, bulging walls closed in menacingly, groaning audibly. My clothes melted onto my body, wax fabric imprisoning my skin. Eyelids drooped, eyes burned, heartbeat quickened. My fingers stuck together, webby, sticky sticky spider wicky, jaw tight, teeth grinding.

"You got that flask?" I asked. The words came out slow and muddled. It was almost impossible to speak, but whiskey was worth the effort.

"Yeah, I think there are still a couple bumps left."

Chris pulled the flask out of his pocket and lobbed it to me. I reached out and I…I missed. I, Paul Mountain, *never* missed an easy catch. I was the reigning two-time all-city all-star shortstop. I fucking scooped up everything, a vacuum cleaner at short. I was the best fucking fielder in Golden Valley, every bit as talented as I was arrogant...close, anyway.

I fumbled for the flask where it landed by my thigh, not feeling good anymore, not about acid, not about myself. Weed weirdness had settled in, self-consciousness laced with stupidity and anxiety. Everything I did felt weird and wrong. I twisted the top on the flask too aggressively, brought it to my lips too quickly, drank too weirdly. Jesus, how does a person drink weirdly? Was I doing anything right? Was I breathing too loud, drooling, noticeably sweating?

"We need music," Chris stated casually, standing up and stretching. "Any requests?"

"The Doors," I answered immediately.

"You always pick The Doors."

"I *need* to hear The Doors, Chris."

What the fuck did that mean? Nobody *needs* to hear The Doors. Or do they? God, what a stupid thing to say. Or maybe not. No-yes. Okay, yes. Yes, it was dumb as fuck. I was young and dumb and not very cool and I proved it by saying stupid shit like *I need to hear The Doors*. That wasn't as bad as missing an easy catch, but it was still pretty bad. Everything was bad and getting worse. I hit the whiskey again, then chased it with a huge gulp of beer.

"Alright, Paulie," Chris said, watching me and chuckling a little. "No need to panic. I'll throw on some Doors for you. Preference?"

"Absolutely Live."

I powered through my beer as Chris prepped the album, and then I cracked another bottle. Beer would get me past the motherfucking weed. Why did Chris have to love pot so much? Pot sucked ass. It was the worst drug ever invented and it

The walls exhaled. My god, I saw them breathe. I felt the wind. The walls were gigantic lungs, breathing when I breathed. I tilted the flask and the last small swallow of Windsor lodged in my throat. It felt like glue, coating my esophagus, closing up the airway. I dumped beer on the problem, and magical beer loosened up the windpipe globs just as the familiar drumbeat of "Who Do You Love" started on the turntable.

Oh God, thank you for familiar sounds, familiar places in my brain.

"Feel better?" Chris asked.

I stared at him, the walls taking gigantic breaths behind his head, his face melting, the entire room tilting hard to the right. A thousand complicated responses bolted through my brain each millisecond but only one seemed PROFOUND enough to address his question. With great profundity, I breathed deeply and solemnly announced:

"I need to sit down for a while."

Chris cackled, his laughter slashing across the music. I saw his voice gash the air, swirling green blades of sound slicing through empty space.

"You *are* sitting down!"

"Over there," I explained, pointing at an open spot on the floor next to the couch. It looked very safe in that corner, a little cubbyhole of Pablo sanity. "I need to sit there for a little while and just…just…you know…"

"Just listen to The Doors?"

My eyes grew wide in astonishment, and I nodded my head slowly. I'd always known my brother was a fucking genius, but until that moment, I didn't realize he could read minds.

"Yes, that's *exactly* what I need. That okay?"

"Of course. I assume you'd like to be alone?"

I nodded again, awestruck. How did one man know so many things?

"Yeah, alone. Just a little while, long enough to, you know, get control of…control the shit, you know? Just the shit, man, control the shit." I wiped thick saliva off my lips. "I'm *really* high, Chris."

My brother reached out and patted my leg. "No problemo, hermano Pablo. Everyone needs a little alone time during an acid trip, especially their first one. I'll go upstairs and hang with Charlotte for a bit. Cool?"

"Cool. Just give me one album side, maybe two."

"You got it."

Chris stood up, took one of the beers I'd brought, and left the room.

I rose to my feet shakily and grabbed a couple cushions off the couch. I threw them haphazardly toward my cubbyhole corner, then carried over two beers and set them on the ground. The bottle of Windsor was still on the table, so I latched onto the neck and carried it to my safe little corner of the universe.

Ah, so much better.

The world was almost manageable on the floor, protected by couch and breathing walls. I hit the Windsor hard, a full mouthful, maybe two shots. That helped immensely and immediately. I cracked a beer and drank a third of it, then took a few breaths and let the alcohol attack the weed. *Fuck you, weed, you're no match for liquor.* Closing my eyes, I watched the whole battle in my veins, a booze battalion charging fast after a slow-trudging marijuana militia. The weeders didn't know what to do, stoned and clueless, as whiskey warriors jumped on their backs, smashed empty beer bottles into their baked faces. The alcohol army was impressive, aggressive, jabbing, stabbing, badass motherfuckers in Molly Hatchet t-shirts unleashing a twelve-pack of whoopass on pacifist stoners.

"Try this on for size, you pussies." I sent another Windsor wave into my veins, then tossed a beer battalion into the melee. Belching loudly, I slammed my hand over my mouth so that I didn't lose any of my armed forces.

Hiding on the floor, my hand clutched over my mouth to keep imaginary alcohol soldiers inside my body on an interior battlefield, it suddenly dawned on me that I was, officially, ridiculous. I was as ridiculously far out of my mind as I'd ever been. I'd lost total connection to reality, and *that* concept struck me as the funniest fucking thought I'd ever had.

I started to laugh, and once I started, I could not stop. I sat in my little corner and laughed and laughed, laughed and laughed. I howled until it hurt, clutched my sides when they started to ache. I tried to swallow more beer to drown the hilarity, but I coughed it out in a huge spasm of laughter, spraying my own shirt with beer foam. I laughed and hacked and coughed and finally, after ten solid minutes of internal hilarity, I was able to take another massive swallow of whiskey. The laughter slowly dried up, and my eyes stopped watering long enough for me to reassess reality. Unfortunately, my reassessment instantly revealed that the living room was now spinning.

No.

Yes.

Oh, no.

Oh, yes.

Oh, shit!

The room picked up speed, and I recognized the motion. Only nine months into what I hoped would be a long and illustrious drinking career, I already knew all about the spins. I clamped my eyes shut, ground my teeth, and prayed for it to stop, but prayer failed me. Again. The booze bounced against my stomach lining, crawled up my throat, and banged on the escape hatch.

"Uh oh." I shoved myself off the ground, feeling the volcano rumble. Slamming my hand over my mouth, I puffed out my cheeks and staggered toward the hallway, blasting my shin into the coffee table on the way past. I soldiered on, lurched into the hallway, crashed into walls, and at the end of my sightline, like an entrance to the afterlife, I saw the chipped and faded kitchen door that led into Chris's small back yard. I dashed for it and burst through. Falling over the two small steps that led down to the grass, I collapsed on my knees and unloaded the entirety of my stomach. It flowed out in spectacular color, long streams of green and red and yellow. It felt as if I were yakking up so much more than mere stomach contents, though, as if I were unloading sins and dumbass ideas and teenage rage and maybe even a hope or two. Shapes appeared in my puke puddle – baby animals, baby babies, liquor bottles, seashells, seahorses, and holy shit, was that my old transistor radio? When the fuck did I eat *that?* It all poured out of me, a mile of bile, and when it mercifully ended, I collapsed on my side and panted like an old dog after a short walk. I lay there, my expanding puddle of vomit a couple feet from my head, the stench overpowering.

"Feel better?"

I rolled onto my back and saw my brother's face gazing down upon me. The city stars outlined his head, making him look almost angelic, a messianic figure against the night sky.

"Much," I answered. "When did you get here?"

"A minute ago. Heard you crashing through my house."

"Sorry 'bout that, had to barf."

"A man's gotta barf sometimes."

I ran the back of my hand across my mouth, hoping to clear off any chunky stragglers. "You got a smoke, man?"

Chris fumbled in his shirt pocket and handed me one. I placed it between my lips as he bent down with his lighter. Cigarette smoke curled up into the sky, smearing the stars.

"I don't ever want to leave this spot," I said.

"You probably should."

"Why?"

"Well, you may need a bath. Hate to tell you, Pablo, but you have a fair amount of puke in your hair."

"Wow. Total bummer." I stayed in the grass and took another long drag off my smoke. The hair barf could wait until I gathered my strength. "You know what I need more than a bath, Chris? I need pizza, dude. I'm *starving*. It feels like I haven't eaten anything in a million years, and I just lost whatever was left of my birthday tacos from last night."

"Yeah, I'm pretty hungry, too. I'll cook us up a couple pies while you take a bath. You need a hand getting up?"

"I think I need a hand breathing right now."

Chris reached down and pulled me up. The second I was on my feet, all the blood rushed to my head and I browned out, almost collapsed again. Chris held me upright. My legs were jelly, my brain and body no longer on the same team.

"I think I'm toast, man," I slurred.

"No worries. A quick bath and a stomach full of pizza will set you right."

My head wobbled in a pseudo-nodding motion. "Fuck yes, stomach full of pizza. Pizza is the best fucking food in the whole world. I'm serious, dude, the *best*."

Ah'm shearius, do, th' besht.

Chris laughed. "Come on, drunky, let's get you to the bathroom, sober you up a tad."

"Thanks, man, you're awesome." I tried to slap him on the back, missed, and almost fell out of his grip. "You know something, Chris? You're my favorite brother, way, way, *waaaaayy* cooler than Dane. He just beats me up all the time. Says he's teaching me a lesson, but he never tells me what the fuckin' lesson *is*, you know?"

"Well, Dane certainly has an aggressive streak, no doubt. But he learned it from our lovely father, so I cut him a little slack. But what about Barry? You two are super close, right?"

"Ah, Barry." I waved my hand dismissively. "Barry's my bud. We're just like, you know, *friends*, not like brothers and shit. Too close in age. He can't *teach* me anything, you know? He's not like a…a…what's the word?"

"I don't know, Paul. There are millions of words."

"*Mentor!*" I yelled excitedly. "Barry can't be a *mentor,* know what I mean?"

"I do."

"And I can kick his ass in any sport." I tugged on Chris's shirt and forced him to stop moving us toward his house. "Seriously, I can kick Barry's ass in *any* sport, even the fake ones – foosball, air hockey, fucking *anything.*"

"Um, okay. But I'm sure you can kick my ass in any game, as well."

"Well, yeah, of course, but…" I waved off the thought. "You're not supposed to be, like, a *sports* guy. You're supposed to be like a…like a…"

"Like a mentor?"

"Like a mentor! Like teach me shit and shit." This time, I actually did manage to slap him on the back. "You're awesome, buddy, totally fuckin' badass."

Chris rolled his eyes and dragged me toward his back door. We staggered into the house and eventually made it to the bathroom. He placed me carefully on the floor, and I leaned disjointedly against the wall, my body swaying back and forth to stay somewhat upright as Chris ran the tub.

"Don't fall asleep, Paulie. I can't eat all that pizza myself."

I pointed at him. "Righteous, bro. Don't you worry, I won't fall asleep before my pizza, that's for sure."

Chris disappeared and I waited for the tub to fill. The weed and acid were fading, but the alcohol had its hooks buried deep in my soul. I was now drunky drunk, slobbering, slurring, off-balance, fucked-up drunk. There was nothing left to puke, but I was fairly certain I'd puke the pizza after I chowed down. Oh well, it would be worth it to have it inside me, if only for a little while. God, I loved pizza. I'd rub pizza slices all over my body if I could, coat myself in grease and let the flavors seep into my flesh.

When the tub seemed full, I wrestled myself onto the toilet and undressed clumsily. Rolling into the water, the warm womb bathtub embraced me. I ran wet hands through my hair, washed away the remaining puke. I generally didn't like baths – something about floating in a puddle of my own filth seemed counterintuitive – but Chris didn't have a shower, so I leaned back and wallowed in my dispersed vomit and teenage funk. After five minutes of silent soaking, a soft but startling knock landed on the bathroom door.

"Yep, I'm alive, Chris!" I called out. "Let me know when the pizza's done!"

The doorknob jiggled, and then the unlocked door cracked open just a hair. "Can I come in for a second, Paul?"

I sat bolt upright in the water, my heart racing. That wasn't my brother. That was Charlotte.

"Um, I…I'm kind of in the tub right now."

The door pushed open a little further, but she still didn't enter. "It's okay." She giggled a little. "Trust me, there's nothing in there that I haven't seen before."

I looked down at the thing she'd seen before, knowing she'd never seen one quite so pathetic. It was acid penis, whiskey dick, and weed willie all wrapped up into one cowering cock. I couldn't let Charlotte see my frightened little boy dick and thin crop of pubic hair.

"Gimme a sec!" I looked around feverishly for a washcloth and saw one crumpled into a ball at the end of the tub. I got it wet and hurriedly spread it over my crotch. "Okay, you can come in."

Charlotte pushed the squeaky door wide enough to finally peek her head inside. She smiled prettily at me. "I'm *really* sorry, but Chris is in the upstairs bathroom and I need to wash my face. You sure it's okay if I come in?"

"'Course, no problem," I answered casually, as if I regularly bathed naked in front of grown women.

"Thanks so much. You're so sweet."

Charlotte stepped into the bathroom and, oddly, flipped the lock after closing the door. When she turned back around, I saw a mischievous smile on her face. And then I saw something that nearly made my eyes pop out of my skull. Charlotte wore only a thin negligee, untied at the waist, and she apparently forgot her bra and panties. My eyes crawled over the round outline of her breasts beneath the flimsy fabric, walked down the flat curvature of her belly, and finally landed on her triangular patch of brown pubic hair. *That's* REAL *pubic hair,* I thought, *a* LIVING *bush!* And underneath that living bush, there *had* to be a living vagina.

My nonexistent penis grew tiny.

"I figured you wouldn't mind having me in here," she said coyly, leaning against the door.

"'Course not – " *happens all the time, babycakes* " – why would I mind?"

Charlotte sauntered over to the tub and kneeled down, her tits *almost* exposed. It was an excruciating *almost,* so much boob in sight, but no uncovered nipple. Damn. In my fourteen-year-old circles, a guy couldn't boob-brag unless he saw at least one nipple.

Charlotte's voice grew sultry. "Paul, I have a confession to make."

"Should I call a priest?"

A surprised giggle fell out of her. She reached over and squeezed my shoulder – god, I loved her touchy-feely nature – and this time, she left her hand in place. "You're funny," she said. She tilted her head to the side and held my eyes. "But no, Paul, I don't need a priest. I think you're qualified to hear my confession."

Is she acting? I suddenly wondered. *Is this what she was rehearsing upstairs, some audition for a mature seductress role or some shit?*

"Um, okay, confess."

"I don't actually need to wash my face." Her hand slid off my shoulder and began caressing my arm. Up and down, up and down, my skin tingling.

My tiny penis grew pudgy.

"No?"

"Nope." She shook her head, smiled, caressed me. "I just thought you might want to take one more step toward manhood tonight."

Aha!

I cocked my head and squinted at her. "Alright, alright, did Chris put you up to this?"

She shrugged off the question. "No one makes me do anything I don't want to do," she sort-of answered.

I studied her face for further clues but came up empty. "Did he tell you what I said earlier about wanting a girl?"

Again she only offered a shrug and her flirty smile. "Maybe I just think you're cute." Her hand moved from my arm to my stomach. She stroked my skinny torso with her fingernails, all the way up to my neck, all the way down to my waist. It felt wonderful. No woman's hand had ever been that low on my body when there wasn't a diaper involved. "But tell me what you said about wanting a girl. Trust me, no judgement here. You can tell me *anything*, Paul."

My pudgy penis grew plumpy.

"I just…just…want them. You know, want to be *with* them." I stared at Charlotte's nearly naked body. "I think about girls all the time."

"That's perfectly normal." Her hand slid even lower, toying with my thin pubic hair. "Have you ever seen a girl without all her pesky clothes on?"

"Only in magazines."

Charlotte nodded, smiled, and stood up slowly. And then, God bless her, my brother's girlfriend shimmied her nightie off her shoulders. There she stood, naked before me: WOMAN. Holy Mary, those were NIPPLES. She must have seen my eyes widen at my first verified nipple sighting, because she pushed her breasts up for me.

"Do you want to touch these, Paulie?"

I glanced at her eyes for the first time in quite a while and saw she was dead serious. I nodded my head fiercely up and down. Did I want to touch a boob? I couldn't imagine a scenario where I *wouldn't* want to touch a boob. If I saw a freshly severed boob lying on the road, I'd give it a quick squeeze or two before kicking it into the ditch.

Charlotte kneeled back down next to the tub. She guided my right hand out of the water and set it carefully on her left breast. Her hand on top of mine, she slowly began moving my hand in a circular motion. She guided me to her nipple, then let my fingertips explore that central feature of every woman's breast.

"Mmm, that feels wonderful," she whispered, her eyelids dropping down. "Do you like touching me, Paulie?"

"Uh-huh."

"I like it, too." She offered me her best seductress smile of the night. "Would you like me to touch *you?*"

"Uh-huh."

My plumpy penis finally achieved full-on boner status. *Captain, we have attained erection!* Fourteen years of sexual frustration – well, more like two – bulged beneath a dirty washcloth, anxiously awaiting the first sexual encounter with the female species.

Charlotte gently removed my hand from her nipple. She ran her fingernails down my skinny chest and stomach once again, but this time, she didn't stop at my thin patch of pubic hair. She brushed aside my crotch-cloth and sensually wrapped her fingers around my penis.

"Don't be scared," she whispered.

I exploded.

Right then, right in her hand, I let 'er rip. Didn't need a single stroke. *THUMP THUMP THUMP!* My insty-ejaculation startled us both. I released a surprised yelp and Charlotte actually recoiled a little.

"Shit!" I said.

My jizz oozed into the water, joining my puke remnants and teenage body funk. Charlotte stared at it in surprise for a second, and then very carefully, very gently, she pulled her hand out of the water. She brought her other hand up to her mouth, stifling a giggle.

"Oh my god, Charlotte, I'm so sorry. I–"

She waved me off. "Don't be sorry, Paul." And then she did actually giggle a little. "You just surprised me is all. But it's totally understandable. The first time with a woman can be pretty…um…*overwhelming.*" She stood up, picked her slinky nightie off the floor, and wrapped it back over her shoulders, tying it at the waist for the first time. "Don't worry, though. You're a little cutie, Paul. That won't be the last time a woman touches you there, believe me."

"I sure hope not."

She stepped over to me, placed her hand under my chin, and lifted up my face. She brought her lips down to mine and kissed me sweetly. It wasn't particularly lusty, just sexy enough to imply our relationship had evolved.

"You're a sweet kid, Pablo. Hope I got you a little closer to manhood."

With that, she exited the bathroom, leaving me stupefied. Wow, someone other than me had finally touched my wiener. I knew I'd beat off to the experience *for sure,* milk it for all it was worth…so to speak. This one was going straight into my all-star collection, that velvet-draped room in the back of my mind where I kept the best jerk-off gems.

I drained the tub while running the water, using the washcloth to wipe away whatever scum still clung to my body. I suddenly felt much better, apparently shocked into some semblance of sobriety by Charlotte's quarter-second hand job. Wrapping a towel around my waist, I walked to the living room and slipped into my sleeping clothes. A minute later, Chris appeared with two steaming hot pizzas, edible trophies for cumming in his girlfriend's hand.

"Hungry?" he asked.

"Oh man, I've never been so hungry in my life."

I gorged for fifteen silent minutes, stuffing as much food in my face as my mouth could hold. I felt pepperonis parachute into my stomach like care packages dropped from friendly forces, and I washed it all down with a gigantic glass of water, the first non-alcoholic beverage I'd consumed in twelve hours.

"So, how do you feel?" Chris asked after we polished off the pies. He raised his eyebrows oddly, but I couldn't tell if he knew about my Charlotte experience. *He has to know,* I thought. *She wouldn't risk something like that right under his nose, would she?* Fuck, I didn't know. They were actors, both of them, weird artists I could never fully understand. I'd probably never know if Chris sanctioned the whole act, and I certainly wasn't going to ask. That one would have to remain a lifelong mystery.

"Feel good," I replied, wiping my mouth and lighting a delicious post-pizza ciggie. "I'm totally wiped out, but I feel pretty damn good. Feel older. After tonight, I think I actually *am* closer to manhood, don't you?"

Chris shrugged. "I hope so. I guess it all depends on how you process the experience over the next several weeks, how you incorporate whatever you've learned into your life. But we'll have plenty of time to talk about it and dissect it later. Right now, I'm every bit as exhausted as you are." My brother stood up and stretched, took a step toward the hallway. He turned, waved, and flipped off the light. "Get yourself some sleep, Pablo."

"Will do," I said. "Oh, Chris?"

"Yessir?"

"Thanks, man," I said. "Seriously, thank you. This was, by far, the most interesting day of my life. Nothing else comes close."

He nodded in the semi-dark room and smiled. "Good, I'm glad. I hope you remember it for a long time to come."

"Oh, I don't think I'll ever forget this one."

Chris waved again, turned, and creaked his way up the stairs toward Charlotte. I wondered if he'd give her the righteous boning she deserved after my pitiful eruption. Probably. She seemed hot for it, and unlike me, I was sure Chris knew what he was doing. My brother always knew what he was doing because he was a real man. I wasn't quite there yet, but I was now significantly closer. Shit, I'd taken my first trip on LSD, fondled my first boob, and ejaculated into a woman's hand. Those were some pretty big steps toward manhood, in my opinion, and I could hardly wait to do all three again.

6.

The Pomp and Circumstance of Monogomy

E L D O R A ,   C O L O R A D O

1 9 9 1

"Your father is selling the van," my mom told me.

So that's why she called. On the rare occasions she did, conversation was always a little awkward, but still a thousand times better than chatting with my dad. Talking to my father on the phone was as painful as pulling pubes, and not the thin curly ones up front, but the ingrown ass clusters in back. Chatting with him in person was tough enough, but without body language to gauge his complete lack of interest at any given time, phone calls were excruciating. With my mom, I only had to endure a short stretch of stilted chit-chat before we got to the point: *Yes, I'm fine, Lonnie's fine, Rummy and Evie are fine. Yep, still delivering pizza. Nope, not back in school.* I could never share the interesting aspects of my life with my mother: *Yep, still tripping acid, trying to write, and yes, still drunk most of the time. Oh, by the way, I'm hooked on speed pills now, too!*

"He's really selling his van?" I asked.

"Yep, finally decided he's ready to give it up. We never use it anymore now that we have our trailer at the lake. He thought you might be interested."

"I'm *very* interested."

It was a little ridiculous that I had to deal with my mother, a go-between, on something that was so clearly in my dad's purview. That old van was his baby, his most loved child. If he wanted to sell it to me, he should have called and offered it himself. But that's how the Mountain world worked best – everything went smoother when Sally Mountain acted as intermediary between Christopher Mountain and his children.

"How much does he want for it?" I asked.

I could visualize my mom placing her hand over the phone's mouthpiece – I'd seen it a hundred times before – as she turned to my dad and relayed the question. *Paul's interested in buying the van; how much do you want for it?*

Mmmrrph mmrrph, mrrmph-mrrmph-mrrmph.

"Your dad says blue book value. Do you know what that means?"

"I do. Does he know what that is, off the top of his head?"

Christopher, Paul wants to know–

Mmrph-mrrph-mrrmph–

"Thirty-five hundred," my mom duly reported. "Does that sound fair to you?"

"I trust it. Dad knows his blue book."

"Yes, I'm sure he does. He knows everything about cars."

"Very true." I paused for a second, stared at my ceiling, and did some quick math in my head. "I don't have that kind of money on hand right now, but I can easily pick up a bunch of extra shifts. It'll probably take a month or so to get all the funds together. Is that a problem?"

"No, we'll hold onto it for you," she said without consulting the living room oracle, "so long as you *definitely* want it."

"Yes, I definitely want it."

"Okay, great, I'm glad it's staying in the family. Just call when you get the money together and you're ready to come back and pick it up."

"Cool. Thanks for thinking of me, Mom."

"Of course. I know how much you loved that van. Take care of yourself, Paul."

I hung up, thinking of all the extra work I'd just committed to. Damn, all those extra shifts were going to eat into my early summer, the best time of year in the mountains. It was only the first week of May, but it might be June by the time I got the funds together. I decided right then to go on the work bender of benders, ask Joel to book me as many open-to-close shifts as he could, back-to-back-to-back for two weeks, if possible. It would be worth the pain to get the funds together quickly and be back in Colorado in time to enjoy the entire summer in the Rockies.

As a childhood passenger in my dad's van, silently staring out the back window while Minnesota farms flowed past, it would be weird to actually drive the thing, no less *own* the blue beast. My mom was right, I loved that van. It was a deep blue '79 Ford Econoline 350, and at age forty-five, it was the first new vehicle my father ever purchased. He bought it bare, nothing inside. Once he got it home, though, he poured his considerable mechanical talents into that stripped-down husk. It took him the better part of a year, but by the time he was done, he had a conversion van with all the luxuries – convertible table/bed, wood paneled walls, tinted windows, carpeted floors, electric outlets, bedside reading lamps, porta-potty toilet walled off in back. And, of course, there was an ice-box refrigerator for beer up front, perfectly positioned within a driver's easy reach. Throughout the '80s, Minnesota law required drinking while driving for anyone travelling over one hundred miles, especially if there were children in the vehicle, and my military father was not one to disrespect authority.

After renovations, the blue beast was the ultimate camping cruiser, and since it was my dad's, I knew it had been loved in the way other men reportedly loved their children. My old man babied his cars, used only synthetic oil, diligently fixed every tiny issue that arose. For me, buying that converted van at blue book value was a steal. Sure, he'd charge me full value for a '79 panel van, but he wouldn't factor in all the upgrades he'd done. And that's how Christopher Mountain's children gauged our father's feelings for us: by the depth of the discount we received when purchasing our family heirlooms. Oh well, fuck it. I was twenty years old, at least twelve years beyond caring about my father's feelings, least of all towards me. I'd buy his pristine van and try not to think about how, in an alternate universe, some fathers actually *gave* shit to their sons once in a while.

After two weeks of nonstop, fourteen-hour pizza shifts, I was back on a plane to Minneapolis, drinking free beer as fast as my attractive stewardess could sling it. White picked me up at the airport and the two of us drank all night, reminiscing about our initial move to Colorado, even though he bailed back to Minnesota after only six months. Following a night of suds at White's apartment, I predictably showed up at my parents' house the next day with an Econoline-sized hangover.

After approximately thirty seconds of awkward chit-chit following my arrival at the family homestead, my dad asked, "So, you ready to go over the features, learn what's what?" My old man actually looked younger, fresher, every time I saw him. Living without children suited him. His salt-and-pepper hair looked thicker, his father-fury anger wrinkles slightly less pronounced without daily use. I knew he'd still be a bit of a limp dick toward me – emptying one's house of children can't solve every problem – but his overall calmer demeanor might keep him from going full-scale erection on my ass.

It wasn't only a childless existence that helped mellow my father. Now in his fifties, my dad delivered motor homes from a factory in Iowa to RV dealerships all across the United States. A heart attack at age forty-six effectively ended his stressful dual careers in the Minneapolis Fire Department and United States Navy – not to mention vaporizing all the health certificates on his pilot's licenses that he'd hoped to parlay into a flight instructor career later in life. Cruising the open road in an RV as a private contractor was calming, and it was also the right financial move. It allowed my dad to pay himself the bare minimum income required by the state and fed, thereby maximizing his tax-free pensions from both.

"I'm as ready as I'll ever be to learn about the old beast," I said, pointing at "my" van down in the driveway.

"You sure you'll remember any of it?" He squinted at me, the disapproval of my glaring hangover obvious in his scrunched eyes. "You know, Paul, you can't soar with the eagles in the morning if you hoot with the owls all night."

It was possibly his favorite line from all his years as a Navy Air radio operator, trolling the skies in P3 airplanes in search of Russian subs and catchy sayings. If I had to ballpark a number, I'd guess he'd rolled his "soar with the eagles" wisdom nugget my direction at least 37,422 times... maybe even 37,423.

"Yeah, so I've heard, Dad. But I'm fine."

We walked down to the Econoline in the driveway, and my father began the tutorial. Turns out the van's operations were significantly more complicated than I imagined. Eventually, I realized my hangover was no match for the endless details, so I started taking written notes.

"All those connections can run on twenty-amp plug-in power," my dad said, pointing at three outlets in back by the porta potty. "But don't overload the circuit."

"Got it."

He stared at me. "You have no idea what twenty-amp power is, do you? Twenty amp, say, as compared to twelve-volt DC power?"

I stared blankly back at him, feeling ten years old again.

He sighed irritably. All instruction to his kids was a source of great annoyance to Father Mountain. He was convinced children should race out the womb possessing the requisite knowledge to disassemble and reassemble an internal combustion engine.

"Okay, Paul, let's try again," he continued deliberately, condescendingly, "and this time, try to focus. I'll even talk slowly for you, if that helps." He shot me a fake, tight-lipped smile. "Now, different electrical components require different current based on the load they need to operate, and if you direct the wrong—"

The young man stared at his father, nodded at all the appropriate times, and dreamed of beer-soaked vaginas and clear mountain ponds and softball trophies and The Grateful Dead singing "Don't Ease Me In" and ephedrine speeders fueling manic mountain ski runs and many, many other things that did not involve his father or brake pad lining or electrical current or Minnesota or the United States Navy.

I tried to make notes, but my dad quickly scribbled them out with irritated slashes before replacing them with *appropriate* notations I would never understand or even consult. I fantasized about that first beer of the day, so many painful hours away, and I stopped listening in any real sense of the word. When we moved on to the engine itself, I regressed back to ninth-grade auto shop, my dad drowning me in cam shaft specs, spark plug gaps, and proper distilled water levels for battery longevity. My father performed all his own auto repairs, only turning his vehicles over to a certified mechanic when the repair required a floor lift or some other enormous apparatus my mother forbid in their one-car garage. He kept copious notes of every repair, as well, and after explaining all the van's idiosyncrasies, he proudly broke out the ECONOLINE REPAIR LEDGER. He focused in on the oil change chapter, the dates, the exact hue of old oil – too dark meant bigger issues afoot, of course – estimated viscosity, exact amount of missing oil before each change down to the eighth of a quart, even the cost of synthetic Mobil 1 at each oil change interval. I slowly realized he actually believed I would *continue* documenting this rich history of the van's oil consumption. For the millionth time, I was shocked at how little this man knew me after eighteen long years under the same roof.

Then, before releasing the title to me, we retired to the kitchen table for the ceremonial reading of Rand McNally. My father worried over his road atlas like religious men deliberated over those particularly troublesome biblical passages that seemed to condone slavery and polygamy. He even showed his atlas the same respect as a holy text, kept it in pristine condition in his den – he had a lesser atlas in each vehicle, of course, a pocket bible of sorts – and he escorted the Rand McNally out to the kitchen table like a Hebrew scroll.

"Do you have your route mapped out?" he asked.

"Didn't give it much thought, to tell you the truth."

He sharply raised his eyebrows in shock and horror, then shook his head. "Well, you do *have* an atlas with you, right?"

"I rolled mine up and stuffed it in my suitcase, yeah."

"*Rolled it up?*"

My mother, the only person my father listened to, reached out and squeezed his arm. She gave him her patented *don't be an asshole* look.

"Well, I suppose it's your atlas, after all," he sighed, acknowledging my mother's silent warning. "Not my problem if you have to buy a new one every year."

We poured over his pristine map for the next hour, discussing interstates versus state highways, dirt roads, county roads, roads to avoid, scenic roads. My old man loved rolling down the open road all by his lonesome, consulting his atlas, scribbling copiously in his ROAD NOTES LEDGER, which he and I now consulted. Delivering RVs had turned him into a true encyclopedia of the Great American Road, so I listened and tried to remember, knowing I might put a few of his suggestions to use. I had my own plans for the ride home, of course, a strategy that involved LSD, alcohol, and little white ephedrine speeders. Strangely enough, those three crucial ingredients were never mentioned in my dad's LEDGER.

Eventually, I turned over a fat check, he handed me the van's title, and my mom gave me a cooler packed with enough food for a drive to China. I shook my dad's hand, waved goodbye to my mother, and successfully avoided all physical displays of affection for yet another year.

The ride home was the single greatest road trip of my life to that point. The van was freedom incarnate, everything I thought it would be and more. I rolled through South Dakota's empty back roads, checking my battered atlas for lakes and reservoirs. Whenever I closed in on a body of water, I scanned for an attractive dirt road, drove down it, and parked wherever I damn well pleased. Flinging open the van's sliding door, I drank beer, blasted the Econoline's kickass stereo, and stared at the empty prairie or shimmering lake. Whenever I felt the urge, I whipped out my dick and whizzed freely all over God's green earth, just as Man was meant to urinate on His creation. I carried the van's bed/bench cushions onto the roof and lay under the stars until the LSD insisted every aspect of my life was finally perfect. And when bad weather rolled in to challenge that perfection, I laughed at lightning and crawled into bed in the back of the van. I read beneath the reading lamp, safe from rain and wind and thunder, listening to the storms rage outside. All the tents of my life suddenly seemed like wispy, bad dreams, cardboard shacks compared to brick walls, and I felt vastly superior to everyone who still owned tents and sleeping bags and thought of that as "camping."

Still, it wasn't until I wiggled my wheels between the Chadron Formations in the South Dakota Badlands that I took a long, deep breath and firmly announced to no one: "I could live this way."

The sound of the words surprised me, the first I'd spoken or heard in two days, but also because I'd stated them with such certainty. I *could* live this way. I sat on a folding chair with a bowl of soup that I'd heated on my one-burner propane stove, wondering what geological upheaval occurred in the distant past to create the wild-ass Badlands of the present, and I knew for a fact that I could live the travelling life for a long, long time. I loved my Ayn Rand as much as any other red-blooded, libertarian nut job, but I was no Hank Reardon workaholic. I wanted to wander, sometimes purposefully, sometimes aimlessly. I had no desire to devote any more time than absolutely necessary to any job.

"But you need to do *something* for money," I said out loud. "You need to write, man. It's the only way."

The *only* way. To live the life I wanted, the full and complete life, I had to be a writer. It would be a life without excess, but it would also be without abject poverty. Most importantly, it would extricate me from the soul-crushing chains of the forty-hour work week. I knew of no other occupation that could do that, not even any of the other artistic pursuits. Comedians had to travel from tiny club to tiny club, trading cleverness for drinks and cheap hotel rooms. Painters needed a gallery to sell their art or at least a studio to create it. Rock stars had to actually perform, had to jump up and down in front of strangers. I never felt like jumping up and down, *especially* in front of strangers. And rock stars had to deal with fame, life's true poison apple, the figurative fruit Eve gave Adam from which humanity suffers to this day. How horrible and imprisoning to lose one's anonymity in the world. There was journalism, of course, men and women who trotted the globe, inserted themselves into interesting and dangerous situations. But journalists *had* to be somewhere, had deadlines, editors, worse alcoholism than my own, and a slew of venereal diseases contracted in miserable, distant lands from miserable, affordable women. I didn't want any of that. I wanted no rules, no laws, no restrictions, *total* freedom, and I wanted all of it in the prime of my youth. I wanted to write books at my leisure, ignore all deadlines, then casually slip a masterpiece in the mail once a year or so, placating my publisher's irritation for another twelve months. The rest of the time, I could travel the continent in my van, reveling in my one and only life.

"And then maybe you could start boning the entire Denver Broncos cheerleading squad," I said as I finished my soup. I shook my head sharply. "Stop dreaming, fuckface, and get your ass back to Colorado."

While writing was my possible future, pizza was my actual present, and pizza was a harsh mistress, demanding I return home. Even more important than pizza delivery – as if there could be anything more vital – I had social commitments back in Colorado, beginning in exactly one week. Lonnie finally graduated from CU, and as the daughter of wealthy divorced parents, she had twice as many expensive celebrations to attend as her fellow students from intact families. Lonnie's parents intended to outspend each other, a passive-aggressive battle over who could best purchase their daughter's love. As The Boyfriend, I was expected to escort Lonnie to each and every elaborate family event.

"He's home, he's home, he's home!" Lonnie called out as I strolled down our elevated walkway in Eldora a couple days later. "Yay!" Her smile split her face, and she clapped her hands excitedly beneath her chin. Rummy and Evie blasted out to greet me as if I were a soldier emancipating them from a concentration camp, their joy nearly knocking me off our walkway.

"I made it," I said to Lonnie after giving the dogs their due.

Now it was Lonnie's turn to greet me elaborately. She fell on me like a waterfall, drowned me in her love. She kissed my lips, cheeks, necks, foreheads, held me tight to her body, ran her hands through my hair, giggled in my arms. Suddenly, the grand freedom of the empty, lonesome road seemed less appealing, and the stability of women and animals and cabins took on greater significance.

"Miss me?" I asked.

"Can I show you how much?"

I didn't answer, just let her lead me by the hand into our bedroom at the back of our cabin. I was glad to see she was her normal, horny self. As per usual, my irritating jealousy had suggested that maybe Lonnie had a backup penis for when ol' Pablo wasn't in the picture. I'd been gone ten days, and Lonnie had been mysteriously absent a couple times when I called, calls I purposely made when she *should* have been home. Oh well, that was Lonnie, always straddling the fine line between slightly sneaky and blatantly untrustworthy. Pressing her on her weird absences would only bring out her predictable lies of omission and other sidestepping tactics that would get me no closer to the truth.

Back in our bedroom, she showed me three times how much she missed me, further assuaging my suspicions. She also proved, definitively, that masturbating in the back of my dad's van was not the pinnacle of human sexuality. When my penis finally demanded an extended timeout from Lonnie's love, I brought her and the dogs out to see my new wheels.

"Oh my god!" Lonnie said, squeezing my arm as she stood outside the van's open sliding door. "This is *so* cool! We need to take a big road trip ASAP!"

"Agreed. But we'll have to wait until after all the family festivities."

"Oh yeah, that. Thanks for reminding me."

"You don't sound very enthused, Lon. Is Andy coming, at least?" Andy was her fifteen-year-old brother, clearly a *Whoops!* child. He was a cool kid, already a drummer in a high school rock band. Both Lonnie and I loved hanging out with the little shit.

"I told Andy he *has* to come. I need at least one person there that I really like."

"Only one? What about Zack?"

Lonnie shrugged. "You know Zack. He said he was coming, but that was three weeks ago. He may show, he may not. Probably depends on the inner earth vibrations or whether Jupiter is in ascension or something."

I laughed. Lonnie's oldest brother Zack was certifiably insane, no hyperbole necessary. Her dad, William, bought a small plot of land in southern Colorado out of pity or guilt and let Zack squat there. Zack lived a free life, both financially and spiritually, his "home" an actual teepee. He heated his teepee with poorly ventilated wood fires and slept on a mat on the ground with a sleeping bag. Zack sort-of worked, occasionally, at some odd jobs for his equally bizarre hippie neighbors, but I suspected William still fed Zack's accounts, just as he did Lonnie's, but with better reason – Zack simply could not handle reality on reality's terms. He was a run-of-the-mill, hard-core Colorado stoner, but talking to Zack was more like talking to the pot itself, as if I were having a conversation with a joint while it was being slow-sucked. But Lonnie's oldest brother was so damn weird, so far out of his mind, that he was impossible not to like. There were no conversations like Zack conversations – twisting, ethereal trains of thought that led into the cosmos or nowhere at all, regularly abandoning logic as dead weight, linear thought as dull and unimaginative.

Predictably, Zack was the embodiment of flaky. He'd pop into town unannounced, drink all my beer, smoke all Lonnie's pot, then disappear for months without a word.

"Are the other siblings coming?" I asked.

"Oh, of course. Ella and Richard never miss a chance to annoy me. Now that Rick's four years out of college, I'd think he'd finally abandon his high school football mentality, but he never will. Same old bully he was as a kid."

"Some high school football studs never stop being high school football studs," I said. "Still, I'll take Richard over Ella any day. Ella is a total c–"

"Stop!"

I laughed. "I was going to say *conniver*. Ella is a total conniver."

Lonnie rolled her eyes. "Right." She called the dogs out of the van and slid the door closed. "Enough of this nonsense. Let's go eat and stop talking about my family. It's depressing. Come on, I made you your favorite green chile."

We went inside and Lonnie served me her awesome green chili that she'd been slow cooking in her crockpot all day, and then we drank too much beer and danced on our deck to old Grateful Dead tunes as the sun went down and the dogs tore around our yard. Since Lonnie hadn't seen me in nearly ten days, she laughed at all my jokes, even the gross one about Astroglide and farm animals, and I'd never felt more at home than I did in my little cabin in the mountains by the stream in the woods.

* * *

I headed back to Pizza Place the following day to resurrect my van-decimated bank accounts. When I emerged from five ten-hour workdays, Lonnie's family descended on Boulder like a well-financed downpour of upper-class judgment. I tried my best to go along to get along, but my efforts went mostly unappreciated. Her family and I were different ducks, plain and simple. They were wealthy, I was not in their social stratosphere, and the tribal distinction was palpable. I didn't blame them; their dislike for me didn't even feel personal. By birth, I just wasn't a member of the club. Many Jewish mothers want their sons to marry Jewish girls. Sabrina once told me her father would only accept a black man for a son-in-law. Lonnie's family didn't care about blood or race or religion, but they did expect a certain social standing – a man who would complete his studies, advance his career, and sire future generations of blue bloods to inherit the family's wealth. Conversely, I drove pizza. I didn't want children. My parents had no money. Strike one, two, and three. In baseball, three strikes only meant one out. In Lonnie's family, those three strikes earned me a game-ending ejection and lifetime suspension from the sport.

It was only three days of tedious dinners, ridiculously polite conversations, and furtive trips to the restaurant bar – *two shots of Beam, bartender, and I mean NOW! No, I don't have an I.D., but this is a family emergency, dammit!* – but every second of those three days was excruciating. It was like being back in high school, trying not to look at the clock again, *promising* yourself you won't look at the clock again, then looking at the clock nevertheless and realizing only two minutes and twenty-two seconds had passed. Time is a loose theory, experienced subjectively. Happy peoples' lives pass in an instant; the truly miserable live forever.

"Thank you so much for tolerating my family," Lonnie said after it was all mercifully over. We sat with our pups on our peaceful deck under the early summer stars, drinking away the memory of a long weekend with too much family.

"I did my best."

"You really don't like them, do you?"

I laughed and tipped back my can. "I like Andy. I like Zack."

"Andy's fifteen and Zack's nuts."

"Exactly."

She sighed. "I know, the rest of my family are such snobs. I can really see it when they're around you. I guess it's just how I grew up, luck of the draw. Don't get a say in where we come from, right?"

"No, we definitely do not. If we did, I probably would have picked a father who didn't hate his kids."

Lonnie shook her head. "God, I just don't see it. Your dad is so nice to me. And he seems nice to you, too."

"He is now, for the most part, especially when you're around." I shrugged. "But that doesn't mean shit. Now that I don't need him, yeah, he's decent enough. But kids need fathers early on, need some kind of positive guide, mentor, whatever. My dad was the opposite, actually, liked to take us down a notch."

"What do you mean, exactly?" she asked, turning to me. "I mean, you never give me any details about any of this stuff."

"I guess I don't like to dwell on the past, things I couldn't control then and definitely can't change now." I thought about it for a few seconds, which was a couple seconds longer than I ever wanted to. "It's kind of hard to explain, Lon, if you don't experience it yourself. Like, for example, my dad *refused* to go to our sporting events, refused. And then he'd tell us about how much he hated being in the stands for youth sports and how he'd never be caught dead watching one of our games."

Lonnie shook her head. "That is so weird. Wasn't he an athlete himself?"

"He was a stud athlete!" I said, then laughed a little sickly. "The dude was a semi-pro hockey player – never once skated with any of his nine kids. He was a third-degree black belt, taught martial arts on the side – never showed a single one of his kids a single self-defense move."

Lonnie stared at me for a few seconds, brow furrowed. "God, it's like being a pro baseball player and never playing catch with your own kids."

"Yep, it's exactly like that." I looked at the sky, thinking back, remembering. "Actually, I'm pretty sure my dad just felt a boatload of resentment toward his kids, lot of things he wanted to do in his life that he couldn't do because he started a family too young. I don't think I told you this, but my dad was accepted for some elite fighter pilot training when he was like nineteen, some program only twenty people or so in the whole country got accepted into each year. But then he got my mom pregnant. Whoops! Back then, the Navy's fighter pilot program didn't take anyone with kids, since fighter pilots had this weird habit of dying on the job and sticking the military with the tab for raising the kids."

"Wow, that's too bad."

"Yep, bummer for him and bummer for the nine of us who had to live with his resentment for the next thirty-five years." I shook out a ciggie and lit up. "Oh well, things could have been worse. I could have been born into the Manson family – father in jail, six moms on acid, all that Helter Skelter bullshit."

"Yep, you gotta look on the bright side," Lonnie said, rolling her eyes.

The stars popped into the sky like alien craft, their cloaking technology dimming them from view whenever I stared at one for more than a few seconds. I drank my beer and tried to stop thinking about family. I'd had way too much family brain drain recently, whether my own back in Minnesota or Lonnie's in Colorado.

"Well, growing up in a world of snobbery wasn't that much fun, either," Lonnie said, apparently not as eager to move on from the subject, "but it definitely has some perks!"

I looked over at her, hearing the upbeat change in her tone. She was smiling back at me now, radiantly. Oh god, I knew that grin of hers. That was Lonnie's "happy-child" face, the one she wore whenever her father dumped an unexpectedly large sum of cash into her checking account.

"Uh-oh, did your dad buy you a new car for graduation or something?"

Lonnie laughed excitedly and pressed her hands together beneath her chin. "It was my mom this time!"

I rolled my eyes. "Your mom actually bought you a new car?" I tried to mask the jealousy in my voice. The Catholic Church taught me all about *ENVY*, one of the seven deadly sins. Envy bought a man a straight ticket to hell for an eternity immersed in freezing water…after a quick stop in Purgatory, that is, to have his eyes sewn shut with wire, if Dante could be believed. But damn, envy was a tough sin to avoid, possibly the hardest of them all. That some people had it so easy, simply by dint of birth, was a reality that gnawed at the human soul throughout all of history. That blatantly unjust arrangement routinely destroyed entire nations, the infantries of *ENVY* racing toward the armies of *ADVANTAGE*.

"Oh, no, nothing like that," Lonnie said quickly, still smiling. "Why would I need a new car?"

"You don't."

Lonnie placed her hand on my shoulder, gave it a little squeeze, and held my gaze. "Okay, Paul, *pleeeaaase* don't hate me for this, but…"

I waited for the rest, but it wasn't coming. Lonnie bit her lower lip to keep her happiness from erupting.

"But what, Lonnie?"

"My mom is taking me on an eight-week trip to Europe!"

Jesus, I should have guessed. Europe. The old country. The old *countries*. That was real travel, a giant leap off the Econoline's roof onto international rails. I wanted to go to Europe. Hell, I wanted to go to Mexico. I'd studied up on Europe, the wild old Europe of Hemmingway and Fitzgerald, the dorky modern Europe of Rick Steves and PBS specials. I would have traded a limb to travel overseas. But a trip like that was not financially feasible unless I wanted to scrimp and save for at least a year of my life. Nope, my realistic travel dreams ended somewhere around the Oregon coastline.

"Wow, that is an unbelievably generous gift," I finally said, whistling low. "I hope you realize how fortunate you are."

"Oh, I do, trust me."

I doubted that. Only the children of the *have nots* truly understand the wild ass good luck of the children of the *haves*. It's one thing to work and earn and grow wealthy; it's an entirely different matter to stumble blindly into wealth at birth.

"When are you leaving?" I asked.

"Three weeks, beginning of July."

The second Lonnie gave me her departure date, envy and spite joined forces in my mind and started scheming for all the sex I'd score while she was away. Without Lonnie limitations, Sabrina and I could have marathon romps at her place in Boulder. Maybe I'd even invite her up to the cabin for a weekend of clean, nature sex, the kind two people can only have while breathing crisp, Rocky Mountain air. Then I'd hunt the leather chicks at the Sundown Saloon, ply them with pitchers of PBR, impress them with my badass AC/DC t-shirts. I'd loiter on the barstools of the Pioneer Inn in Nederland, see if some of the older hippie chicks wanted to relive their youth with some of that Free Love they were always bragging about.

"Wow, July is right around the corner," I said. "Where are you two going, anyway?"

Lonnie giggled excitedly. "*Everywhere!* My mom bought us Eurail passes so we can take the train pretty much anywhere in Europe. I guess she's been planning this trip for the last year or so with her travel agent." Lonnie glanced over at me, and I thought I saw a hint of guilt on her face, a slight acknowledgment of how easy she had it. "I don't know if it's even of interest to you," she said a little sheepishly, "but my mom left me all kinds of guidebooks for a bunch of different countries. Do you want to see them, see where I'm going?"

I nodded, sighing a little. "Sure, Lon, I'll give them a look. But only if you promise you'll ditch your mom and take your poor, broke boyfriend instead."

We went inside and Lonnie gave me a firsthand look at what it meant to be a Spoiled American Princess. The SAP lifestyle involved wineries in southern France, weekends in Paris, castle tours through Tuscany. Lonnie would drink huge mugs of suds in the beer halls of Munich, and she'd drift slowly through the canals of Venice, her flowing blonde hair flapping like a flag of surrender to all the swarthy Italian dudes. She and her mother would spend nights on a Greek island, days on a Swiss mountaintop. They'd ride the double-decker buses of London and, god dammit, they were even going to Abbey Road Studios. That was about all I could handle without getting visibly angry. *I* should be visiting Abbey Road Studios, not Lonnie. I was the one who sat through all the Beatles albums, even the cheesy, early stuff about chasing underage girls. Shit, I was one of the only people I knew who had listened to the entirety of Revolution #9, and not just once, either. I took it for a spin while sober, on acid, drunk out of my mind, always searching for why the Beatles ever released the most annoying "song" ever recorded.

"I wish you were going," Lonnie said.

"Well, someone's gotta take care of the dogs. And that damn pizza isn't going to deliver itself." I lit up a ciggie to calm my growing irritation. "Let's face it, Lon, I don't have the money for a trip like that and probably never will. I have no idea how much it's going to cost your mom, but I'm betting my calculator doesn't go up that high."

"My mom has the money," Lonnie said, waving off the cost with a flick of her wrist. "She walked away with a massive settlement from my dad in the divorce, and then she inherited a fortune when her own dad died. This is nothing to her."

Wow, so casual, so dismissive. The chasm between the haves and the have nots is more than money, I realized, it's an impassable mental gorge. Lonnie would never know financial hardship, would never feel so much as a glancing blow from poverty, and it showed in her detached demeanor toward wealth. From my perspective, her wealthy world seemed like something out of an F. Scott Fitzgerald novel. Fictional luxuries invented by authors – new cars for sixteenth birthdays, season ski passes to Vail, train rides through the fields of France, nights in castles, rent paid, tuition paid, random cash dumps into dwindling bank accounts. Wealth is an absurdity to the functionally poor, and the functionally rich can't conceive of living any other way.

"Well, it should be one hell of a trip," I said.

She reached over and squeezed my forearm. "It's going to be hard being away from you for almost two months. I'm going to miss you so much."

"I'll miss you, too, babe," I said reflexively, envisioning spite-sex with random women and all the gritty, inexpensive pleasures of the *have not* world. Lonnie put her arms around me and hugged me tight. I hugged her right back, a little more aggressively than I intended.

* * *

It was a beautiful night for Lonnie's "real" graduation party, the one she and I planned for friends only at our little cabin a week after the formal ceremonies. NO FAMILY ALLOWED, DAMMIT! The liquid acid I'd taken to celebrate having liquid acid rolled clean and strong through my brain. At least a half dozen other acid adventurers were at the party, but I'd lost track of them somewhere. Throughout the night, partygoers wandered into the woods when the drugs came on too strong or when a surge of lust inspired young couples to check out the creek. Sabrina had been at the party, but she'd left early, thankfully. With three gallons of beer coursing through my veins, I knew I'd eventually sneak off with her if she stayed. And if I couldn't keep my dick in my pants when celebrating a party specifically in honor of my girlfriend, then I was an even bigger S.O.B. than I already suspected.

I was peaking hard, so I stepped away from the festivities for some alone time in the woods to come to grips with the trip. I strolled down to Middle Boulder Creek and the sanity of running water. It was beautiful, the splish-splash subtle symphony of a mountain stream rolling over rocks on an LSD-infused summer night. A nearly full moon speckled the drifting creek, and I stood and wondered if I should go back to the cabin, grab my gear, and do some fishing. I'd never fished my stream at night. Was night fishing for trout even possible? More importantly, was it ethical to drag a fish from his cool water home in the dead of night, or was that just too cruel? Acid morphed the simple question into a grand philosophical undertaking, one of fish, of water, of death, of being plucked from an assumed reality and violently thrust into a greater truth, like being abducted by aliens and flown to Alduburon where molten beings communicated telepathically and could not understand feeble human squawking. Damn, there was so much to contemplate in the universe – theorems, chasms, multi-layered spaz-masms. All reality was a Dr. Seuss riddle-rhyme, all in time, mine for a dime.

"Stop it," I said…and shook my head…like a ball of lead. "Seriously, dude, knock that shit off."

If a weird mental rhyming pattern took hold while peaking on acid, I could easily see an onslaught of dumb limericks forcing me to get in my car, drive to Nantucket, and find out once and for all if that man really could suck it. I decided to keep moving and walk the voices out of my head. I turned upstream, strolled quietly, and let the sound of rolling water wash away the rhymes. After five minutes of wandering through the forest, I thought I heard actual voices up ahead, but I couldn't be sure. LSD was weird in the woods, so many soft sounds merging into confusing patterns that often sounded like voices but were not.

I slowed and quieted my footsteps, straining to hear. Yep, those were hushed voices, alright. I grinned, curious who it might be. It was always fun to find out who locked legs at a party. Sometimes they were cheaters like me, which was always nice. Those little liars helped reinforce all my philandering excuses. Sinners need sinners to justify sinnin'. Other times, it was only an innocent drunken fling, two people who would never get together had they not poured twenty beers down their throat that particular night.

I crept closer, avoiding twigs, the voices growing crisper. The male voice became more audible, and it began to sound familiar. I moved in even closer. Ducking behind a tree, I listened as clearly as my acid ears would allow until I finally recognized the voice. Sweet! It was Phil. Of all the guys I knew, Phil was the one dude most desperately in need of a good lay. In the year and a half I'd known him, he'd never so much as mentioned a woman outside of Ayn Rand, and I was objectively, rationally, and logically certain he wasn't banging her.

"Oh, I gotta see this," I whispered, grinning, curious as hell which woman Phil plucked from the party.

I moved stealthily to a slightly closer tree. Now I could see the couple's outline against the water, the two of them sitting on a carved bench some Eldora resident had long ago placed along the creek. It was a great spot, the trees opening up to a commanding view of the valley mountains, especially tonight under the nearly full moon. Lonnie and I stopped there regularly to smoke pot and cigarettes respectively while walking the dogs. I watched Phil's silhouette close the space between the two bodies, and the girl's silhouette met him halfway.

"Nice, dude," I whispered. "Go for the tits, bro."

After a minute or so of intense necking, Phil did exactly that. I watched the female silhouette pull her shirt over her head, and Phil's face ducked down for a taste of flesh. The girl leaned her head back, her hair drifted down past her shoulders, and a soft moan fell from her lips.

Wait a second.

I stood up sharply, almost backpeddled into a thick pine. I knew that moan. *No way*, I thought, *no fucking way*. My heart galloped as I peered through the darkness, but the swirling acid hallucinations kept me from completely making out her face. But I knew that moan, goddammit. And as I watched closer, I recognized those body movements. Long ago, I'd memorized the intensified gasps that fell from this young woman's mouth as she clutched a man's head between her very large breasts.

I had to know for certain. I snuck in as close as I dared, using the couple's passion for cover. This time, when the woman pulled Phil's head up, I distinctly heard Lonnie say, *"C'mon, one more time before I leave, okay?"*

Phil stood up and reached for his waistband. Then Lonnie stood up. She quickly raised the cute new flowered skirt she'd bought specifically for her party. I'd complimented her on it, was looking forward to sliding it off her hips after all our fellow partiers lay passed out on our living room floor. I couldn't get my eyes off Lonnie's silhouette. I would know the outline of that body from space, even as it swirled within the multi-colored pool of psychedelic hallucination. And I knew that when Lonnie hiked her skirt hurriedly instead of slowly removing it, she was hot for the action *right now*.

Eyes wide, I stepped slowly backward, and a very strange thought took hold: *This is none of your damn business, Paul.* It was a weird thought to have when a good friend of mine was about to pork my live-in girlfriend. But that's exactly what I thought, exactly how I felt. I did not need to see the grand finale, because it was none of my damn business. I did not need to break up their passion, because it was none of my damn business. I did not need to hold it over her, did not need to make a scene, did not need to come crashing through the woods to attack Phil with a downed tree branch. I did not even need to tell Lonnie I was wise to her ways, not that night, not ever. Maybe it was the peaking acid, maybe it was a rare moment of clarity and wisdom, maybe it was my own acknowledged guilt for the same crime committed multiple times, but I decided right then and there that this romp in the woods was one-hundred percent Lonnie's business and none of mine.

Retreating into the woods, I finally knew, *knew*, that Lonnie and I had an expiration date. I always believed we'd be done some day, but now I knew it in my bones. How liberating. Two years' worth of suspicions and jealousy about Lonnie's disappearing antics, her countless lies of omission, and her endless vagaries turned out to be well-founded. She was a sneaky little cheat, just like me. Right on. We were even-steven, regardless who cheated more often. One cheat or ten, what's the difference? The bond is broken at the first dalliance. Besides, I distinctly heard her say, "one more time." That implied a previous pounding, maybe a whole history of backwoods boning, perhaps dating back years. And why *shouldn't* Lonnie sleep around? She understood the score, saw the writing on the wall. She and I weren't forever, and like me, Lonnie was young and dumb. And now, Lonnie was officially young, dumb, and full of Phil's cum.

I made it back to the main path without alerting them. Lonnie's moans were still audible, but they swooshed and swirled back into the distant sounds of the psychedelic forest. Good, didn't need any more of *that* nonsense, thank you very much.

I couldn't help giggling a little as I put some distance between myself and the crime scene. People often laugh at tragedy, especially when tragedy strikes at the same time LSD peaks. Maybe I was laughing in relief, the weight finally falling off my shoulders, all that old Catholic guilt no longer strapped to my back. Now that I knew Lonnie was also a little cheat, I could carry on with my life without all the pomp and circumstance of monogamy.

"We're practice partners, that's all," I muttered as I closed back in on Lonnie's graduation party. "Just learning how to love, warming up for something bigger down the road."

I liked that. Everyone has to learn with someone. Best to get all the bad mojo out of our systems before our actual life partners arrived on the scene. Best to make all kinds of horrible mistakes before horrible mistakes result in horrible divorces or broken families or destroyed businesses or all the other manifestations of general ruination.

I walked through my back gate and saw Franzen sitting alone on my deck, his legs dangling in air. He stared intently at the ground four feet below, as if studying a rare form of soil never before discovered. The acid he took at the same time I did was obviously roaring through his veins.

"Dude," I said.

He lifted his head slowly, his mouth agape, his eyes wide with wonder. "Jesus, man, where the fuck have you *been?*"

"Wandering the water, bro, just wandering the water."

He nodded, understanding the urge. "That's cool, but you've totally been missing out on everything."

"Yeah?" I walked up the stairs to my elevated deck and plopped down next to him. "Like what?"

He swooped his arm across his body, then pointed down at the dirt he'd been studying. "Like *everything.* Did you know that the whole world is contained, like, in that single patch of ground? Or any patch of ground, really, any small patch of ground in the whole fucking world. I mean, do you realize that if you dig into any one thing deeply enough, you'll eventually understand *everything?*"

"I guess I haven't thought about it." I reached over and poured myself a beer from the full pitcher Erik had at his side. "Explain."

Erik explained to the best of his acid ability, and I listened and laughed and tried to give it real thought. It was a typical LSD exploratory conversation:

confusing, enlightening, disturbing, and at times, hilarious. The summer night wore on in Eldora, Colorado, and Lonnie emerged from the woods roughly thirty minutes later. I didn't ask any questions, simply kissed her quickly – didn't want to taste Phil's dick on her lips – and gave no indication that anything was wrong. Phil strolled in from the street side of my cabin ten minutes after Lonnie, claiming he'd gone for a long walk up the road. I invited him to grab a beer and take a seat, then Phil, Franzen, and I carried our conversation way further than it probably warranted. That was cool by me. Even though I accepted the backwoods boning I'd recently witnessed, I still needed a little time to fully process it, needed a distraction from the imagery. Weird acid chat was so much better than picturing Phil pounding his penis into Lonnie's sopping wet pussy. Pounding it. Pounding it. Lonnie's moans mounting, her hands clutched around Phil's neck, begging him for more and more and MORE as he stuffed his cock way up deep inside the only woman I'd ever loved.

Yes, weird acid chat was so much better than that.

7.

An Enigma Wrapped in a Belch

"I'll miss you, Lon," I said.

"Not as much as I'll miss you."

"Bullshit. You'll be too busy exploring Europe to think about me."

She pushed herself up on her toes and kissed me one last time. "I gotta go. My mom's waiting. I love you."

"I love you, too." I flicked my wrist, shooing her away. "Go thou, go thou, and of this world report you well and truly."

"Huh?"

"Nothin'. Have fun, Lon."

She turned and wheeled her suitcase toward where her mom waited impatiently at the jetway, both of them anxious to board the plane and plop their pampered asses down in first-class seats. Nothing but the best for that family. I smiled and waved at Lonnie's mom. She waved back briefly with an involuntary grimace. Ah, the unintentional pettiness of the upper classes.

Driving away from Stapleton International Airport a half hour later, I felt great. Liberated. Free as homeless shelter soup, wild as…wild rice soup. I'd been stapled to Lonnie's side for almost two years, cohabitated with the girl for a year and a half, and even though I was only twenty years old, I suddenly felt my youth come roaring back into my bones. For the first time since White, Chuck and I crossed the Colorado state line, I felt like the whole world was open to me.

I drove straight to my buddy Eddie's place in Boulder, ready to kick start the party. Eddie was always up for drink and drugs, even if it occasionally resulted in him barfing in my sink in Eldora, as it had on my twentieth birthday. He was from TEXAS, where everything was BIGGER, capitalized, even the ALCOHOLISM. Eddie was probably the only thing out of Texas that wasn't big. He was small and skinny, in fact, way too small and skinny for such a gigantic Texas thirst, and he often outdrank his short, 140-pound frame. But what he lacked in stamina, he made up for in *Let's Go, Cowboys!* enthusiasm. Besides, as an extremely talented musician, he had a built-in excuse for any and all excess that regularly occurred in his large garage where his band practiced. Eddie manned the keyboards, our fellow pizza driver Len throttled the axe, and All Night Diner was getting better and better by the day. With the help of a solid bassist, drummer, and their hot, female lead singer, they were starting to open for some of the bigger bands around Boulder. I could think of no better place than Eddie's garage to launch a brain-rattling bender in celebration of my newfound liberty.

"He's not here," Eddie's younger sister, Allie, told me when she answered the door.

"Really?"

"Yes, Paul, really."

"He told me he'd be home today."

"What, do you think I'm lying to you?" Allie scoffed. "You think I'm trying to trick you into leaving?"

Eddie's little sister Allie was the single best-looking girl I'd ever met in person. There wasn't even a close second. She was jaw-dropping gorgeous, dangerously hot. A man needed oven mitts to touch her. She could brand a steer with her palm. Her long brown hair fell in rolling curls onto her perfect tits, bear's porridge tits, not too warm, not too cold, *just right*. She had a perfect ass, perfect legs, perfect weight. Everything about her body was proportionally accurate, a sculptor's finest vision of WOMAN. Her face was a painting, beautiful hazel eyes that appeared equally intelligent and cruel, full and inviting lips, shapely nose, high cheekbones, groomed eyebrows.

Sadly, Allie was also the biggest bitch in Boulder County, and with so many qualified contestants, that was not a trophy easily earned. She was just plain mean, born bad, raised in a lion's den. She was angry and dark, the polar opposite of Eddie. And Allie wasn't the typical "hot girl" bitchy, either; she was a bitch at some deep-seated root level, something wrong in her core programming. She'd relocated to Boulder from Fort Worth, Texas to go to CU, a move that horrified Eddie. He thought he'd left his little sister's insanity behind down in the Lone Star state. Now at nineteen and only in her second year at CU, Allie had already gone through four roommates. Finally, Eddie's parents told him that if he didn't let Allie live with him, he could forget about the tuition assistance they promised if/when he ever decided to go to a serious music school. After laying down some very strict ground rules, Eddie relented and let her move in.

Oddly, I kind of liked Allie, and not just for her waves of brown hair, hypnotic hazel eyes, and super sexy, softly southern Texas drawl. Allie was unique. Uniquely horrible, true, but still unique. I enjoyed messing around with her to see what made her tick, as if performing some kind of weird chemistry experiment on bitchiness. *If I add three parts sarcasm to two parts subtle insult, will this highly combustible young woman explode?* Allie was a vanguard of the no-smoking fascism soon to sweep the nation, so I chain smoked around her, sending her into a tailspin. I made crude jokes, because she found crudity and comedy equally unrefined. I told her pet ferret – yes, Allie had a ferret – to bite her, to hide behind the furniture, to crawl into the wash machine. Strangely, it almost seemed like Allie enjoyed all my teasing. Or maybe she respected that I wasn't afraid of her. She was so impossibly good looking that most men morphed into mice the instant she entered a room. Had she not been Eddie's sister, I'm sure I would have squeaked and scurried away as well, but with Eddie providing friendship cover, I had the necessary confidence to engage his gorgeous little sister.

"Well, he *could* be here," I said. "I wouldn't put lying past you."

"Why would I lie to you, Paul?"

"Because you don't like me being so close to your big brother."

Allie's eyebrows furrowed. "What are you talking about?"

"You know *exactly* what I'm talking about, Allie." I pointed my finger at her. "Your Texas homophobia isn't lost on me."

"Oh my god, you're so weird." She stepped aside from the door. "Do you want to come in and see for yourself?"

"Don't mind if I do." I moved right past her and walked up a short flight of stairs to the living room. Without looking for Eddie, I took a seat on the couch and lit a smoke. "Well, I guess you weren't lying, he's not here. Oh well. There any beer in the fridge?"

"Are you seriously going to smoke cigarettes in my house?"

"It was Eddie's house first, and he doesn't mind."

"But I do."

"So?"

She shook her head, hands on her hips. "Why do you act like this, Paul? You light those gross cigarettes in my house, and then you actually expect to stick around and drink free beer?"

"Bingo! A-plus, Allie!"

She crossed her arms and glared at me.

"Oh, come on," I said, laughing, "lighten up a little for once in your life. I just want to stick around for a bit to see if Eddie comes home. I swore he told me he'd be here this afternoon. How 'bout you grab us a couple beers and hang out with me for a can or two?"

"I don't like beer," she said, tempting me to slap her for blasphemy. She paused for a few seconds, looking away. "But I suppose I could have a wine cooler. I could use a short break from studying. *Short*, though."

"Amen, Eddie's sister! Break out your weird little wine coolers!"

She walked past where I sat on the couch and continued into the kitchen. I couldn't help ogling her as she passed by. My god, the girl was a sledgehammer of hot, slamming me right in the dick. That image cracked me up, seemed like a great scene in a short story: *The brunette's hotness slammed Johnny right in the dick, forcing a feeble "Ouch" from his lips. Someone constructed that chick in a girl factory deep in the Magic Mountains, he knew, but that was exactly why he wasn't particularly intimidated by her — she was not a real human being. Johnny could not accept a reality where human females were that stunning. Her existence seemed impossible, laughable even, like meeting Jesus while not on acid or deciding to domesticate a ferret.*

Allie returned from the kitchen and gave me a Budweiser, a wine cooler in her other hand. Good lord, she even smelled perfect. Whatever light wisp of perfume she wore accented her overall appearance expertly.

"So what are we drinking to?" she asked.

"Do we need a reason?"

"I do. Derelicts like you and my brother may not need a reason to drink in the middle of the afternoon on a weekday, but I do."

"Fair enough." I rubbed my chin and gave it a few seconds of thought. "Okay, let's drink to freedom."

"Freedom? Like the United States or something?"

"No, to *my* freedom. I'm free as a goddam bird for the next eight weeks, Allie. Just dropped Lonnie off at the airport. Her and her mom are trekking all over Europe for the next two months, so I'm a wild and crazy bachelor once again. Now drink!"

I held out my beer bottle and Allie clinked it, then she took a sip off her wine cooler before settling into the recliner across from me.

"Most guys would be sad to see their girlfriends leave for two months," she said.

I laughed loudly and took a second big belt of beer.

"What, you don't think so?"

"Would you be sad to see your boyfriend leave for that long?"

"You know I don't have a boyfriend."

"Yeah, I guess I do know that." I sucked on my Marlboro and blew the secondhand smoke in her general direction. "Why *don't* you have a boyfriend, anyway? That surprises me."

"I'm too big of a bitch." She shrugged and tilted her wine cooler. "That's what everyone says about me, right?"

I smirked but didn't answer. I'd heard many, many stories that attested to her chronic bitch-itis. Allie poisoned her previous roommate's prized houseplants, for instance, which led directly to her now living with Eddie. There had been some dispute over the electric bill, and Allie felt shortchanged. So when her roommate was away at class one day, Allie wandered through the apartment and poured bleach into all the potted plants. Her roommate loved plants, apparently, had a dozen or so exotic varieties. *Had* exotic varieties. Not anymore.

"Don't worry, Paul, I know what everyone thinks, and I don't really care. They're wrong. It's not that I'm such a bitch deep down, it's just that I get so…so…" She trailed off and stared at the ceiling, looking for the right word. "*Infuriated*. People *infuriate* me, all the stupid things they do, stupid things they say. I can't help reacting to all that stupidity. I have a real problem controlling my temper, and so many things drive me nuts, that's all."

"Do I drive you nuts?"

She laughed in surprise. Allie was usually so sullen or angry that when she smiled, her full beauty was startling. *Damn*, I thought, *this girl truly is the prettiest creature I've ever seen.*

"Of course you drive me nuts," she said, "but I know you're driving me nuts on purpose, more like teasing me, so I let you get away with it. Besides, it's kind of nice that you actually *talk* to me. You're one of the only people in Boulder that gives me the time of day. Sure, you're usually only chatty when you're shitfaced drunk, but at least *someone's* talking to me."

"Wow, I'd think men would trip all over themselves to talk to you."

Allie sighed, then leaned forward in her chair, elbows on her thighs, and stared intently at me. "Look, Paul, I know what you're saying. I'm not stupid. And I don't mean to sound conceited, but I know how I look. It's not something I'm proud of or arrogant about because what I look like has nothing to do with me as a person. I didn't earn it or anything, don't deserve it or not deserve it. We look how we look, good or bad, that's all. It's just dumb luck, and in a lot of ways, being on the plus side of that equation isn't so lucky." She paused and rolled her wine cooler between her palms. "See, that's the problem, guys are scared of how I look. Other than you, guys don't *ever* talk to me. And if I say a word to them, they regress back to nervous little boys or else they become pompous windbags, always trying to impress me." She cocked her head, as if considering whether to share more. "Actually, I'll tell you a secret, Paul: no one ever asked me to prom, not once in three years of high school. I haven't even been asked out on a real date since early in my junior year of high school, and I found out later that he only asked me out on a bet. His buddies didn't think he had the balls."

She shrugged, then hit her wine cooler.

I was surprised to hear a genuine note of loneliness in her voice, almost a touch of human tenderness. She'd erected so much barbed wire fencing around her persona that I didn't think Allie cared about anything, least of all dating.

"Jesus, Allie," I said, "that sucks some serious donkey dick."

"You have a real way with words, Paul."

"Thank you." I crushed my cigarette in one of Eddie's ashtrays and tipped back my beer. "Look, Allie, don't take any of that crap personally. Men can be cowards, true, but when it comes to women, it's usually learned cowardice. After you're rejected two-thousand times before your eighteenth birthday, you get a little gun-shy." I puffed out my cheeks and blew out a long breath. "But hey, fuck all those guys. What do you say I take you out today, right now? We can grab a bite wherever you want and then maybe we can go catch a movie or do whatever you like to do when you're not shaking your fist at the whole damn world. My treat, Allie, a real live date with a real live dude." I flashed her a big smile and spread my arms wide. "And damn, *what* a dude!"

She almost smiled back at me, lips making it about two thirds of the way up before flattening again. She cocked her head to the side and stared at me out of the corner of her eye. "Paul, are you messing with me? Please don't tease me about stuff like this."

I shook my head. "I'm not messing with you, Allie, not this time. I'm honestly asking you out on a date."

"What about Lonnie?"

"Who is this Lonnie person you reference?"

Allie laughed a little. "Fair enough." She studied me for several more seconds. "But I have to know, do you actually *want* to take me out or is this just some kind of pity date?"

"Mainly pity." The most beautiful girl I'd ever seen was worried about pity dates. Wow. "Come on, Allie, there's not a man in Boulder who wouldn't want to date you if he thought there was a chance you'd say yes." I shrugged. "At least until he got to know you."

"God, why do you always *do* that?" she asked sharply, slapping her leg. "Why do you always ruin every nice thing you say with sarcasm, turn everything into a joke? My brother does the same stupid thing. Why does everything have to be funny to guys like you?"

I pointed a finger at her. "Because everything *is* funny, Allie. This life is comedy, baby, nuns with shotguns, goggles on donkeys." I drained my beer and belched loudly because belching loudly in front of ultra-hot chicks reinforced everything I just said about comedy. "Look, Allie, do you want to go out with me or not?"

Her face slowly softened, and then she finally smiled at me, almost shyly. It was an innocent girl smile, one who just received an unexpected gift. "I'd love to," she said, grinning. "Can we go play miniature golf after getting a bite? I love mini-golf."

"Mini-golf, maxi-golf, whatever you please."

She laughed and stood up. "Then yes, I'll go out with you! Give me a half hour to clean myself up, okay? Have another beer while you wait!"

Given thirty whole minutes, I had two more beers while I waited and nearly cracked a third. I sat in Eddie's living room, guzzling his beer, trying to grapple with the fact that I was about to go out with his sister, the most beautiful woman in the world. Lonnie hadn't even boarded her connecting flight in New York yet, and I was already heading out on the town with another woman. But I had an awesome alliteration of an excuse: Phil's plump porpoise powerfully penetrates Lonnie's labia. It only took seven days to create the universe and only seven words to set me free from my adulterous guilt. Besides, Lonnie would bone someone in Europe, I was certain of it. Her veneer of innocence was gone, lost in a sticky glob of Phil's man-goo, and no hot twenty-two-year-old blondie was going to run around Europe for eight weeks without sampling some German sausage, some Italian noodle, a little French baguette. Her bitch mom would probably encourage Lonnie every step of the way. *Honey, go straddle that swarthy Salvador and forget all about your indigent little pizza driver. He's not worthy of your lineage, baby girl.*

Allie reappeared thirty minutes later, stepping off a magazine cover and strolling into the living room. The girl was primped to perfection, miraculously more attractive than I'd ever seen her. She'd curled her hair in long ringlets, made up her face just a touch, and donned a thin, high-necked, long-sleeve red shirt that hugged her in all the right places. She wore a tan skirt and leggings, fashionable black boots with two-inch heels. She was the sexiest thing I'd ever seen without appearing even slightly slutty. Until that moment, I didn't think it was possible to decouple slutty from sexy, but Allie pulled it off masterfully.

"Allie, I know you're probably sick of hearing this, but you are an absolute knockout."

She spun around, smiling, showing herself off. "You like?"

"I like." I suddenly felt very self-conscious about my t-shirt and shorts, Pizza Place baseball hat, two days of stubble.

"So you won't be embarrassed to be seen with me?" she asked.

"A little, but with a few more beers, I'm sure you'll get prettier."

She rolled her eyes. "Let's go, Paul."

Allie chose Tom's Tavern, a popular Boulder burger joint, because she said she wanted to celebrate her first date in three years with the fattiest, most unhealthy food she could think of. Every man in the restaurant did a cartoonish double take as Allie walked by, and then they studied me with obvious confusion. *How on earth did that dude manage to…* Once we were served our sodas – no underage drinking at Tom's Tavern, unfortunately – Allie opened up about herself. She told me she didn't chase her brother to Boulder, she was actually given a full-ride academic scholarship to CU. I knew Allie was bright, but I didn't know she was *that* bright. More surprising, she said she was starting pre-med classes in the fall on her way to becoming a surgeon.

"You're going to be a doctor? You?"

She looked at me curiously over her swiss and mushroom burger. "Why do you sound so surprised?"

"Because you hate people."

"Right, but this way I can hack them to pieces and I won't go to jail."

I burst out laughing. "Sweet Jesus, Allie said something funny! I don't think I've ever heard you make a joke before."

"Who says I'm joking?"

I laughed again.

"I'm actually really funny, Paul."

"No, you really are not. You're way too serious to be funny."

An hour later, we waited in line to tee off on Hole #3, a little roundabout circling a small fountain. A perfect bank shot would deliver a hole in one, but a conservative roll play would damn near guarantee a two. So many gut-wrenching decisions to make in the hardscrabble world of miniature golf. As I stood weighing my options, I felt Allie's hand slip into mine. I looked down into her spectacular hazel eyes and immediately felt weak, vulnerable. *This girl could make me do anything,* I thought. Beautiful women are like clinical hypnosis, and young men are highly suggestible patients, ready to cluck like chickens at the trigger word.

"This is so much fun," she said, giving my hand a quick squeeze. "Thank you so much for taking me out."

"Any time, Allie."

"*Any* time?"

I shrugged. "Sure, why not?"

"So are you saying you might ask me out again?" She smiled up at me.

Again, I was shocked at her self-doubt. "Of course. I'm actually surprised you're so eager to go out with me again."

She bit her lower lip cutely, her big eyes flirting with mine. "Well…" She trailed off, then let out a long breath before continuing. "I'm going to let you in on a little secret, Paul: I've always kind of liked you. I never really showed it, but ever since the first day I got to Boulder and you helped my brother move me into the dorms, I had a little crush on you."

I paused, trying to remember that day almost two years in the past. I couldn't recall much beyond hauling all her stuff up to her dorm room with Eddie and thinking his little sister was scary hot, way too good looking for the likes of me.

"Seriously?" I asked. "Why?"

"You really need to ask why some young, impressionable girl might have a crush on her big brother's friend?"

"Yep."

"Then you don't know much about girls, Paul. Big brother's buddy is always attractive. Maybe it's because we look up to our older brothers, so his friends have an automatic stamp of approval or something."

"I'll be damned. Didn't know that." I glanced away from her, embarrassed.

She giggled at me. "What, does someone having a little crush on you make you uncomfortable?"

I had to think about that for a bit before answering. "I don't know that I'd use the word *uncomfortable*, exactly. Disbelief is more like it. I come from a huge-ass family, Allie, nine kids, and a person kind of disappears when there's so many other people around. After a while, it's hard to believe anyone really gives a shit about you or that anyone ever thinks of you at all." I shrugged. "And besides, I know I'm not some great catch, especially for someone like you, planning to be a surgeon and all."

She smiled. "You know what? That's exactly why I like you, I think. You're honest about who you are, and you're not trying to impress me. You're not trying to impress anyone, as far as I can tell, almost the opposite, actually. It's like you're purposely keeping your own and everyone else's expectations low." She held my eyes, again nibbling her lower lip. "But if you *are* trying to impress people, you're doing a really shitty job of it, mister."

"Wow, I take back what I said at dinner. You actually are hilarious, after all."

She squeezed my hand tighter. "And you're sweet." She pushed herself up on her toes, and without warning, Allie kissed me quickly on the cheek.

I was dumbfounded. I'd just been kissed, however lightly, by the most beautiful woman in the world. I stood still for a second and waited for the horseman of the apocalypse to gallop across the horizon.

"Thanks, I think," I said.

"You're welcome." She held me fast with her smile. "Now, if only we could do something about that cigarette smoking…"

"Don't start in on me, woman, not on our first date." I lit up a Marlboro in manly defiance, then pointed at Mini Hole #3. "We're up, go tee off. Use your driver."

* * *

"You got the rush shift tonight?" Eddie asked.

"Yep."

"Any big bachelor plans afterwards?"

I studied him for hidden implications behind his words. I hadn't mentioned anything about my date with his sister a few days before, but I was curious if Allie had said something. Had Eddie known, it wouldn't bother him, but I was certain he'd wonder if I'd lost my motherfucking mind. Eddie had a healthy dislike of his bitchy little sister, almost a fear of her volcanic personality. He wouldn't wish Allie on his worst enemy, let alone one of his good friends.

"Nothing in particular," I said. "Probably head back up the hill, suck some suds."

"Cool. Wish I could pound a few with you, but I'm closing tonight. We gotta do some hiking up there while Lonnie's gone, maybe drop some acid."

"Sorry, dude, I'm not into drugs."

"I know, me neither, but I've heard that LSD stuff is pretty wild." He laughed, stuffed a few pies into a warming bag, and headed out Pizza Place's front door.

"Paulie!"

I turned to see Phil standing at the office door.

"Yes, sir?"

"Pretty slow around here. I'm going to cut you loose. Bring me your bag and tags. Hammer out some dough trays while I check you out."

I washed up a stack of trays as directed, and fifteen minutes later, Phil called me into the office. I took a seat next to him as he paid me my commission and mileage. It was weird to think that the man seated next to me was slipping my girlfriend the long, hard, and drippy. It was even weirder that it actually wasn't so weird at all. I liked Phil. I loved Lonnie. Part of me knew the two of them were a better fit for each other than me and Lonnie. Phil's staunch libertarianism would clash hard with Lonnie's blossoming leftism, but other than that, he was the superior suitor in almost every way. I got the impression that Phil's family back east had some money, making him far more acceptable to Lonnie's family. He was finishing his business degree, as well, and he had the personality and drive that would undoubtedly usher in financial success someday. On top of that, Phil did not smoke cigarettes or constantly drop acid or bang every woman west of Nantucket. He was a solid backup cock, ready to cum in off the bench at a moment's notice. No wonder Lonnie fucked him. Shit, the more I considered all Phil's awesome qualities, the more I thought maybe *I* should fuck him.

"Big night planned tonight?" Phil asked. "Got the whole world to yourself up there on the mountain these days, don't you?"

I shrugged. "Yep, just me, myself and I. Maybe I'll go home and see if I can drink myself to death. Lonnie can't stop me this time."

"Yeah, she'd probably frown on that if she were here." Without looking at me and with strained casualness, he asked, "You hear from her yet?"

"She's only been gone a few days, dude."

"Right, right." He stared at the books, inserting my numbers into the Pizza Place totals. "Just thought she might call to say she landed in London or wherever."

"Paris."

"Oh yeah, that's right, one of you mentioned she was going there first."

You know damn well where she landed, I thought. *And you want to know she's safe. Aww, that's so sweet of you, Phillip.*

"I actually don't expect much contact while she's away," I said. "She told me that international calls are a total pain in the ass, not to mention expensive. I'll probably just get a few postcards here and there." Since I couldn't resist needling him a little, I added, "Besides, she'll be too busy boning all those Euro-dudes to think about some idiot pizza man back in the States."

Phil scoffed in surprise, but he played it cool and never looked away from Pizza Place's books. "Lonnie doesn't strike me as the type to casually fool around, Pablo."

I laughed, then stood up and clapped him on the back. "They're all the type, dude, just like we're all the type."

Phil grunted, but didn't take the bait. He was good at secrets, had to hand it to him. I walked to the front counter and pulled one of the phones over, dialed Eddie's number. After three rings, Allie answered.

"Is this Allie of the clan Texas?" I asked.

"Um, yes."

"Missus Allie, I'm calling about your son, Malcolm. Seems he's been swording the other clanskids, swording 'em right in the haggis."

"Ouch, that sounds awful."

"More awful than you can imagine. I have to say, Missus Allie, you are a terrible parent and you need to be punished. I better come over there and give you the ol' what for."

I heard her laugh on the other end of the line. "I've been *waiting* for you to call me, Paul. I thought maybe you changed your mind about wanting to see me again."

"Nope, just didn't want to seem too eager."

"Trust me, you don't seem too eager, kind of the opposite, actually," she said. "So do you really want to get together tonight, or are you just calling to say hi?"

"I'm actually just getting off work, thought maybe we could hang out a bit if you're available. You interested?"

"Yes!" Her excitement was immediate and obvious. "I mean, I can get together for a couple hours or so. I've got all kinds of homework I need to get done."

"Homework? It's summertime, Allie."

"Pre-med and med school students don't take breaks. I'm enrolled in a bunch of summer school classes. But come over and spend a little time with me, okay?"

"On my way."

Just thinking of Allie's insane hotness as I walked to my car made me pop a boner straight enough to toss rings around at a small-town carnival. I didn't know if people still played "Boner Toss" in rural America, but if they did, I'd provide the pole. I pulled into Allie and Eddie's driveway ten minutes later and walked up to the front door. I heard her race down the stairs after I knocked. She pulled open the door, threw her arms around me, and hugged me tight.

"I'm so glad you came over!"

"Wow, that's quite a greeting, Allie. Wasn't expecting that."

She hugged me even tighter. "I think I'm lonely." She pushed herself back from me. "After the other night with you, I realized how nice it was to have a guy around."

"Yeah, once you get past all the farting, we're pretty awesome."

She rolled her eyes, stepped back, and let me inside. "Let me guess, you want a beer?"

"Allie, you must be psychic. Do you have ESPN or some shit?"

"Yes, yes, you're so hard to predict, Paul, an enigma wrapped in a belch." She smiled, reached out, and touched my arm. "I had my brother buy me a whole case of Budweiser, hoping you'd come around from time to time."

"He didn't ask what it was for?"

She shrugged. "He hardly talks to me, acts like I'm going to explode if we ever exchange more than three sentences."

"Now why would that be?" I grinned at her.

She slapped me lightly in the chest. "I'm not *that* bad. Maybe a little high strung, but not totally awful."

I did not respond. No matter how nicely Allie was currently behaving, I thought it wise to never forget The Tale of the Poisoned Plants.

"I'll go get you a beer if you'll do me a big big favor," Allie said, her tone so sweet I could hardly imagine her pouring bleach into *anyone's* planters.

"Lay it on me."

She tilted her head to the side, reached out for one of my hands. "Will you please please *pleeeease* take Roger for a walk with me?"

"Roger?"

"My ferret."

"Oh yeah, Roger." I furrowed my brow. "Are you talking like a walk walk? Like on a leash and shit?"

She smiled and nodded.

"You want me to walk a ferret in public?"

She smiled and nodded some more. And then she stepped even closer, put a hand on each of my shoulders and pushed herself up on her toes. Her lips were only an inch from mine, her beautiful hazel eyes gazing into my soul. "I'll be soooooo thankful, Paul."

Shit. Allie's promise of gratitude could get the baddest hombre in the world to drink a wine cooler. It could get Clint Eastwood to star in a soap opera. For a young woman with no almost dating experience, she certainly was skilled in the art of feminine manipulation.

"Fine, we can walk Roger," I said, "but I will *not*, under any circumstances, hold the leash. That's where I draw the line, Allie. Too much testosterone in these veins for that shit."

"Deal!" She ran up the stairs to the kitchen to fetch me a beer before I could change my mind.

Twenty minutes later, I walked next to a ferret named Roger through a middle-income neighborhood in east Boulder. In my weirdest acid imaginings, I never envisioned a romantic stroll through the suburbs with the most attractive girl in the world and her pet rat. I avoided eye contact with other pedestrians, but I heard them laugh after they passed, their dogs too confused to even bark at the two weirdos and their leashed rodent.

"Let's go take a seat on that bench," Allie said, pointing into a neighborhood park. "I like it there. I go there to calm down sometimes when my temper gets the best of me."

We walked over and Allie tied Roger to the bench. He sat down and calmly sniffed the air. For a glorified rat, he certainly was well behaved. Sitting down next to Allie, I reached for my ciggies and stuffed one between my lips. Allie snatched it out of my mouth. I would have abandoned almost any other woman on the spot for such a move.

"Alright, Allie, what the fuck?"

She smiled but didn't say a word. And then, as if making a tough decision, she sighed loudly, scooched over quickly, and kissed me. I kissed her back. She kissed me more assertively, almost desperately. Her hands went up behind my head and she pulled herself over and onto me, straddling me on the park bench. I couldn't believe it. I was instantly as hard as I'd ever been. My boner was like two boners taped together, Siamese boners, as big a boner as I'd ever birthed. Allie's passion spilled through her and rolled over me as she pressed her crotch lightly down upon my conjoined boners. I felt a pre-ejaculate thump roll up the shaft of my penis, and a small wet dab drizzled down toward my balls.

Then, as abruptly as it began, it ended. Allie broke our lip-lock, rolled off me hurriedly, and planted her hot ass right back on the bench where she'd been. She looked at me sternly. "No," she said.

I laughed. "No, what? You kissed me."

"I know. I'm telling myself no." She was breathing hard. "It's been *soooo* long since I've even kissed a guy, Paul. Oh my god, I feel like I could jump your bones right here, right now, right on this bench."

"Allie, you have my full consent. I'll even sign a waiver."

"I can't. If I do that, you'll make this a sex thing. Or I'll make it a sex thing. Either way, as much as I want to jump you right now, I don't need just a sex thing in my life."

I shrugged and put a new cigarette in my mouth. I lit it quickly before Allie could yank it away. "Well, I'd think that after I walked your ferret in public, a little sex is the least you could do for me."

"Don't do that!"

I laughed. "Do what?"

"Don't make light of this, Paul! Stop joking around! Sex is not some little thing to me. It's a *big* deal. I've only slept with two guys in my entire life, and I didn't even really want to be with the first guy. That I'm even thinking of sleeping with you is an enormous decision for me."

I sighed. "Allie, you're a very odd duck."

Her fist flashed out and punched me in the arm, punched me a little too hard for playfulness, I thought.

"Don't *say* that!" she demanded.

"Jesus Christ, Allie, don't say what?" I rubbed my sore arm.

"Don't say I'm odd! I've been hearing that my whole life. I'm weird, I'm mean, I'm odd, I'm a bitch, I'm stuck up, I'm strange, I'm different. After ten billion times, that stuff gets annoying as hell." She stood up and started untying Roger from the bench. "Let's go. I have stuff I need to do."

I shook my head at this sudden turn of events. "Are you serious? Thirty seconds ago, I could have sworn you really liked me."

"I did, thirty seconds ago."

"But now?"

"I don't know, Paul." She stood in front of me, arms crossed. "I'm just angry, okay? Everything's always so damn complicated. But I need to go. I have homework." She stared at me angrily, then pointed at my cigarette. "And I wish you wouldn't smoke around me. I *hate* that about you."

I took a big hit off my cigarette. "Hate is a pretty strong word, Allie."

"It's the right word for smokers."

I shrugged. "Well, I'm a nicotine addict, and I have no intention of changing that. That's something you may want to think about."

"Oh, trust me, I'll think about it."

With that, she turned and stormed off. I stood up from the bench, dumbfounded, and watched her walk away from me. She didn't even glance over her shoulder to see if I was following. Still, my father did not raise me to be the kind of man who lets a beautiful woman storm off into the night with only a leashed rodent for protection. I jogged until I caught up with her, but we didn't speak until we reached her house. She stood on the front stoop of her door, physically barring my entry.

"Can I assume I'm not invited in for another beer?"

"Wow, Paul, you must be psychic. Do you have ESPN or something?"

"Fair enough." I scratched my chin. "Allie, did I do something to you?"

She sighed hotly. "Yes. No. I don't know."

"Are you mad at me?"

She threw up her hands. "Yes, no, *I don't know!*" She breathed in deeply, let it out slowly, and visibly tried to calm herself. "Paul, I need to do my homework. That's all I should focus on right now. I'm under a lot of stress, okay?"

I stared at her. Allie was beautiful, even while angry, even while confused, even with a ferret clutched tightly to her chest. Still, I preferred the Allie of twenty minutes ago, the one balanced on my crotch, her perfect lips crawling over my chin, her teeth nibbling my ears.

"I guess I'll go then," I said.

"Yes, I think that's for the best."

Allie turned, opened the door for Roger, and the two of them scurried inside. No goodnight smooch for ol' Pablo. I was too confused to leave right away, so I stood on the stoop and watched Allie's silhouette through the frosted glass. She moved downstairs, and when I saw the light in her bedroom flip on, I knew she was not coming back to the door to apologize. Bummer. There would be no makeup sex after our very first, very confusing argument.

I shook my head, walked back to my bland Subaru wagon, and drove to the nearest gas station. Digging for a quarter, I headed for the payphone.

"Yeah?"

"What's up, hottie?" I asked.

I heard a half-snicker, half-laugh from the other end of the line. "Damn, that didn't take you long, boy," Sabrina said. "Your little Lonnie's only been gone a few days, right?"

"That's right."

"And I already get the booty call?"

"Right again, girlie."

"Then quit talking, get your skinny ass over here, and fuck me good and proper."

I laughed. "See you in ten minutes."

Sabrina was great. She didn't sweat the small stuff, didn't have weird emotional outbursts, didn't own a ferret. We had the greatest fuck buddy relationship in all of Boulder County, just two horny youngsters with no expectations. Cock and cunt, prick and pussy, all the good, none of the bad.

An hour later, I boned Sabrina long and thoroughly, toying with her, visualizing Allie all the while. It was strange to fuck a woman as gorgeous as Sabrina and still think of another woman even more gorgeous, but I was twenty years old and there was no end to my sexual greed. I wanted to fuck it all, everything, well aware that everything was still not enough. Sabrina moaned beneath me, her beautiful lips sucking my nipples, her tongue teasing, her pussy embracing my cock like an old friend on a chance meeting. She was everything I should've wanted in the "other" woman, or even in the primary woman, but I was too damn selfish to understand such a simple truth. When Sabrina screamed out her first orgasm, I unloaded inside her, and then we both lit cigarettes without any stupid arguments about tobacco.

"You want a drink, baby?" Sabrina asked.

Jesus, Paul, WHY are you chasing after Allie when you have this perfect woman who loves to fuck and smoke cigarettes and drink alcohol and crank heavy metal tunes? What is WRONG with you, dude?

"Of course," I said. "What's on tap in this here establishment?"

"You know I always keep some of those skanky Budweisers around for you. You think I'd let my man go thirsty?"

I pushed myself up on one elbow in her bed on the floor and watched her perfectly round ass glide over to the fridge. "Your man?" I asked, grinning.

Sabrina stopped suddenly, facing the fridge, not turning around. "You know what I mean, Pablo."

I let her grab me a beer and pour herself a big red wine before pressing the issue. "Actually, no, I don't. You saying you think of me as your man?"

She walked over, crawled back into bed, and took a long hit off her wine. "Don't be an idiot. You're not my man in any literal sense of the word. But you're as much of a man as I have right now."

"Seriously?"

"Yes, *seriously*. If I met someone else, like a boyfriend, you and I would have to stop all this fucking. I'm not some cheatin' S.O.B. like you."

I laughed. "Are you saying you don't go out with other guys?"

Sabrina shook her head sharply and glared at me. "What's with the twenty questions? Fucking my fine ass ain't enough for you? Now you need to get all up in my personal shit?"

"Sorry. Just curious."

She reached over and placed her hand on my chest, her tone softening. "If you must know, yes, Paulie, I've been on a few dates in the time we've been together. Unfortunately, none of them went anywhere. Dudes were dull. And if you need to know whether I fucked any of them, no, I did not. So don't you worry, baby, I've been perfectly faithful to you since the first time you stuffed that big ol' dick of yours way up inside me."

I laughed.

"And I know you've never touched another woman besides me and Lonnie since we started all…" – she twirled her hand in the air – "…all *this*, whatever this is."

"Of course not."

"Bull-she-*ite!*" Sabrina said loudly, then sighed. "You know, maybe if you weren't…"

I waited for several seconds, but nothing followed. "Maybe if I weren't what?"

She shrugged, tamped out her cigarette, and set her wine on the nightstand. Then she stretched out her beautiful naked body alongside mine and rested her head on my chest. "Maybe if you weren't such a cheating scumbag, I'd take all our fucking a little more seriously. You never know, there might be more here than just sex. And now would be my chance, I suppose, what with Princess Lonnie traipsing all over Europe for a couple months."

I paused, caught off guard. I smoked instead of speaking, hoping something would come along to change the subject. It didn't, unfortunately, so I finally had to respond. "I have to say, Sabrina, I'm surprised to hear this from you."

"What's so surprising, you little shit?" She lifted her head off my chest and gazed up at me, her huge brown eyes holding mine. "We get along great. We fuck great. We love the same music. We have fun together. Why is it so surprising that I might want to go out, you know, on a normal date once in a while and stop all this silly sneaking around? Is it really so hard to believe we could actually be together like a real couple?"

"Sabrina, I never thought—"

"Of *course* you never thought." She slapped my chest irritably and looked away. "'Cause you don't *think*, Pablo, certainly not when it comes to women. That's not your strong suit." She sighed again, but it sounded more like a growl. "Fuck it, dude, forget I said it. You ain't there yet, probably never will be."

She was probably right, so I remained silent. At times like these, I knew that anything I said could and would be used against me in a court of Paul. Almost a minute passed in silence – other than the Iron Maiden pumping out her stereo speakers – and then I felt Sabrina's hand crawl down my stomach and tightly grip my penis.

"Who gives a shit, though, right?" she said, her voice switching gears, back to a sultry dominance. She looked up at me from my chest, grinning fiercely, animalistically. "We should probably just get back to the fucking. Fucking's what we do best, right?"

I yanked her on top of me and kissed her as if I were kissing her for the first time, all the passion and lust of surprise and anticipation. She escalated aggressively, gyrating against my cock with noticeable anger, and seconds later, I was ready for her. Stuffing my prick way up inside, I fucked her solely, not thinking of Lonnie, not thinking of Allie, boning only Sabrina because Sabrina was more woman than any man should ever want, need, or expect in this world.

8.

Eyes Trap the Dick, Dick Tricks the Heart

E L D O R A ,   C O L O R A D O

1 9 9 1

"I'm coming to Colorado," White said.

"Huh?"

"You heard me, bitch."

Jesus, White coming back to CO? I'd only seen him a couple times since he returned to Minnesota almost two years before. Considering we'd been virtually inseparable in our last couple years of high school, even moved out to Colorado together, it was hard to believe how small a part of each other's lives we'd become.

I wiped the sleep out of my eyes and walked the phone over to my front door. The dogs needed out, so I pushed open the screen door and they blasted past. It had been two weeks since Lonnie left for Europe, and although I promised myself I'd use the alone time to dive headlong into my next writing project, I'd only turned out ten pages or so. I spent the rest of the time drunk, tripping, or boning Sabrina every chance I got, often all three at once. There was some pizza delivery in there, as well, I think, but it was hard to remember between all the drinking, tripping, and boning. In fact, I'd spent the previous night guzzling Budweiser and banging Sabrina every

193

which way we could twist ourselves. She fucked with particular aggression these days, perhaps unleashing the sadness and frustration of screwing the same man for almost a year who was too much of a boy to take her as seriously as she deserved.

Conversely, I'd only seen Allie once since she chose anger over sex, forcing me to share my lust with Sabrina instead. Allie had agreed to meet me for coffee before a shift at Pizza Place, but when we got together, she was as cold as a shivering ferret, unresponsive as a poisoned plant. She complained about tests and homework, and forty-five minutes after we met up, she stormed out of the coffee shop, angry at nothing and everything simultaneously. I assumed my short time with Eddie's volatile sister had reached its confusing conclusion.

"Don't you remember inviting me out there?" White asked. "We talked on the phone a few weeks ago. You said Lonnie was going to England or some shit."

"Uh, that conversation sounds vaguely familiar."

White laughed. "Yeah, you were pretty liquored up. You really do drink too much, you know."

"Thanks, Dad. How's that weed addiction coming along?"

"Touché." I heard a crackle through the line as he lit something and inhaled. "But I took your offer seriously, dude, so I'm coming. Already took the time off work. Can't wait to see the mountains again, man! Fuckin-A, I need a break from all this Minnesota melodrama."

"Yeah? What's the melodrama?"

"Too complicated to get into over the phone. I'll tell you when I'm there."

"Right on," I said. "Alright, this sounds great, I could use the company. When you comin'?"

"Leaving crack of dawn tomorrow, should be there by tomorrow night."

"No shit?"

"Not even a stubborn turd on a Monday morning," White said. "Tell your liver to limber up. He better be ready for a serious fucking onslaught."

"Oh, he's limber, believe me."

I gave White directions to my cabin from Boulder and we hung up before the long-distance charges grew imposing. Sweet! I missed White's weird, dark camaraderie. My life got significantly stranger when White was around, which was exactly how I liked it.

I stared around at my cabin. After a three-second assessment, I decided to add a few extra speeders to my standard morning dosage and clean up the pigsty, pronto. Lonnie-less for only two short weeks, I'd turned my place into a hazardous waste site. My filth was like nature's wrath – left to its own devices, it would quickly engulf the world. There were dishes everywhere, clothes strewn about as if a rare indoor tornado had recently ripped through the cabin. Half-forgotten stories, pizza crusts, and shot glasses covered my desk, all of it protected by Bud bottle sentinels that lined the perimeter. I fell into cleaning, but only an hour into the task, the phone rang again.

"Paul?"

I didn't recognize the young woman's voice. It wasn't Sabrina, the only girl I could think of who would call me at home. Uh oh. Dread passed over me. I didn't remember the details of many drunken nights, especially when I overdid it on the ephedrine. I was usually careful not to pass along my phone number to random women, but discretion sometimes vanished while immersed in an alcohol-speed fog.

"Um, yes?" I asked carefully.

"Do you know who this is?"

"Um…"

"Come on, what young lady besides Lonnie would call you at home?"

There was only one young lady I knew who would refer to herself as a "young lady."

"Hi, Allie."

"Good answer!" she said excitedly, giggling.

"Wow, you sound so upbeat for a change. What, did someone close to you die?"

"Ha-ha, you're really funny, Paul," she said. "But yes, I am in a great mood. I just finished some *brutal* tests, and I'm pretty sure I aced them. I want to celebrate!"

I stood in my living room and scratched my chin. Allie confused the fuck out of me. I'd given up on her, figured she'd thought better of whatever brief interaction we'd had. But here she was, laughing excitedly on the other end of the line.

"I have to tell you, Allie, this call is a little surprising. I'm kind of shocked to hear from you, to be honest."

"I know, I know." I heard her take in a big breath and exhale in a long sigh. "I'm really sorry for how I acted the last couple times I saw you. I was a total bitch. It wasn't anything you did or said; it was all the pressure of these tests I just finished. I felt like I was so far behind in everything, and anything other than studying seemed like an imposition on my life. Seriously, Paul, I'm really really sorry."

"Hmm."

"Can you forgive me? Pretty please?"

She used her cutesy-cute voice, the one I assumed got her smoking hot ass out of a thousand smoking hot jams throughout her smoking hot life. I felt that cutesy cuteness worm into the forgiveness quadrant of my brain, however small that sector may have been. I couldn't help imagining Allie standing in her bedroom, begging for forgiveness, nibbling her lower lip, smiling beautifully. In my vision of her apology, she wore something skimpy, maybe lace lingerie, maybe nothing at all, her pubic hair trimmed into an arrow that pointed directly at her vagina, the slogan "Enter At Your Own Risk!" tattooed across her lower abdomen in bold, red letters.

I sighed. "Well, I guess—"

"I'll make it up to you," she interrupted, and I heard her giggle again.

"Really? What does that mean, exactly?"

"Take me camping. Take me camping tonight, right now, while I still have the nerve. I love being in the mountains, and you have that great van.

I'll meet you somewhere up Boulder Canyon this afternoon, and we can go from there. You pick the campground."

I whistled. "Ah, Jesus, Allie, your timing is terrible. My buddy White is coming out from Minnesota, supposed to be here tomorrow."

"That's fine, we'll just camp one night. We can head back in the morning."

"I gotta clean my cabin. It's filthy."

"Paul," she said, letting that one word dangle on the line for several seconds, "I don't know when we'll have another chance. I don't know *if* we'll have another chance. As you may have noticed, I'm moody. But right now, my mood is perfect. So *pleeease* take me camping in your van tonight."

My penis plumped at the prospect, throbbed at the possibility of exploring Allie's moody vagina. I wanted to find out what it hated, what made it laugh, and most importantly, why it couldn't be more reasonable and control its fucking temper. My filthy mind overwhelmed my filthy cabin, and I knew any further resistance was futile.

"Ah, fuck it. Count me in, Allie."

"I knew I could talk you into it! How soon can we meet up?"

We hammered out the specifics, and two hours later, I pulled my van into a dirt park n' ride lot in Nederland next to Allie's little green Chevy. She was waiting for me, leaning against the hood of her car as if posing for the cover of a softcore porn magazine, the kind where the girls come so tantalizingly close to disrobing that a man tries to peel the gloss off the pages in hopes of removing that final flap of clothing. Allie wore tight, tiny, jean-short cutoffs, the pockets dangling below the impossibly high, ragged cut line. A black and red half-shirt flannel top caressed her shoulders, ran halfway down her arms, and was tied in a loose knot beneath her perfectly proportional breasts. Her flat, tan stomach and smooth upper chest lay exposed, not a single blemish or line anywhere to be found on her pristine, nineteen-year-old flesh. Atop her head sat a black cowboy hat, matching the black boots on her feet, two dark bookends holding the most beautiful novel ever written between them.

"Good god, Allie, were you made in a fucking factory somewhere?" I asked out the window of my van.

She smiled. "I was hoping you'd like this. It's my cowgirl camping outfit! Used to wear it all the time in Texas."

"Jesus fuck," I muttered beneath my breath, opening the door and stepping out of the van. "You look gorgeous, but I hope you brought more clothes than that. You ain't in Texas no more, Dorothy. Gets cold in these here Colorado mountains at night."

"Isn't it your job to keep me warm?"

She stepped up to me, wrapped her arms around my neck, and unloaded a kiss on me with all the firepower of a shotgun blast. Her tongue in my mouth, her body jammed into mine, she released all the frustration of studies and tests and a celibate youth. Allie was suddenly all things lusty and darkly beautiful, strippers in Paris, prostitutes in Moscow, first night on the job, pussies like pastries. I'd never touched something so aesthetically perfect as Allie in a cowgirl outfit, and I sincerely doubted I ever would again.

"Allie, we won't make it to our campsite if you kiss me like that again."

She laughed, walked to the back of her car, and opened the trunk. "Help me load my stuff."

We moved her wine coolers and a small duffle bag of heavier clothes into my van. After finagling her few groceries in between my twenty-seven beers in the mini fridge, we set out.

"Where did you decide to camp?" she asked.

"Brainard Lake." I made the mistake of glancing over at her while answering, and my eyes refused to go back to the road. I hit gravel on the side of the Peak to Peak Highway, then swerved sharply back into my lane. "It's not that far from here, maybe ten, fifteen miles."

We drove along the stunning highway, chatting easily, lightly. Allie talked about childhood trips into the Texas hill country with her parents, places in the world she'd like to see, and she offered overly intricate observations of Roger the Ferret that proved the girl desperately needed a social life. Still, it was very close to having a normal conversation with a normal person. Allie laughed at jokes, even made a few of her own, and she didn't suddenly lash out at nothing or explode at imagined slights. Smart and insightful, Allie actually made for an interesting conversationalist. *If only she could sustain this*, I thought, but I quickly buried the idea. That was not how the world worked. The most stunning mountains suffered the most violent winters, the majestic oceans masked millions of monsters, and every living thing in the surreal rain forests competed to murder each other. God did not dispense beauty lightly. He attached enormous caveats, and Allie was no different. Today, she was the perfect mountain in the middle of July, no wind, no snow, warmly astounding. I should enjoy it while I had it. It would not last. It could not last.

Brainard Lake was a spectacular camping area situated just above the paradoxically disturbing town of Ward, Colorado. Ward was junked cars and strange, sagging houses, hippies wandering around aimlessly, dirty, all of them searching for 1967 and a way back to San Francisco. Thankfully, the road up to Brainard Lake wound quickly away from that old hippie encampment, and before we could say "Woodstock," we were pulling into our spot.

"Oh my god, this is stunning!" Allie said, stepping out of the van. "I never knew a place like this existed so close to Boulder!"

I followed her outside. A small lake shimmered in front of us, encircled by mountains still streaked with snow. The sun was hot at 10,000 feet, that conman sun of the high Rockies. Almost sweating, a person falsely believes the temp will remain warm well into the night. Not so. At that elevation, the second the sun slips behind a mountain, all the warmth races after it, sprinting across the Rockies to the deserts of Utah. Since I knew alcohol made even perfect afternoons a million times better, I pulled open the van's sliding door, reached into the fridge, and grabbed a drink for each of us.

"Let's walk down to the water," Allie suggested, accepting her wine cooler.

I nodded and grabbed myself a second strolling soldier to avoid the profound, soul-sucking pain of the One Beer Blues. I drank deeply from my first can as Allie took my hand and walked me toward a path that led to the lake. A few minutes later, we stood on the shore of that pristine pond and stared quietly at the sun-splashed ripples, wallowing in all the majesty of Colorado.

"Do you love her?"

I turned to Allie, but she didn't look back at me. She had a faraway face, gazing and thinking well into the distance.

"Lonnie?" I asked.

"Yes, Paul, of course. Who else?"

"I thought you meant Evie."

"Paul…"

"Alright, alright." I lit a cigarette. Cigarettes were great distractions, the perfect way to buy time during life's awkward moments. "I suppose I do."

Allie nodded, no judgment visible on her face. "Then why are you here with me?"

She was too temperamental to answer with total honesty. Truth is a dangerous flame when applied to combustible personalities. Instead, I rubbed my chin a while, trying to massage out an answer. "Because you're beautiful," I eventually said, a fairly decent approximation of the truth, "and I'm weak in that regard. Most men are. Also, I find you fascinating in your own way."

Allie still didn't look at me, simply stared off into the distant mountains. "Do you think you'll marry her?"

A surprised laugh jumped out of me.

"What's so funny?" she asked, finally turning to look at me.

"It's complicated." I suddenly pictured Phil pounding Lonnie on the bench by the creek, Lonnie demanding deeper and deeper thrusts, and I thought maybe it wasn't so complicated after all. "But god no, Allie, Lonnie and I will never get married."

"How can you say that with such certainty?"

"Well, first and foremost, she wants kids. It's probably what she wants more than anything else in the world. Lonnie's family is filthy rich, she'll be a full-blown trust funder soon enough, and she'll never want for anything. I suppose children are the only thing daddy can't give her. Not without some really sick shit going down, anyway."

Allie didn't laugh, so I laughed enough for two.

"Actually, it makes perfect sense when you look at it that way," I continued. "We all want to make our mark on the world, I guess, bring something into it that wouldn't exist if we didn't exist."

"And you don't want kids?"

"Fuck no."

"Why not?"

"Fuckin' hate babies." I pulled on my smoke. "You know, smiling babies, sunsets, puppies, purring kittens, can't stand any of that shit."

Allie gave me a patient stare instead of the laugh I was gunning for. "You don't want kids because you have a bad relationship with your father," she said. "I don't know what happened there, but I know you're thousands of miles from where you grew up, you're completely on your own financially at twenty years old, and you almost never mention your huge family in any conversations we have."

I smiled. "You're a very perceptive individual, Allie."

"Thank you." She raised her wine cooler and took a good pull. "By the way, I don't want kids, either, not in the least. I'm interested in practicing medicine, not raising children. So it's theoretically possible you could marry me."

I must have recoiled, based on the laughter that finally fell out of her.

"Don't worry, Paul, that particular theoretical possibility would be a long long *long* way down the road for us." She stepped in closer to me and dropped another of those Allie makeout bombs on my face, then pulled away a bit. "I mean, you haven't even made love to me yet. We should probably do that first, see if we're compatible physically."

I didn't need any further coaxing. I grabbed Allie's hand firmly and marched her directly back to the Econoline. I slid the door open and she climbed right onto the van's bed. Pulling off her cowboy hat, she shook out her flowing brown hair.

"Leave the door open," Allie said, "I want to see the mountains behind us."

I followed orders, loving her subtle exhibitionism, and then I crawled in next to her. Pressing my body down upon Allie felt like a fantasy, not quite real, impossible actually. I, Paul Mountain, did not bone women who looked like Allie. I slept with attractive girls, sure, but I never had sex with a woman who could inspire rows of hard-ons as she walked by, the Queen's guards raising their phallic rifles to salute their stunning monarch. *Rise, penises, rise!* Nevertheless, here I was, and there she was beneath me. That was *my* penis plumping against Allie, however confused he was about the mission. I forced myself to ignore my doubts, suspend my disbelief, and fall into the moment.

Allie wasn't tentative, per se, but she was slow and curious. She needed it all, I realized, the whole sexual buffet, not some quick appetizer followed by a big ol' scoop of super sexy mac and cheese. She wanted to sample everything, even that gross dish on the end with the white gravy and curry. We kissed for a long, long stretch, rolled on top of each other, under each other, her tongue exploratory without being aggressive. Her hands touched my face, tickled my neck, caressed my chest. Slowly, there emerged a palpable desperation to Allie's lovemaking. She clung tightly to me, almost hugged me as she licked my neck and applied pressure to my crotch with her own. It was obvious I needed to lead, so I took over methodically, seeking her stated and unstated permission for each sexual escalation.

"Ready?" I asked, slipping my hand underneath her pretty red and black flannel top.

She nodded, so I slipped off her shirt and went to work on her breasts in a way I hadn't done in a long time. It reminded me of early high school, back when the breast was the best I could test. In those days, I'd linger on a girl's tits for impossibly long stretches, rubbing them, sucking them, slurping up the cleavage sauce. Now spoiled by Lonnie, Sabrina, and a series of other less meaningful encounters, I'd forgotten how much fun it was to work the boobs. Allie moaned and squirmed just from the boob work alone, all those little nibbles, all that foreplay. When it was time for more, I treaded carefully. I knew she had minimal experience with the demon penis, so I pretended he was actually an angel and presented him gently, methodically introducing her to the root of all evil. It didn't take long before she demanded more. Then more. Then more. She jammed her crotch firmly against mine as I lay atop her, and I felt both her hands clutch my hair.

"*Now*," she insisted. "There's a condom in my back pocket. Hurry!"

It wasn't easy yanking off her skin-tight cutoff jeans, but I managed, almost laughing when four condoms fell out of her back pocket. God damn, the girl came to party. Who did she think I was, P.H. Mountain? I stood up in the cramped van to dress my dick in latex and survey the scene. Wow, there lay Allie, naked, waiting for me to fuck her, *begging* me to fuck her in the ol' Econoline lust palace. It wasn't a dream, and it wasn't some roofie-fueled sex scheme. The world was full of wonders. I dropped my drawers, strapped my sex-crazed cock into his raincoat, then guided the little monster back to his favorite hiding spot.

Allie inhaled sharply as I entered, then squeezed me tightly everywhere at once. "That feels *wonderful*," she moaned in my ear. She wrapped her arms around my shoulders, legs around my ass, and she fucked me slowly, almost languidly, trying to really *feel* that Paul penis way up deep inside. I kissed her chin and slid myself in, out, in, hold-hold-hold, in, out, in, hold-hold-hold. I maneuvered my crotch to better press against her clit, and her quickened breath told me she felt the pressure.

"Oh my god, oh my god, oh my god," she breathed. "Cum inside me, Paul, I need to feel you cum inside me."

I picked up the pace. It didn't take long to grant her wish, maybe a dozen more strokes to trigger the geyser. Allie shook below me as I came, close to her own peak, but I could tell she didn't quite summit the mountain.

"You're close, aren't you?" I asked.

"*Yes, dammit!*"

"Can I finish it off for you?"

Her beautiful hazel eyes fluttered opened, almost scared. "I've…I've never had an orgasm with anyone."

"No time like the present, Allie."

"I don't know what to do."

"I do. Lay back and relax; I'll take care of the rest."

I slid down her length, gazing back up the landscape of her perfect nineteen-year-old body the whole time I licked her. It was a gorgeous sight, near pornographic perfection, so I snapped a thousand mental photos for *The Big Book of Fuck* I kept shelved in the recesses of my mind. Allie twisted and writhed as my tongue tasted her. She cried out with shock and awe, and after a dozen more "oh my gods," she blew her stack. The orgasm rocked her whole body. She thrashed on my van cushions as she tore at her own hair, her eyes slammed shut in agony/ecstasy, but I didn't stop. I ravaged her. I terrorized her. I brutalized Allie's clitoris. I licked it and sucked it and swirled it around well beyond anything resembling kindness, dragging every final screaming speck of orgasm out of her until, finally, she shoved my head away violently and yelled at me to stop. Reluctantly obeying, I drifted back up her body, rolled over, and gently pulled her head onto my chest. Allie lingered there, panting, sweating, until she was sane again.

"I never…never…" She ran her hand down my chest and stomach, not looking at me. "Is it always so good?"

"Not always." I stroked her hair and kissed the top of her head. "But the first few times you *really* fuck, it's pretty amazing."

"I don't think I like the word 'fuck.' It's animalistic. I think I like 'making love' much better."

I scoffed. "Making love sounds like I'm trying to impregnate my Amish wife."

Allie laughed, lifted her head, and turned her beautiful face up to me. "How about we call it having sex? Is that a good compromise?"

"Fair enough." I pulled away from her and rummaged around my shorts for my ciggies. "And now for the part you'll hate, the ceremonial after-sex smoke."

She giggled. "I don't think I'll hate anything you do right now. After what you just did to me, you have a free pass for a while." She paused, and a curious look arrived on her face. "You know what I want to do, Paul? I want to get drunk. Let's get *really* drunk. I haven't been really drunk in a few years. We should get totally bombed and celebrate my first orgasm during sex."

"Allie, I'm really good at getting bombed and celebrating orgasms. I'm fucking great at it, actually."

She laughed. "Cool! And then I want more sex!"

"How 'bout we make sweet Amish love?"

"Yes! Or let's fuck, or whatever we're calling it!"

I commenced drinking heavily, mainly to keep my liver limber, as White instructed. Allie took off on an alcohol kamikaze mission of her own, but her battle didn't require much of an arsenal. She was good and drunk after four wine coolers, so I made sure she didn't overdo it, scared of all the annoying high school / drunken hot girl short stories my mind could conjure: *The super-hot chick turns her eighth wine cooler upside down, swallows the last of it, then barfs a little in her own mouth. No problem, she's used to the taste of bile. She and her six most bestest friends make themselves puke every day after lunch, taking turns hurling into the bathroom toilets before their super-stupid literature class. Suddenly, though, it doesn't seem right that she should be so self-conscious about her weight. In fact, it* ISN'T *right, dammit. It's super-sad, actually, and the super-hot chick's eyes start leaking big ol' sloppy crocodile tears because she feels totally really super-sorry for herself. Her girlfriends rush over to console her, and, like, oh my god, the super-hot chick unloads a slew of stories detailing the pain and agony that only the smokingest of hottingest girls feel. Cheerleader slights and rich girl fights, the countless dudes who've tried to bone her over the years when all she really ever wanted was a bunch of free shit, like fruity drinks and sportscars and diamond necklaces – never pearl. Is that so much to ask? And then the boys close in to comfort her as well, and they listen intently to her nothing sorrow because the super-hot chick always has an eager audience at her show, no matter how vacuous the performance.*

"Would you ever consider dating me?" Allie asked long after our dinner and drinks at the campfire, and immediately after we'd had a second incredible round of high-octane, Econoline sex. She was much wilder the second time through, and the alcohol was now loosening her tongue as much as her sexual inhibitions.

"I'm not sure what you mean, Allie." I dragged on my post-fuck smoke to stall for time. "I mean, we've already been on a date or two, right?"

She pushed herself up on her forearm and looked down at me. "I'm talking like regularly, like dating dating, like me being your girlfriend."

"Allie, I…"

She waited several seconds for more, but I was at a rare loss for words.

"You what?" she asked.

"I just…"

She waited several more seconds. "You just *what?* You just want to fuck me?"

"Well, yeah. That's the best part."

She slapped my chest. "Very funny, mister." She reached for her wine cooler and took a great big swallow, maybe too big. "I think I'd be a really good girlfriend if someone would give me a chance. I'm smart, I'm ambitious, I'm pretty. I think I'm fairly interesting, even a little funny sometimes. And I *can* be nice, you know. It doesn't exactly come naturally to me, but I can work on it." She leaned down and kissed me sloppily, the sweetness of her wine cooler lingering on my lips. "Why don't you want me to be your girlfriend?"

I laughed. "I didn't say that. To be honest, Allie, I haven't really given it any thought. Up until about eight hours ago, I thought you hated me."

She waved away the comment. "That was then. I was just moody. But now that we've done *this* –" she swept her arm in front of her, indicating the bed and all its magical orgasmical properties "– I think I like you again."

Allie smiled at me, giggled a little, and I felt those weird tentacles between my eyes, heart and dick entwine. Christ, men are so damn visual. The eyes trap the dick, the dick tricks the heart.

"You know, I sort of already have a girlfriend."

"Screw that, Paul!" This time Allie waved her wine-cooler more aggressively through the air. "You already said you're not going to marry her! Rip off the god damn Band Aid and move on to someone where there's at least a *possible* future!"

She had a point. But I loved Lonnie. And Lonnie loved me. But Lonnie fucked Phil. And I fucked Sabrina. And I fucked Allie. And I fucked many, many others, some I barely recalled. But how many others did Lonnie fuck? One, ten, a stripper's dozen? How many are even *in* a stripper's dozen? Jesus, love and lust were so confusing and hard to remember. Maybe I actually fucked Rummy and Lonnie boned Sabrina. Maybe Phil nailed Ayn Rand and John Galt gave Allie an Objectivist orgasm, one she could totally rationalize. I tilted my beer way back, because unlike love and lust, Budweiser made perfect sense.

"*So?*" Allie pressed.

"What, you want me to declare you my girlfriend on the spot, right here and now?"

"Yes!" She smiled gorgeously at me, the persuasive little bitch.

"That's not how this works, Allie." It was hard to ignore her beautiful smile, but I had to set her straight. "Things have to grow. They take time. The whole boyfriend-girlfriend thing isn't a declaration anyone makes; it's more of an unstated agreement."

She sighed, flopped down on her back, and drained her wine cooler. "I hate waiting, don't have enough time in my day for patience. And I don't like uncertainty."

"Nobody does, Allie, that much is certain."

The van grew silent for a couple minutes as I finished my smoke and tilted my dwindling beer. I hoped the wine coolers were getting the best of Allie, working their magic and escorting her off to Slumberland. With any luck, all the booze would erase this boyfriend-girlfriend nonsense by morning, and we could part ways with very sore crotches, very good memories, and exactly zero plans for the future.

"Okay, I'll try to be patient," Allie finally said, her voice much quieter now, "but on one condition."

"Name it, girl."

"That you'll give me a chance. You have to date me while Lonnie's in Europe, treat me exactly as if we were just starting out together and there was no one else in the picture. Then we'll see where we are by the time she comes back, and you can make your decision then." She pushed herself back up on her elbow. Waves of flowing brown hair spilled onto my face. "Deal?"

With all those pretty curls tickling my cheeks, I knew I had no choice. Free will exists; it's just not absolute. Sometimes we simply engage in actions without any thought whatsoever, like farting in the car. Shit just pops out of us.

"Deal," I said. I stroked her hair to the side and saw her radiant grin.

"Thank you." She dropped her lips back onto mine, those lusty, needy lips of hers, so sensual. "Now have sex with me one more time before I fall asleep."

"Christ, Allie, what do you think I am, a machine?"

She reached down and throttled my penis for the better part of four seconds. It rose to the challenge.

"Yes, I think you're a sex machine." She giggled. "That's why I want to be your girlfriend."

I groaned, rolled on top of her, and machined her one final time before falling asleep by the pretty lake beneath the towering mountains as the night creatures crept to the water's edge and drank in moonlit peace.

9.

The Weird Rhythm of My Pleasure

ELDORA, COLORADO

1991

"Dude!"

Hearing the familiar voice, I closed my book, wrestled myself out of my hammock, and strolled down my elevated walkway. White stood at his car, stretching his tall, strong, hockey player's body as he surveyed the Eldora mountain valley. For the first time since I'd known him, he had a short, conservative haircut. I laughed. Given White's personality, the responsible façade looked ridiculous.

"This is fucking amazing!" he said, sweeping his arm in front of him. "If we'd moved here, I probably would have never left Colorado!"

"A tiny cabin in the woods might be a little intimate for two dudes, dude."

"Fuck that. I could wander the woods, start painting again, get back to writing poetry."

"Yeah, it's always been my dream to hunker down in a small cabin with a male poet." I walked out my gate and over to where White stood. We shook hands, as was the heterosexual fashion in 1991. No sissy hugs. "Great to fucking see you, bud." I pointed at his haircut. "What happened, you lose a bet?"

White laughed and ran his hands through his too-short hair. "Nah, man, my new job insists I look the part. Clean cut all-American boy, you know. It's actually been chopped like this for a while, but it still looks weird as hell every time I pass a mirror."

Reaching into his car, he dragged out a large suitcase and a larger cooler of beer. "You ready to launch this fuckin' party or what?"

And just like always, we launched, full speed ahead. Three hours later, we stood on top of My Mountain, Mount Mountain, the first twinges of the acid we'd swallowed beginning to assert itself. Rummy and Evie ran wild on the path, happy to have another man around to throw them sticks and roughhouse in general. I pulled out my flask of whiskey to tame the acid demons that were beginning to poke their heads out of my soul and sniff around my mind.

"This is too fucking amazing," White said, standing in the sun close to the edge of a steep drop-off, surveying the valley thousands of feet below. "I could live like this, I really could. I envy you, dude."

"So what's holding you back? Run home, get your shit, and move back out here. Plenty of places to rent in Nederland."

"No can do. Job's keeping me there. That's the main thing, anyway."

"What is this god damn job, anyway? They got you looking like some kind of Joey Joe Johnson, Andy All American. What, you climbing the ladder, toeing the line, making it happen? You starting to fall for all that douchey doucheness?" I laughed a little. "Douchey." I laughed a little more. "Double douchey doucheness, dude."

White glanced over his shoulder at me. "Acid starting to kick in, Pablo?"

"Oh yeah, it's definitely creeping up on me."

"Yeah, me too." White walked over, took my flask, and had a belt. "I'm actually working for this credit rating and collections company, tracking people down that owe money, trying to explain to them how bad credit will fuck up their lives. Once you get that message through, then you set up a payment schedule with them, get them to cover their debts."

"That sounds so businessy, so responsible. Is it 8:00 to 5:00?"

"Mostly."

"Shirt and tie?"

"Yep."

"Desk and phone?"

"Yep."

"Cubicle?"

"Yep."

"Wow." I hit the whiskey again. "That so very un-White, White."

"I know, totally. I feel like a spy, some kind of weird outsider, like they let the poet in to get a firsthand look at the respectable world so he could squirrel away the info and report back to the asylum." He stared into the distance, apparently contemplating his new, respectable role in the world. "But yeah, it's just like that, an actual legitimate job. I even get benefits. And the money is fucking fantastic."

He gave me the exact numbers, and I didn't have the heart to tell him it was about the same amount I made driving pizza, a job I could do without a tie or a set schedule or an alarm clock or taxes or a cube. I wasn't even required to get a haircut, for fuck's sake. And since I was certain I'd die at twenty-seven like all the other self-destructive narcissists I admired, benefits didn't mean a god damn thing to me.

"And there's a girl, of course," White said, sighing. "There's always a chick, isn't there? That's its own fucked up story."

I raised my eyebrows. "Wow, White's finally got himself a new girlie? Jesus, what's it been, three years?" I raised the flask. "A toast! May your dick forever be bone, but never bone dry!"

White rolled his eyes. "Good one, Paul. I don't know that I can cheers to Gloria, though."

"Can you just drink to her, no cheers?"

"I can fuckin' drink to anything, dude."

I passed him the flask and White fuckin' drank to anything, dude.

"So what's her story?" I asked.

He shrugged. "Unbelievably beautiful. Unbelievably crazy. I'm talking batshit crazy, like fly-off-the-handle crazy, like volcanically volatile. The girl seriously needs medication or therapy or something." He stood silently for a second, then shook his head as if remembering a story about Gloria that he wasn't ready to tell. "But you gotta see her, Paul. It's honestly unfair how good looking this girl is. She stops fucking traffic. If you look at her long enough, you can actually hear your dick whimper."

I laughed, and I suddenly had a perfectly clear vision of my dick sobbing, salty little tears dripping out the pee hole, the entire wrinkly length racked by sorrow. The acid, clearly, was coming on stronger by the second. I started giggling as White rummaged around his wallet, pulled out a picture of his new girlfriend, and handed it to me.

My giggles dried up. "Holy god, man."

"Exactly. Only a holy god could make something like that."

Gloria had aggressive, reddish curls that careened down her head until they almost grazed the nipply zone of her large breasties. She was a full-featured woman without being a pound overweight, full lips, huge brown eyes, large and radiant smile. The longer I stared at her smile, though, the more her teeth began to glow. Domino teeth. Piano key teeth. They were suddenly as white as John Lennon's trademark tuxedo, blaring, glaring, *white* fucking teeth.

"That girl is smoking, no doubt," I said, "and I'm not trying to one-up you or anything, but you should see the girl I slept with last night. Every bit as hot, but in a different way, more petite, more innocent."

"No shit?" White's eyes widened. "Having a little fling while the missus travels, eh?"

I shrugged. "I'm not very good at keeping my dick in my pants."

"No, you most certainly are not." White lit a cigarette, blew a cloud toward the clouds. Even though it was 85 degrees out, a shiver suddenly wracked his body. "Dude, I gotta stop talking about this shit," he said. "The trip's coming on way too strong. I just had a horrible vision of you trying to wrestle your uncooperative prick back into your pants to avoid boning anyone other than Lonnie. Seriously, nothing will spoil this ride faster than a visual of your dick."

I laughed loudly. I felt my laughter hurl out from deep within me and descend like rain upon the mountain valley below. It was happiness rain, a comedy downpour. The pines on the distant mountainsides swayed in time with my breathing, my laughter, all those distant green guys grooving like concert goers, digging the weird rhythm of my pleasure.

"Agreed," I said. "Let's walk. I wanna show you the pond around back. Evie and Rummy love it."

"Perfect, man, perfect." White's voice was airy, far away. "I need to see some water, sit down, maybe be by myself for a bit, you know? Reflect, think, shit like that, man."

The LSD engulfed us. We stayed on the mountaintop for hours, exploring the high-altitude world, losing all perception of time. We made it down before dark, gathered roughly a hundred beers from the cabin, then rode out the rest of our acid adventure by Middle Boulder Creek on the bench where Phil and Lonnie boned. I told White all about it, and he found the whole situation hilarious, which made me see the comedy, as well. Phil. Lonnie. Boning. Groaning. All us weird little mammals engaged in breeding – most of us praying like hell it doesn't actually happen – driven by God or Nature to perpetuate, our primary planetary purpose. Screwing was a huge part of the Grand Comedy, I decided, a critical component. Penises and vaginas slap-splashing around, all thought lost in the moment, weird grimaces, strange pronouncements, regrettable requests hopefully forgotten the second the cum spews forth. *You wanted me to do WHAT with my elbow?* Boning was funny and weird and sometimes sad depending on who was boning who and for what bone-tastic reason, but all fucking seemed oddly warranted and amusing when I considered it through the objective purity of acid eyes.

* * *

I took off for a ride on your motorcycle, like we talked about last night. Don't know where I'm going or how long I'll be gone. Just going to blast around the mountains, man! I'll try to call later. Leave your cabin unlocked if you go anywhere. Thanks, dude!

– White

I read the note taped to my front door as my dogs unleashed an onslaught of morning urine onto the trees in my yard. Wracked by a beer hangover and acid fog, I had exactly zero recollection of any motorcycle conversations or authorizing White to take off on my bike. It sounded like something I'd agree to, though. White was probably the only person I'd let disappear on the machine. He easily matched – if not exceeded – my own athleticism and coordination, but even better, he rode aggressively and without protection, exactly how motorcycles are supposed to be ridden. I wouldn't let some safety-first candy-ass jump on my bike, didn't want the goo of cowardice gunking up my gears.

The phone exploded on my desk, and I almost screamed. Damn, I was jumpy. I didn't want to answer, but it could be White, broken down, not knowing my motorcycle's quirks. Or, if White was as mentally damaged as I felt, the call could be from the Colorado Highway Patrol. *Mr. Mountain, we're sorry to inform you that your motorcycle is totaled. I know, I know, it's a hard ol' world. Please stop weeping, sir, there will be other motorcycles. Oh, and your buddy's dead.*

"Hello?"

"My vagina hurts."

I snickered a little. "Mine, too, Allie. Makes me wish I had a penis."

She giggled. "Did you and your friend White kill yourselves with booze last night?"

"We tried. Barely alive this morning."

"I want to meet him, especially since you said he was your best friend growing up. You can learn a lot about someone from the company they keep."

"Um, yeah." I wasn't sure I wanted to align myself too closely with

White's particular brand of aggressive oddity. "I suppose I could introduce you two one of these days."

"I want to meet him today, like this afternoon. You guys should come down and have lunch with me. We can go get subs or something, maybe hang out on the Pearl Street Mall for a bit."

"No can do, Allie. White disappeared on my motorcycle."

There was a long pause that I didn't know how to interpret. "Hello?" I eventually said.

"You have a motorcycle?" I heard concern mixed with disapproval in her voice. "Please tell me you're joking, Paul."

"Um, okay, I'm joking."

"You are not!"

I sighed. "Allie, can you hold on for a second?"

I didn't wait for her answer. I set the phone down and walked to the refrigerator. There were many, many cans of brain coolant arranged in symmetrical rows, a liquid battalion prepared to outflank all semi-maternal scolding. I pulled one out, cracked it at the sink, and drained it in four long pulls. Much better.

I returned to the phone and picked up the receiver. "Still there, Allie?"

"I'm still here." Her voice was looser but still overly concerned. "Paul, motorcycles are *sooooo* dangerous. You wouldn't believe the pictures I've seen in some of my pre-med classes. They literally scrape young guys just like you off the pavement and hose down the blood. It's horrendous."

"Then it's a damn good thing I'm indestructible, eh?"

"You are *not* funny!" she claimed, falsely. "*Please* tell me you wear protection, helmet, leathers, all that."

"You want me to lie to you twice in the same conversation?"

A long silence held the line. "Paul, I'm going to have to call you back before I say something I'll regret. Bye."

She hung up without waiting for my response. I stood in my living room, surprised but not stunned. Allie had serious anger issues, not to mention an annoyingly bloated sense of self. Did she honestly believe her opinion on motorcycles mattered to me? *Oh, you don't approve of motorcycles, Allie? Well then, by all means, I'll have White tow mine back to Minnesota. Anything else, Princess?*

I returned to the fridge, back to my ice-cold militia, and punched a hole in another soldier's head. His foamy brains tasted even better than the first, and I knew I'd launched a day drinking journey that would end in total annihilation. I swallowed a few morning speeders, then stepped outside onto my deck and played with my dogs. Evie-girl was so much cooler than Allie. Evie didn't give a shit if I drove motorcycles, smoked cigarettes, or drank all day. Evie only wanted me to be happy, just as I wanted her to be happy. That's what made for a strong, loving relationship: two living creatures consistently pulling for one another's happiness. It also didn't hurt that Evie couldn't talk. Most of my problems with women were directly related to the things they said.

Fifteen minutes later, the phone rang again, forcing me inside. Perfect timing. I needed a third beer.

"I'm sorry," Allie said as soon as I answered, "I was out of line."

"I wholeheartedly agree."

"You're a twenty-year-old man; you can do what you want."

"Yes I am, and yes I can." Unfortunately, the goddam phone cord couldn't reach the goddam fridge, goddammit. Why hadn't I bought a longer cord? There I was, standing in the living room, holding an empty beer can like an asshole when there was a whole column of Budweiser in my fridge. "All jokes aside, Allie, thanks for apologizing. That was nice of you."

"See? I told you I could work on being nicer. I just need to control my first impulse." I heard her sigh loudly. "So will you meet me for lunch even though your friend is off on that…that thing? I'd really like to see you again."

I wondered if my blood alcohol level was still sky high from the night before, not to mention my two morning beers. Probably. But getting nailed for drunk driving in the middle of the day required a serious boneheaded maneuver. I figured I was still competent enough to carefully navigate the canyon. I agreed to meet her right away before my alcoholism asserted itself, forced me to drink more, and I became a clear and present danger to all Colorado motorists.

As I approached the Subway sandwich shop on The Hill where we'd agreed to meet, I saw Allie standing inside the entranceway. Her beauty lit up the chain restaurant, turned its yellows to gold, transformed its shabby subway motif into high-speed bullet trains packed full of grinning Asian passengers. She looked summery and unspoiled, as fresh as a toasted foot-long roast beef on Italian herb and cheese bread with lettuce, tomatoes, pickles, black olives, spicy mustard, scattered jalapenos, onions, and pepperjack cheese, just waiting for me to stuff her deliciousness in my face. She smiled and waved as I entered the restaurant. Every young man in the Subway gawked at her, buddies nudged buddies, eyes widened and penises stiffened. I couldn't verify that last one, but I knew what plumped the Paul porpoise, and since all men are precisely 96.7% the same, I felt confident in assuming the room was packed full of boners.

"You look devastating, Allie."

"You look devasta-*ted*, totally wrecked."

"I can only do my best with what God gave me."

"Did God forget to give you a razor?"

I reached up and rubbed my stubbly cheeks. "Yeah, I suppose I could've shaved, eh? Sorry, forgot."

She stepped up and kissed me quickly. "Jesus, you smell like a bar."

"Right on, I love that smell."

She shook her head. "You really need to take better care of yourself, Paul. What you're doing to yourself is not–"

I held up my hand. "Allie, stop, please."

She drew in a big breath and almost disturbed The Force with an onslaught of negativity. But then, miraculously, Allie closed her mouth. Proud of her, I was. She was honestly trying to change her very nature, which is not an easy thing for anyone to do. It's easy to quit eating sugar or stick to beer instead of whiskey or refrain from groping for the puckered penny in the middle of boinking, but it's nearly impossible for people to change their core nature. Most people never even attempt it, way too difficult. But Allie, God bless her, was giving it the ol' college try. Not my college try, of course, but a legitimate college try, the whole four-year degree and possibly grad school.

"Okay, I'll stop," she said.

"Good for you!" I pointed my finger at her. "Just for that, I'll buy you lunch."

She scoffed. "You still have all those antiquated Catholic ideas about chivalry and manliness. You'd buy me lunch no matter what."

"True, but now I won't resent you for it."

She rolled her eyes and moved toward the counter. Fifteen minutes later, I jammed a foot-long tuna sandwich into my face, having once heard tuna fish improved the brain's functioning. Mountain Dew improved exhaustion, I knew, so I ordered Subway's "Obese American" size, hoping to dynamite my mind with caffeine and sugar. Nothing worked, though, not the Dew, not the tuna. What I really needed was another handful of speeders, but that would make me too weird around Allie, probably too jittery to drive. I was already deeply deranged from the night before, still half drunk, and coming down hard from everything.

"Are you okay?" Allie asked.

I glanced at her over my sandwich. "Yeah, fine. Why?"

"You're quiet. You're never quiet."

"Not true. I barely say a word when no one's around."

"You're hilarious, you know that?" She took a sip off her "Waif" size Diet Coke. "Seriously, you seem distant."

"I'm just fried, Allie. White and I dropped a hit of some pretty powerful acid last night, and it's still eating my brain a little, I think."

I took a big bite of tuna fish and followed it with some irritatingly loud kettle chips that sounded, internally, as if someone were chopping hardened sediment off my brain with a pickaxe. It wasn't until I reached for my massive Mountain Dew that I saw Allie's face. I couldn't tell if her expression registered shock or horror or unbridled anger, but whatever it was, she glared at me like she'd caught me pleasuring Roger the Ferret.

"There a problem?" I asked around a mouthful of half-chewed food.

"Did you just say you dropped acid last night?"

I shrugged. "I think so, yeah."

"Like…as in LSD?"

I cocked my head, furrowed my brow, and stared at her for a second. "Yes, of course. What else would I mean by acid?"

"You take LSD," she stated, not a question.

"Of course."

"How many times?"

"I don't know, a million six? Couldn't tell you, Allie, I have a hard time doing basic math these days. Too much acid, I think."

She stared at me hotly, stared right through me for way too long. I couldn't believe this was actually a problem. Her brother Eddie was stoned *at least* 80% of his waking hours, and he was no stranger to acid. Surely, Allie knew about that. And she already mentioned that she could learn a lot about someone from the company they keep. Since Eddie and I were great friends, she had to know we'd have similar habits.

Oh, fuck it, I thought tiredly. I went back to my food. I was too hungover to deal with Allie's roller-coaster anger antics, and that tuna sandwich wasn't going to improve its own brain function, goddammit. At least five minutes of silence followed, and I felt no obligation to break it. I was about to get up and reload my Mountain Dew cavity creator when Allie finally spoke.

"I can't believe you take LSD."

"Believe it, baby."

"I can't believe you're so cavalier about such dangerous activities."

"You might as well start believing that, too." I finished my last bite, then sucked my straw until the ice cubes rattled. "Christ, Allie, I figured you knew all about this shit. Eddie's your brother, me and Eddie are buds, surely you had to figure we'd be into a lot of the same stuff, right?"

"*Oh my god!* Are you saying you smoke pot all the time, too?"

I laughed. "Now that's one bad habit I actually don't have. Never liked being stoned."

"But you like tripping on LSD?"

"I prefer to think of it as tripping *over* LSD."

No laughter, not even a smirk. Obviously, she'd never tripped over acid.

"What other drugs do you take?" She laid a real sneer on the word *drugs*.

"Nothing, really," I lied. Probably not the best time to mention my ephedrine addiction. "Booze, acid, that's essentially it."

She shook her head sadly, staring into my eyes, but all her judgmental sorrow only pissed me off. Good fucking lord, I didn't need this shit. I had a mother somewhere. I had an actual girlfriend somewhere. I had five sisters somewhere. If I needed sorrowful female judgment, I already had all I needed.

"Look, Allie, back off this crap, okay?" I said. "I really don't need any pseudo parental concern in my life. Yes, I smoke cigarettes, lots of them, take acid, lots of it, ride motorcycles, as fast as I can. And yes, I blast down the slopes on my skis, usually while drunk, and I do a whole bunch of other crazy crap I can't think of off the top of my hangover. That's just how I live, the kind of shit I like to do."

"But why, Paul? Why do you do all that stuff?"

"Because it's *fun*, Allie. Danger is exciting." I reached into my pocket and whipped out a smoke, not caring that she hadn't finished her sandwich yet. I watched her grimace at my Marlboro, but she'd gotten under my skin right in the middle of a rough hangover, and that warranted a tobacco retaliation. "I do it because life is dull most of the time. Work is dull. School is dull. Eating is dull, sleeping is dull, pissing is dull, taking a dump is dull. The vast majority of day-to-day living is boring as hell. Our time on earth is primarily consumed with basic maintenance, immediate survival, or setting things up for future survival, and 99% of all that shit is tedious, at best. But you know what? Throw a hit of acid into the mix, and I can sit still in my yard and study a leaf for six hours, one leaf, totally fascinated. I can go places in my mind that no sober person can even fathom. And ripping around the mountains on my bike at eighty miles an hour, pavement flying by, potential death around each corner, now *that's* a fucking rush, Allie. Nothing like it, except maybe parachuting or other adrenaline sports, and I intend to get to as many of those as soon as I can afford them.

"But if you want to spend your life in a classroom or grinding out a residency or working eighty hours a week as a doctor, be my guest. Live for the future, Allie, play it safe, follow the program. I sincerely hope you enjoy it, I really do. But that's not for me, certainly not at this point in my life. So let's just agree to disagree about how to live, okay? As far as I'm concerned, I'm young, I'm free, I'm an American. I can do and will do whatever the fuck I want whenever the fuck I want, and I don't need anyone's god damn permission, certainly not yours."

She didn't reply, simply scooched her awesome ass out of our booth. Without a word, she turned her back to me and walked toward the front door. She paused there, as if waiting for me to chase after her and beg her to stick around a little longer, if only to loudly finish chomping her kettle chips. But I was too hungover for all her silly hot girl shenanigans. I wasn't chasing after anyone, too much effort. Pushing open the door, Allie stepped out of the Subway sandwich shop and merged into the drifting stream of youthful passersby on the streets of Boulder, Colorado.

"Fuck her," I muttered under my breath. I reached out and grabbed the rest of her six-inch turkey on wheat with light mayo, limited toppings, and no cheese. It was a hot girl sandwich, low fat, no flavor, but I paid for the fucking thing, I wasn't about to let it go to waste. I ate it aggressively, ground it between my teeth as if crushing all feminine concern for my safety, and then I chomped down her remaining kettle chips. I even drank her fuckin' Diet Coke, sucking down that sickly sweet, horrible crap simply out of spite. Good lord, the little bitch had dragged me off my mountain, interrupted my alcoholism, and all for what? All for this stupid scene. To hell with her. I was done with Allie, swore I would never screw her again. Not once, not neva'.

Unless she asked me nicely, that is. And if she wore that cowgirl camping outfit again, she may not even have to ask, nicely or otherwise. Outside of those scenarios, though, me and that little bitch were *over*. I mean, unless… or unless…or unless…

* * *

White was gone for two days. He left a hilariously mangled message on my answering machine about how he'd called up his old high-school hockey teammate Ripper up in Breckenridge. He slurred something about how he and Rip were going to party like defensemen – meaning aggressively and without apology – up in Breck for a couple days. When White did finally return to Eldora, he looked like Death on a bad day – unlucky Death, auto-erotic asphyxiation Death, the gun went off while cleaning it Death, AIDS contracted from a blood transfusion Death.

"You look like death," I told White when he walked through my front door.

He groaned. "Fuck yourself. You don't know shit about death. Death is sleek and stealthy, not brash and obvious. Death giggles, man, it doesn't groan." He exhaled loudly. "Jesus Christ, is there any fucking beer in this cabin?"

I laughed and pointed at my fridge. "Plenty. I was just about to get going on it again myself. Worked last night, so I'm starting booze-fresh today."

"God, I haven't stopped drinking since I got to Colorado." White walked to the fridge, grabbed a bottle for each of us, and returned to the living room. "I can't believe I made it back on your bike. I'm fucking wrecked, balance is all screwed up. But damn, what a gorgeous ride." He spun the top on his Bud bottle and tipped it for several long seconds. "Ahhh. That oughta help."

"Always does." I opened my own beer. "You and Ripper tore it up something fierce, eh?"

"Fuckin' blow," White said, plopping down on my couch. "Rip's dealing coke up there to supplement his waiter income. Good god, I've never done so much cocaine in all my life, never *seen* so much coke. That's all those fuckers do up there in Breckenridge. Everyone's doing it, all the restaurant workers, all the rich tourists. Everyone boozes nonstop, and when they crash a little, they stuff their nostrils full of the powder. It's surreal." White finished his beer within ten minutes, then got up for more. "Fuck this inside shit, man. It's beautiful outside. Let's go drink on your deck."

I accepted the second bottle of Bud he gave me even though I was only a quarter of the way through my first. "Sounds good, but gimme about an hour. I was just at a good point in this story I'm working on. Want to finish up."

"Shit, sorry," White said hurriedly. "Yeah, of course, take your time. Working on anything good?"

I see-sawed my hand in the air. "This particular story's pretty cool. My ideas are better these days, the writing's better, but I still have a long way to go."

"Right on. I'll get out of your hair. Actually, I think your hammock is calling me." He went back to the fridge, grabbed a couple extra Buds, then carried his stash out to my hammock. Three minutes later, the sweet aroma of sticky weed wafted through my open front door and windows. Three minutes after that, the sound of deep, exhausted snores rattled the walls of the cabin. White, Party Animal Extraordinaire, had crashed back to Earth.

I threw on some headphones to drown out his thunder and dove into my story. I'd downplayed it to White, of course – humility is crucial to creativity – but I was actually pretty pleased with my recent stuff. This particular story centered around a horribly deformed kid who had talons for fingers, three on each "hand." At the climax, I'd have the boy rip out his own eyes with his talons in front of his peers, purposely horrifying all the classmates who'd teased him mercilessly throughout his life. Talon Boy would die in front of all those bastards, imprint a lasting image in their skulls that they could carry with them for the rest of their hopefully miserable lives. It was a good ol' anger story where everyone I ever disliked became my protagonist's classmates. I couldn't wait to damage their psyches for life, if only in fiction.

I lost track of real time, but in beer time, I wrote for a six pack while White snored two days of cocaine out his nostrils. Just as I was wrapping up

– a little too buzzed to write effectively – the phone rang. I glared at it. White was safely back in Eldora, so it couldn't be an emergency. It could be friends, Len or Phil or Eddie or Erik, trying to drag me off my mountain to drink with the flatlanders. But it could be Allie, wanting to "talk." I didn't want to "talk" right then. I almost never wanted to "talk" if talking required quotation marks. I liked to talk if talking involved the Minnesota Vikings or a stand-up comedian a buddy enjoyed or a great novel someone recently read. Still, my phone rang so rarely in the cabin that curiosity got the best of me.

"Hello?"

"I love you! I miss you!"

Maybe it was the beer, maybe it was the hypnotic rumble of White's snoring, but it actually took me a few seconds to recognize the voice.

"Oh my god, Lon, is that you?"

"Yes!" And then her tears burst forth, proving beyond a doubt it was Lonnie. "I miss you so much! I wish you were here with me right now! I *need* you here with me right now!"

I caught myself smiling the way only Lonnie could make me smile. It started somewhere down in my soul, a deep happiness switch only she could flick. Damn, the girl lit me up inside.

"Holy crap, Lonnie, I didn't expect to hear from you on the phone. Where are you?"

"We're in Rome. But Paul, calling is *sooo* expensive that we have to make this super quick. I just really really *really* needed to hear your voice. Did you get my postcards from Paris and London? I sent them a week ago or so."

"No, not yet." It was hard to talk to someone all the way over in Europe. I tried to picture Lonnie in Rome, but I couldn't imagine an actual scenario. All I could conjure up were the tourist traps, stereotypical locations seen in postcards or travel books. I could only envision Lonnie standing in front of the Colosseum, resting her gigantic boobs on the Spanish Steps, or chucking change into the Trevi Fountain. None of that was realistic at this hour in Europe, probably way too late for her to be wandering around the tourist centers.

"Jesus, Lon, what time is it over there, anyway?" I asked.

"It's super late, like 3:00-ish. But I can't go back to the room where my mom is yet. Need a little more time away. She's driving me *totally* insane, Paul. I'm actually standing at this little pay phone in our hotel lobby just to avoid her for a little longer. And to hear your sweet, melodious voice, of course."

And just like that, Jealousy, my nemesis, popped into my living room for a quick visit. *I'm back, Paul! Did you miss me?* Lonnie was still awake, out and about at 3:00 a.m. in Rome. She was drunk, as well. I'd disregarded it at first, but I definitely heard that subtle Lonnie slur in her voice. And she wouldn't have lingered at the bars all by herself, of course, nor did her mother hammer down the booze until 3:00 a.m. Lonnie's mom barely drank, in fact. The chances were pretty slim that Lonnie even started the night with her mother, let alone finished it.

Knowing all that, my jealous mind quickly concocted its own story: *The hot little blonde rests her breasts on a hip European bar filled with a bunch of dark and handsome – albeit sweaty and swarthy – Italian men. Italians usually talk with their hands, but tonight, they whisper Italian-y things in the blonde's ear, alluring and foreign phrases like "Caesar Salad" and "Spaghetti with Meatballs" and "The Godfather." They buy her wine, that fuckin' Euro-wine that comes in fancy bottles with actual corks, and the young woman sucks down the free wine and laps up the attention, eventually slipping away with her chosen Casanova. But then something goes horribly wrong: Salvador softly slaps her overly-sensitive left ass cheek while they're making sweet, sweaty Euro-love. "Never the left cheek, you perv!" she yells, then yanks his pepperoni right out of her rigatoni. She runs back to her hotel pay phone to call her stupid, gullible, unsophisticated boyfriend back in the States, because that idiot is always there and he always knows which ass cheek to slap and he will always say he loves her, no matter what.*

God damn, I suddenly wanted all the dirt, all the info. I wanted to keep Lonnie on the line for three hours so that I could grill her relentlessly until she barfed up every last detail of her whoring night. But somehow, I resisted every terrible impulse in my justifiably jealous soul and managed to keep the conversation casual.

"Wow, that's really late to be out by yourself," I said calmly, my insides churning.

"Yeah, Europe's late in general, especially in the south where it's hot. It is *roasting* in Italy. It's so scorching down here that people don't even go out to dinner until the sun goes down at like 9:00 or 10:00. But Paul, Italy is *so* unbelievably beautiful. I can't wait to develop my pictures and tell you all about it."

"Tell me all about it right now."

I heard loud footsteps stomp through the cabin door, followed by an even louder voice. "Holy shit, is that Lonnie?"

I turned and saw White tilt back the beer he must have fallen asleep drinking. I nodded quickly.

"Tell her I say hi, dude!"

"Who is that?" Lonnie asked.

"It's White. He says hi."

"White's in town? Wow, tell him I say hi, too! I didn't know he was coming out to visit."

"I didn't either until about four days ago. He needed a drinking and drugging vacation, I think."

"Oh god, you two alone in a cabin in the woods for a week? Seriously, try not to kill yourselves. I'm guessing the liquor store had to double their Budweiser inventory and your dealer had to order an emergency sheet of acid."

"Exactly, Lon," I said. "But hey, who cares about me? Tell me about your trip, where you've been, where you're going."

"Paul, I can't, sorry. I'll tell you everything when I'm back. This call is so expensive, and my mom says she's paying for everything except phone calls back to the States." I heard Lonnie's sniffles start up again. "I just needed to hear your voice, needed to hear you say you love me."

Despite the cheating I knew of and the cheating I suspected, I did love her. I really did. I could not shake that girl from my soul.

"I do, Lonnie."

"Then tell me."

"I just did."

"What, you can't tell me you love me when White's in the room?"

"Umm…" I glanced over my shoulder and saw White leaning against the sink, grinning, watching me. "Okay, Lonnie, I love you."

"Pussy!" White shouted loud enough for Lonnie to hear.

"I'm so proud of you," Lonnie said. "Look at you, expressing your most sensitive emotions in front of one of your oldest friends. You're getting so mature, Pablo."

"Alright, enough. Don't push it."

She giggled. "Well, I love love *looove* you. I'm never afraid to say it. Do you love love *loooove* me?"

"Not anymore, just changed my mind."

She laughed again. "Okay, I really have to go. Please say hi to my puppies and tell them their mommy misses them and loves them to pieces."

"Will do, Lon."

"Smooch them for me."

"I will."

"And give yourself a big smooch from me, too."

"I can't bend down that far."

"Not *there*, you weirdo." I heard her sigh heavily. "Okay, I gotta go, but I'll try and call again at some point. I'll keep sending postcards.

"Sounds good. I do love you, Lonnie. I really do."

"'Kay. I love you, too. We'll be back together before we know it! I'll see you in five weeks!"

I hung up the phone and looked at White.

"You gonna cry?" White asked.

"Maybe a little, out my dick. Just a few sticky tears."

"Cheers to that." He tipped his beer and drained it dry. "Dude, I feel fuckin' *great* after my nap. That's the best sleep I've had in three days. Now I feel like going drinking in that dusty little town down the road."

"Nederland?"

"Yeah, that's it. Any good bars there?"

"There's the Pioneer Inn. Cheap beer, awesome food."

"Cool, I haven't had anything decent to eat on this entire bender. Could use some good grub. Will they serve alcohol to your underage ass?"

"They always have, no questions asked."

An hour later, we sat in a booth at the Pioneer Inn and devoured huge burritos stuffed with eggs and beans, sour cream and guacamole, black olives, a sticky sea of melted cheese. Eggs Sonora, one of the tastiest menu items ever concocted in one of the most unlikely locations in the world. An hour after that, we planted our asses firmly at the bar. Another hour on and a few whiskey shots later, White leaned against the jukebox, crooning along to old Doors songs.

"Your friend is really drunk," Carmen, the bartender, told me.

"Nah, he's just really weird. If he were really drunk, he'd be playing air drums, too." I tipped back my cold Bud bottle. "White can handle a lot of booze before he hits the 'really drunk' phase, trust me. He can certainly handle more than me, probably more than anyone I've ever met."

Carmen nodded as she stared at White. "Well, he is an awfully tall kid. Tall, dark and handsome, actually. *Very* handsome."

I glanced up at Carmen and saw her gazing hungrily at White. She was older, early thirties, and she'd perfected the mountain-plain style, the "looks don't matter" look. Mountain-plain girls had brown, outdoor-work skin instead of beach-body tan, and they usually sported flannel shirts and faded, ripped jeans. Their hair was always smashed up and clipped somewhere on the back of their head, no makeup, au naturale boobs that refused any bra's confinement. Other mountain girls admired the look for its defiance of traditional femininity, but it wasn't a style that grabbed the attention of the typical young male.

"So you like my buddy White, eh?"

She opened her eyes a little wider and nodded. "I have to say, that boy is a pretty strapping young lad. Does he have a girlfriend?"

I nodded, then shrugged apologetically.

"Does he fool around on her?"

I laughed. "Actually, White's oddly loyal. Not sure why. His mom passed away when we were in high school, so maybe that has something to do with it. It might have given him some kind of higher respect for a woman's dignity than the rest of us shitheads have, or maybe he just doesn't have the same level of lust poison rolling through his veins. Fuck, I don't know. But no, I don't think I've ever seen him cheat on any of his girlfriends."

Carmen threw up her hands. "Now I like him even more! Oh well, can't have 'em all." She drifted down the bar to placate a different drunk.

I fired up a Marlboro as White belted out his own rendition of "People Are Strange" at the jukebox, proving, definitively, that people are strange. A couple hours and many Budweisers later, we found ourselves deeply engaged in conversation with a mother-daughter combo from just up the road in Rollinsville. They were a bizarre set, the daughter "mountain pretty" at twenty-two years old, the mother a forty-year-old, hard-drinking sneak peak of the daughter's inevitable future. The mother was all over White, and White tolerated her weird advances so long as she listened to his long-winded opinions on impressionist art, Rimbaud's poetry, and college hockey. That left me with the pretty but already jaded daughter, and after a heroic effort, I managed to extract her phone number. I didn't want to use it – Rollinsville was way too close to Eldora for comfortable cheating – but I wanted to *get* it. Every phone number received was a bizarre masculine trophy, a triumph of testosterone.

"Gimme the keys, bro," White said as we stumbled out of the Pioneer Inn and into the crisp, clear, summer night.

"No way. You're fuckin' wrecked."

"So are you, and face it, I'm the better driver." White pointed at the sky. "Besides, look at that."

"Look at what?"

"Look at the fucking *sky*, man!" He stared at me with big, weird, wasted eyes. "Gimme the keys, Pablo; you'll see what I mean soon enough."

I tossed him the keys. It didn't matter which drunken idiot drove. There wasn't a cop within twenty miles of Nederland, no chance of a DUI bust in the town proper, and even less a chance once we slipped onto the small county highway to Eldora.

White swerved through the silent streets of Nederland, the two of us seemingly the last humans awake in the world, and then he turned onto Eldora Road. A quarter mile up the two-lane, White flicked off the headlights.

"Um, dude, what the fuck?" I asked.

"Give it a second."

"Give what a second?"

"Let your eyes adjust."

"White, this is a bad—"

"Shut up and look up."

White pointed upward through the windshield, and now I saw what he was talking about. A brilliant full moon lit the sky, illuminating the deep dark nothingness between Nederland and Eldora with the power of ten thousand klieg lights. My eyes did adjust, precisely as White said, and now I could see the valley plain as day. Everything was spectacularly lit, the highway included. The scrub brush and trees practically glowed, all the world dunked in moonlight.

"Holy shit," I said.

"Pretty cool, eh? Try this, man."

White rolled down his window and pushed himself up until the majority of his large torso was out the window. He curled his left leg under him, kneeling on the driver's seat, but he was still tall enough to hang onto the wheel and reach the gas pedal. He pressed down on the accelerator, speeding up. I had to join in. Since I didn't have to reach any pedals, I easily wrestled myself out the passenger window and sat my ass on the door frame, my entire upper body exposed to the moonlit night. Adrenaline kicked in as I stared at the gloriously full moon and felt the hard blast of chilly mountain air scald my face. Our car sped across the road as it snaked through the valley, White managing the tight mountain turns without so much as a flashlight for guidance.

"Fuckin' wild, ain't it!" White yelled over the roar of the wind.

"Fuckin-A!"

"You alive yet, brother?!" he yelled.

The wind penetrated my pores, the moonlight bathed my brain, and death flitted through the forest, waiting to pounce on the slightest wrong move. White jammed the gas pedal down even further. We whipped around every curve, one stray deer away from certain death.

"I asked if you're fucking alive!" White screamed at me across the car's rooftop.

"Maybe for a few minutes longer!"

White laughed and shook his head in the wind, clearly missing all the long, flowing hair his big-boy job eliminated. He threw his free left arm high in the air, embracing the night, saluting life itself. I watched the forest fly by as the massive mountain silhouettes slinked across the horizon like slow, lazy elephants, the full moon drowning my little slice of the world in radiance. I knew I had to die, dammit, but since I had to die, I decided there could be no better moment to do so, and the intense awareness of perfect death made me suddenly fall madly in love with life. The moon, the night, the cold sting of mountain air, a madman at the wheel, his wailing scream penetrating nature's wildly illuminated darkness. Damn. It was worth it, enduring all this long life, all the hidden terrors just over the horizon, the heartache and heartbreak, the hard work and easily achieved misery, if only for ten minutes as such.

10.

Immature Walking Penis

ELDORA, COLORADO

1991

"What's up, girl?"

Sabrina glared at me, and without a word, she turned her back and stomped into Pizza Place's tiny office.

"What's with her?" I asked Len.

"You know Sabrina. She's moody."

It felt like more than that, though. I'd just arrived for my shift, and while I was curious about Sabrina's behavior, I didn't want to approach her with Len and Erik in the store. Long ago, Sabrina warned that if our affair ever hit the Pizza Place airwaves without her permission, all that fantastic fucking would come to an unceremonious end. She was in charge at the store, and she didn't want all the drivers snickering behind her back or thinking maybe they were next in the sack. So I waited until Len and Erik's pies slid out the oven and the two of them headed out on their runs.

Stepping cautiously back to the office, I peeked my head in. "Um, is there a problem?"

Sabrina turned angry eyes on me. "Oh yeah, there's a fucking problem, Pablo. You and me have a *big* fucking problem."

233

I watched her, waiting for more, but she apparently needed to see me squirm a bit. I squirmed dutifully for her, but then I grew impatient. "Mind letting me know what the big problem is?"

"Like you don't fucking know?"

"Sabrina, I–"

She reached onto the desktop, grabbed an envelope, and threw it at me. "That's the problem, Mountain. You're holding the fucking problem right there in your slimy little hands."

"I don't even know what this is, Sabrina."

"Oh yeah? Well, I do. It's a little love letter from your *other* side girl. Eddie's cutesy little sister bounced her tight little ass in here today, big doe eyes all wet and sticky. She asked me to tell you how sorry she was, told me to make sure you got her lovesy-wuvsy wuv-wetter, and she made sure I knew it was for your eyes only."

"So you read it, of course."

"You're god damn right I read it!" Sabrina threw up her arms. "Jesus Christ, all that sappy shit practically made me barf. *I miss you, Paulie, I care about you, Paulie, I need to see you, Paulie.* Jesus, girl, grow a spine." Sabrina glared at me, her chest heaving with adrenaline and frustration. "What the fuck is wrong with you, Paul? It's not enough to have Lonnie, have me, have occasional other side action that I *know* you chase down from time to time? Now you gotta go gettin' yourself a third steady lay?"

I shrugged and smiled guiltily at her. There was no good response. I flipped the letter around in my hand, stared at the ground, and waited for more verbal punishment.

"*Say something!*" Sabrina insisted. "I want to hear your goddam cheap excuses so I can remember them the next time I think of doing something as stupid as getting all involved with an immature walking penis."

I had to forcibly restrain myself from laughing. *Immature walking penis.* I liked that. What a great way to start a short story: *The immature walking penis sat at the bar, broke again. "Balls!" he said, wishing he could afford just one more drink, or at least a small sack of nuts…*

I shrugged again. "Look, Sabrina, I don't know what to tell you. This isn't an excuse, but I'm actually surprised you care. Never even crossed my mind that something like this would bother you, to be perfectly honest."

"You didn't – it didn't – you really…" She shook her head, brow furrowed. "I seriously can't believe you just fucking said that, I seriously can't. Are you honestly that crass, or are you just that stupid?"

"Probably a combo of both. Throw in a scoop of horny, and you've got yourself a Pablo casserole."

"God dammit, you are *NOT* funny, Mountain!" She stood up and stormed out of the office, but then she stopped at the double-decker oven and pointed at me. "You don't talk to me for a while, boy, not a single god damn word for a good long stretch. I don't want to hear your voice. And don't you even *think* about trying to worm your skinny ass back into my bed. Go off and fuck your new little girlie, the little tramp." She looked at the ceiling and threw up her hands. "Jesus, what was I *thinking!*"

Even angry, Sabrina looked smokin' hot as she stomped over to the prep line. Her jeans were ripped right below her right ass cheek, a little sliver of panty showing. I knew those panties well. They were baby blue, laced, beautiful against her chocolate skin, especially when she lay stretched out on her bed, gesturing me over. *Come crawl inside me, Pablo, get way up deep inside, baby.* Damn, did I really just blow that perfect setup for a shot at the tightly-wound Allie? Yep, I sure did. That second elusive bird in the bush was every man's downfall.

Still, I hadn't lied; I honestly didn't believe Sabrina would care. In fact, it seemed absurd to me that *anyone* would give a shit about anything I did. I was so obviously a lecherous drunken buffoon. It's not like I was hiding it. I reveled in my assholery, cultivated it, announced it boldly to the whole damn world. How could Sabrina see me any differently?

I didn't have any answers, so I did what I did best: I walked to the warming rack and routed myself a three-delivery pizza mission. I may have been a lecherous drunken buffoon, but I was one helluva pizza man, and three scattered drops way up in North Boulder would keep me out of the store for a good long stretch.

I dropped off all the pies before the thirty-minute delivery guarantee expired, and then I pulled over and extracted Allie's letter from its envelope. Damn, it smelled like her. She'd perfumed it just for me…just for me and Sabrina, apparently. I suddenly wanted Allie again, no matter how angry it made Sabrina. Allie was a drop-dead gorgeous young woman, and drop-dead gorgeous young women always dismantle the more practical instincts of horny young men.

Paul,

As I write this, I feel sick to my stomach about how I acted the other day at Subway. I've been going over it and over it in my head, and I guess when I heard about you being so reckless, it scared me, so I lashed out. I don't want to think about anything bad happening to you because I really care about you, Paul. I shouldn't be so protective so early in our — whatever we are — but I guess I'm no good at being with a guy. I know I need to control these stupid outbursts if I expect to be your girlfriend — I hope you're still considering that! — and I know I can if you'll give me another chance. I realize it's only been a few days since I saw you, but I REALLY REALLY miss you and would love to see you again as soon as you're ready. Please call me! Let me make it up to you!

- Allie

Wow, she wanted to make it up to me. Hot shit. My penis certainly didn't need any further convincing; he was ready for immediate make-up sex. He raised his little head high, his single eye scanning over the Levi Strauss horizon for Allie. But no way, fuck that, the little bitch needed to stew on it another day or two. I had to scare her straight. Besides, she'd filled her letter with real and honest emotion, and between Sabrina, Allie, and Lonnie, all the good vibrations flowing my direction were getting uncomfortable and annoying. What was with all the care and affection lately? They needed to talk to my father; he'd learn 'em right quick how to not give a shit about me. And then maybe one of them would write me a letter I'd actually respond to:

Dear Pablo,

I want to fuck you a whole bunch and buy you a shit-ton of beer. Please call the next time you're horny, thirsty, and broke.

- Dream Girl

I'd set the fuckin' land speed record responding to that letter.

I took too many ephedrine speeders, stayed out of Sabrina's way, and blasted my way through the rest of that awkward work shift, feeding all of Boulder's hungriest citizens. Well, maybe not the hungriest. The truly starving continued to starve, and I sailed past them on the streets, not giving them any pizza, because starving people never tipped for shit. When business slowed, I hid in the back of the store and washed dough trays and folded pizza boxes. At the end of my shift, I accepted my mileage and commission from Sabrina without a word between us, and then I slunk out of Pizza Place, rolled into Boulder Canyon, and flipped off my headlights. I navigated most of the canyon by moonlight, only turning on the lights on the rare occasion another driver's headlights approached from the opposite direction.

By the time I got home, I was flying high on moonlight adrenaline and far too much ephedrine. Although it was 3:00 in the morning, White was awake on the porch with my dogs, wrapped in a blanket to ward off the increasingly chilly, late summer mountain nights.

"I'm really fucking drunk," he said by way of greeting.

"Your secret's safe with me, dude."

White slowly turned his blurry eyes up to me. "You want to get really drunk with me, stay up all night, maybe hike your mountain and catch the sunrise like we used to do in Boulder when we lived there?"

"Hell, yes. Is there any other answer?"

"No, my friend, there really isn't."

* * *

White stayed two weeks, a full week longer than he'd planned. We decided to repeat our first day on his last day. We dropped acid in the early afternoon, drank like unfulfilled, mentally-damaged poets – as opposed to all the well-grounded, sober poets of the world – and hiked the high hills of Eldora. As the sun drifted toward the tips of the Continental Divide, we settled onto My Rock, ready for the sunset spectacle.

"I can't leave, man," White said sullenly. "I can't leave this place."

"Then don't."

"I have to."

"Then do."

He laughed. "It really is just that simple, isn't it?"

I nodded. "It really is. Life's a breeze, brother. Do what you want, live how you want, where you want, when you want. You're a young American, White, the possibilities are endless. Want to live in the mountains? Do it. Want to live in an enormous city? Do it. Want to live in the desert, by the ocean, live poor, get rich, hide in an isolated cabin in the fucking forest, live on a lake, by a stream? Do it, all of it, any of it. Fuck it, man, write all day, drink all night, do as you please. Money is the only real issue, and you can pretty much make however much or little you want, just depends on how many hours you're willing to put in. But as far as your cash will take you, seems to me you can do whatever the fuck you want in this big ol' country of ours."

"God damn, that's so true. And so simple." He lit a cigarette and blew a cloud into the evening air. "I've let myself get all confused and fucked up, made everything complicated. A lot of it's Gloria, but it's mainly me. She kind of pushes her version – or her version of the world's version – of normalcy on me, but I'm the one who falls for it. Dude, she's just so fucking hot, that's all there is to it. Her hotness scrambles my goddam brains. I start living the way I think she expects me to, even if she doesn't come right out and demand anything." He shook his head with disgust. "Seriously, Paul, I now spend forty hours a week hunting people down to scold them for credit violations. Can you believe that shit? I'm a collector, like the tax man, except I'm collecting from the poor and irresponsible and giving to these colossal mega-corps that bury weak people under a mountain of debt and insane interest rates. That's not me, man. That's some weird, foreign version of me that I've convinced myself I'm supposed to be right now. Seriously, what the fuck am I doing with my life?"

He glanced over at me and shook his head, looking bewildered. I stared back at him for a few seconds, and then I laughed right in his face. Loudly. I couldn't help it. It took White several seconds, but he eventually got it and joined in the hilarity. White, of all people, was now a shirt-and-tie, 8:00-to-5:00, glorified bill collector, hounding the poor for a pound of flesh. It was absurd, and the acid in our bloodstream cemented White's ludicrous life firmly in its proper position within the Grand Comedy.

"Seriously, *what the fuck am I doing?*" he asked again. "I want to be a poet, a painter, live in nature, live *with* nature. I want to find a woman who will wander the woods with me, inspire me, a real muse, man. Gloria can't even leave her apartment until she's spent two hours prepping in front of the mirror, for fuck's sake. She likes nightclubs and fashion, celebrity magazines."

I laughed even louder at that, laughed my ass off. Nightclubs. Celebrity magazines. Fashion. Jesus motherfucking Christ. Tripping acid at sunset on a rock atop a mountain in the Colorado Rockies brought out the full hilarious insanity of all that meaningless shit. I laughed so hard I actually slapped my knee like some old-timer in overalls on an Arkansas porch.

"Jesus, you *should* laugh. Or cry. Same fucking thing," White said. "Damn, I gotta break free before it's too late. She'll suck me in, man, suck me straight into her vagina like some inescapable black hole. I'll pop out the other side as a seventy-year-old man with a solid retirement account, house in a nicer suburb of Minneapolis, couple kids. But no paintings, no poetry, no travel tales, my whole life wasted, hypnotized by a beautiful face and perfect body, neither of which will last."

I nodded slowly, considering. "You know, I think you can have it all, man, you just can't have it all at the same time. You can have Gloria and you can have the poet's cabin in the woods, just not simultaneously. Sucks, but that's life. Doing some things makes doing other things impossible, you know? I mean, you *can* live a smorgasbord life, try a little of this, a little of that, a little time doing this, a little time doing that. But that's never really going to get you anywhere, and if you ever go *all in* on one thing, whether that's painting or writing or chasing wealth or whatever, you can kiss a bunch of other shit goodbye forever. You just can't load a ton of conflicting flavors on your plate at the same time. Makes everything taste kind of shitty, if you follow me."

"Yeah, I follow. And that's exactly what I've been doing. I want the smoking hot vain chick at the same time I want the poet's retreat in the forest. Whenever I have one, I crave the other. Gotta stop doing that, man, gotta make some firm choices and be comfortable with whatever other parts of my life those choices eliminate."

"Exactly." I flicked my wrist, waving the conversation away. "But there are bigger things, more important things." I pointed to the west. "Like that, man. Remember this scene next time you start to feel trapped."

Our eyes wandered across the mountains to the Continental Divide in the distance. Atop Mount Mountain, plenty of afternoon LSD still in our veins, we had the best seat in the world for the most spectacular sunset in the western hemisphere. Soft, scattered clouds aligned in the west just above the horizon, acting as backsplashes for the falling sun's color explosion. The giant yellow yolk cruised gently toward craggy rock mountaintops, their upper third naked and stark above timberline. Yellow light dove between the peaks, the treeless mountainsides striped orange and red. Through the clouds, sunlight splashed the sky in long, wandering tentacles that stretched to the east. We watched the whole show, watched the sun drop steadily, further and further, until it finally burst across the jagged peaks as if an explosion had occurred within the sun itself. I actually *felt* our star detonate, waves of energy blasting through me, past me, a solar wind that ripped across the Rockies, over the plains, all the way to the dense forests of middle America.

When it was over and only an eerie glow illuminated the distant peaks, White finally spoke. "I think that was the most beautiful thing I've ever seen."

"Remember it, dude, hold onto it. And then come back for more when you're ready."

He reached into his pocket, extracted a flask, and hit it hard. "Don't you worry, Pablo, I will. Someday."

When White left the following morning, I had no doubt he'd be back in Colorado before long. He had a determined, focused look in his eyes that I knew well. It was how he looked when he was playing hockey and some opponent got under his skin, or when he was painting, or when he spoke of all the things that truly moved him. White was not done with Colorado. Or maybe Colorado was not done with White. Either way, whenever he decided to give life in Colorado a second shot, I hoped I was around to see it.

11.

A Boner in One Hand and a Beer in the Other

ELDORA, COLORADO
1991

"Make me cum again," Allie whispered.

I slid down her perfect body, past her perfect breasts, and buried my face between her perfect legs. Allie came quickly and aggressively now that she was accustomed to a tongue on her clitoris. She came with the ease and ferocity of someone wound far too tight for far too long, like the first time an inmate laughs after being released from the gulag, then keeps laughing and laughing until finally bursting into tears at the horror of it all.

"Oh my god, I think I could do that ten times," she said after I finished her off.

I slid up on her bed, lit a cigarette, and blew smoke at her bedroom ceiling.

"You know I hate it when you smoke in my room."

"You know I hate it when you complain about me smoking in your room."

She laid her head on my chest and endured my addiction. It was the third time we'd been together since our Subway fiasco, and while we never revisited that tortuous tale of turkey and tuna, it loomed over us. Allie was now on her best behavior, barely bristling at my secondary addictions while feeding my primary addiction: sex. In fact, we were learning together

243

that Allie loved a good romp almost as much as I did, loved exploring it, pushing it to new heights. She liked being held down submissively, then instantly flipping the switch to wild dominance. There was a little demon buried in her soul, I realized, and if I stuck around long enough, I knew we could unshackle that strange bastard and unleash his full potential upon the bedroom. Her future patients would thank me for wrestling out Allie's darkest devils in the bedroom. Hopefully, that would keep her from grinning weirdly, eyes narrowed, as she sharpened her scalpel in the operating room.

"We're running out of time, you know," she said. "There's only about two weeks left."

I felt her light breath roll across my nipples, and somehow, that little nipple-tickle made me want her again.

"I know, Allie."

"What do you think you're going to do?"

I dragged on my smoke silently because smoking quietly was easier than talking.

"Well?" she pressed.

"I don't know."

She pushed herself off my chest, sat up against her headboard, and folded her arms across her perfect, naked chest. "How can you not know?"

"God, Allie, not again, please?"

"I don't understand. You *have* to know, Paul. I mean, seriously, there's so much potential with me and you, but you can't get yourself to try something new? You keep saying there's no future with Lonnie. Why on earth would you stay? Even if it doesn't work out between us, at least you'd be out of that dead-end relationship."

"You're ruining this, Allie." I looked over at her pouting face, saw her angry, almost childlike frustration, and I felt overwhelming sympathy for her. Just a girl who wanted a boy, that's all. And she deserved one, too, especially since she was trying so hard, probably for the first time in her life.

What I couldn't get myself to tell her was that I was probably not that boy. My time with White left a sort of sticky residue on my brain. All his stories of Gloria stuck with me, her beauty, the hypnotizing effect she had on him. He was desperate to escape her and her expectations, but he seemed oddly unable to do it. It was dispiriting to witness a full-blown woman addiction in one of my best friends, and I noticed the striking similarities between his Gloria and my Allie. Doctor Allie. Healthy Allie. Light-drinking Allie. Ambitious Allie. Would light-drinking, non-smoking, drug-free, career-oriented, Doctor Allie accept writer Paul, pizzaman Pablo, the drunk who sped up mountain canyons using the full moon for headlights? Fuck no. Once she leapt over the Lonnie hurdle, the whole damn contest would change. She'd stuff me into White's cubicle before the snow flew that winter, or worse, goad me back into some goddam college classroom, corralling credits, laying the groundwork for a respectable, responsible future. Allie would have my motorcycle impounded and my beer confiscated, and being powerless over sex, I'd consent, just so long as I could invade her perfectly pretty pussy from time to time. I'd spooge out all my artistic ambition and badass attitude in one giant glob of male subjugation.

Lonnie, on the other hand, didn't give a shit about the practicalities of my life. For all the downsides to staying with her, Lonnie wanted a writer, so she tolerated a maniac. Maybe that's why I had such a fierce and complicated love for her: she loved me. *Me.* Lonnie had no interest in playing Mold a Man, Design a Dude. There was no future with her, true, but the present was exactly what I needed: a judgment-free zone in which to live like a lunatic.

"Look, Allie, it's a big decision. Lonnie and I signed a lease together, have a history. We have pets, for fuck's sake. Our dogs would be heartbroken if we split them up."

"Oh, please. That's such a lame excuse. It's actually pretty cowardly."

"Excuse me?"

"You heard me, Paul. *Cowardly.*"

"That's not my favorite word, Allie, especially when referencing me." I snubbed out my cigarette in the ashtray I now made her keep in her bedroom.

"I know you don't, that's why I used it. You're always talking about fearlessness and living aggressively and all that crap, but you're thinking of staying with Lonnie because you're afraid to change. I get it; change is hard. Takes courage to change, takes fearlessness and aggression, all the things you say are so important to you. It doesn't take any balls whatsoever to stick with something that you know is going nowhere just because it's comfortable. That's not courage; that's apathy."

God dammit, why did I always date smart women? Why couldn't I pick a know-nothing bombshell? Everything about me was obvious to Lonnie, transparent to Sabrina, and self-evident to Allie. Someone once said you can fool some of the people some of the time. Really? Like who, and when?

"Fair enough, Allie. It's just that I have other things to consider. And please, don't force it tonight. I'm not making a decision right now." I pushed myself off the bed and scrounged around the floor for my underwear. "In fact, I gotta go."

"So now you're running away?"

"Nope, not running. I told you I have to work in the morning. Took a day shift."

Allie pouted. She had a beautiful pout, especially when she was naked, her hair all mussed up from fucking, the scent of sweat and tobacco and vagina in the air.

"You can stay here, you know."

"Dogs, baby. Those little monsters need me."

She sighed loudly, but I could see she wasn't going to press it any further. "Will you at least stop by after your shift tomorrow and say hi? I have a lot of studying to do during the day, but I'd like to see you afterward."

I grinned. "You'd like to see me or my penis?"

"I, well—"

"It's my penis, right? Admit it, Allie, you can't get enough of the dirty little prick."

Her face shifted from a pout to an embarrassed smile. "I did *not* say that."

"You don't have to. We woke the sleeping sex beast inside you, and now it rules your life. Take it from me, you'll get used to your monster after a while. I certainly have."

She laughed and everything felt lighter for the moment. "Get out," she said. "We'll see how I feel tomorrow."

I dressed, crawled across the bed, and kissed her warmly. She gave it right back to me, a subtle promise for the following day.

Sitting in Allie's driveway as my lame Subaru warmed up, I couldn't resist reaching inside the glovebox and pulling out the postcard I'd received that morning, a beautiful impressionist depiction of Paris. Lonnie was too complex a woman to send a simple tourist shot of the Eiffel Tower, Notre Dame or the Louvre. Instead, she chose a painted postcard of a simple street – long rows of old, squat, blue-topped buildings, cafes at street level, Parisians drinking, smoking, reading novels at tiny tables. It was dusk, and the scene promised a night of mystery, beautiful women with intriguing accents, strong drinks prepared with proper reverence. Every figure in the postcard was warming up for the grand adventure of a City of Light night. They were getting their first few belts in, cramming their heads full of literature, ready to disappear into some hidden speakeasy where too-cool musicians played too-cool blues or too-cool jazz.

Damn, I wanted to be there. I wanted to be in Paris with Lonnie, wanted to wander from watering hole to watering hole, take in the streets and smells. I'd even tolerate the B.O. of all those French dudes if it meant I could experience a few nights in Paris. There was a whole world out there to see, Hemmingway's world, Fitzgerald's world, Joyce's world. I wanted to be a writer, for fuck's sake, and writers were supposed to travel. *"Travel is fatal to prejudice, bigotry, and narrow-mindedness... Broad, wholesome, charitable views of men and things cannot be acquired by vegetating in one little corner of the earth all one's lifetime."* Mark Twain said that, and then he dropped the N-bomb a couple hundred times. Travel may be fatal to prejudice and bigotry, but it sure ain't fatal to racial epithets, apparently. Nevertheless, the point was valid;

any writer worth his B.O. should travel far and wide. *I* should be in Paris, London, Rome. I should be anywhere other than Allie's driveway, reading Lonnie's words off a postcard from the other side of the world.

I miss you SO much! I love you, love you, love you! You should be here. WE should be here together. You could really write here, Paul, all the history, all the beauty, all the artists. They even name their streets after writers. Give Rummy and Evie big kisses from their Mommy and tell them I'll be home soon! Love and miss all of you!

— Lon

I suddenly wondered if Lonnie had sent Phil a postcard from Paris, too. Did she also love him, love him, love him? Or did she just want his cock, his cock, his cock up inside her cheating little vagina? For some weird reason, sending Phil a postcard almost seemed more disloyal than boning him. Unable to recognize – and thereby overcome – my own hypocrisy, I felt a wild stab of jealousy at the prospect of Phil receiving a postcard. Even as Allie's juices slowly dried on my penis, I smoldered with idiotic anger at this potential "betrayal." How dare Lonnie do as I do? What a bitch!

As I entered Pizza Place the following morning, I saw Sabrina's perfectly round butt sashay into the walk-in cooler. Bummer. Had I known she had inside duties that day, I wouldn't have signed up for the shift. Summer day shifts entailed one driver and one inside person, lots of food prep work, and usually several hours without any orders, time when two people who enjoyed each other's company could shoot the shit and kill an afternoon together. Sabrina and I could no longer do that. It had been almost two weeks since Allie dropped off the poison letter, and while Sabrina would now bark out pizza commands at me, our conversations never went beyond dough trays, folding boxes, or other pizza-related topics. Sadly, when Sabrina and I now talked about sausage, we were actually talking about sausage.

"We need peppers, 'shrooms, and onions, two buckets each," Sabrina said, emerging from the cooler with a tub of ham in her left hand, a tub of pepperoni in her right.

"Can do."

I set my book down on the front counter, then stood in place for a few seconds. I really didn't want to have a "conversation," but I was sick of sidestepping someone I liked so much. And until very recently, I was under the impression she felt the same about me.

"Hey Sabrina, we ever going to talk about all this shit, maybe clear the air a little?"

She slid the ham and pepperoni tubs into place in the prep line, then turned to look at me. "What do we need to talk about, Mountain?"

I shrugged. "This. Me. You. Whatever's going on."

"Are you still fucking Eddie's cutesy-cute little sister?"

I opened my mouth, then closed it quickly before the lies fell out. Word had gotten around the store, I knew, so there was no point in trying to cover my ass. When Eddie found out, he told me I must be some kind of insane masochist and not to come crying to him when his sister inevitably set my dog on fire. Even Phil knew about Allie. He didn't say anything to me, but I saw it in his eyes, the knowledge of my expanded adultery and the contempt he felt for it or me or both. I wondered if he'd tell Lonnie once she got back. Phil was a hard one to figure, but if he told her, he'd probably be doing me a favor, ending what should end that I could not seem to end on my own. Still, squealing on your buddy went directly against The Man Code…almost as much as boning your buddy's girlfriend.

"Yeah, I've been spending some time with her," I admitted.

"Then that's all there is to say, lover-boy. I'm not going to be a part of your goddam harem."

I released a long breath. "I suppose that's fair. But can we go back to being friends? Or at least be civil to each other?"

Sabrina laughed once: "*HA!*"

"Why is that so funny?"

"You just view life in such simplistic terms, Pablo, such a basic color palette," she said. "But sure, maybe we can be friends again, maybe when I'm done with you."

"Done with me? What does that mean?"

"Never you mind. Now get in back and chop up those veggies. We have a couple lunch orders already. I need those toppings ASAP."

Things felt easier for the next couple hours, a slightly lowered tension level. Without CUs full student body in session, the summer lunch rush was pretty light, finished within an hour. I returned from my final lunch delivery, saw there was nothing new on the warming rack, so I walked back to Pizza Place's little office and peeked my head in.

"No orders?" I asked Sabrina.

"Nope."

"Cool. You need me to fold boxes or do some line prep?"

"I need you to go lock the front door," she said, staring down at Pizza Place's daily financial sheet.

"Huh?"

"You heard me." She didn't look up. "Lock the front door, then come back here to the office."

I stared at her curiously, but she wouldn't meet my gaze. I strolled up to the front of the store, flipped the lock on the entrance, then returned to the office.

"Okay, we're all locked up."

"Get your ass in here and close the door," Sabrina ordered, still plugging numbers into the daily financials.

When the door clicked closed behind me, Sabrina pushed all the papers on the desk off to the side. Standing up, she reached across the desk and closed the slatted shade on the single office window. She turned around and finally looked at me.

"We're going to end this on *my* terms, Paulie."

"I have no idea what that means."

"Oh, I think you do."

She stared hard into me, her eyes hot and angry. But there was something else there, too, another fire I recognized.

"How many times did I tell you I wanted a good fuck right here in the office?" Sabrina asked.

I raised my eyebrows. "You can't be serious."

"Oh, I'm serious, boy. You're going to fuck me right here, right on this desk, and then I'm done with you. This is over when *I* say it's over, not because some cutesy little floozy ends it for me. That little bitch needs to know I had you first and can still have you whenever I want."

"Jesus, Sabrina, I–"

She reached out with both hands and grabbed me by the waistband of my shorts. Yanking me toward her, our crotches connected, hard. And then her lips were on mine – those soft, full, Sabrina lips that I wanted to devour every time I felt them graze my own. Ah, shit, she was right, I was powerless over her. She unzipped my shorts aggressively, reached for her own zipper, and both pair fell to the ground with alarming speed. My dick was a girder, no hints of hesitancy there. I jammed it against Sabrina's panty-covered crotch, and I could already feel the wet warmth of her.

"You're going to fuck my fine ass one last time, baby, and you better do me good," she said. "No soft shit. You fuck me hard, Paulie, you got it?"

No need to answer. I hoisted her up on the desk, ripped off her panties, and then I dropped to my knees and stuffed my face into Sabrina's glorious pussy. I ate her alive, gorged on her. She screamed, wrapped her legs around my neck, drove her heels into my shoulder blades. She was merciless. I was merciless. God damn, she was absolutely correct; *this* was the way to go. Go out screaming, go out mauling, go out in pain and pleasure and anger and lust. Get it all out, all the angels and demons. Don't whimper away into the night nursing hurt feelings and betrayed emotions. Go out like we came in – dogs in heat, rabid, foaming.

Finishing her first orgasm, she plunged her fingers into my hair and yanked me upright by the roots. "Fuck me one more time, baby, make it count!"

I rammed it in, grabbed Sabrina's beautiful ass and slid her forward onto my full length. My balls scraped painfully against the sharp edge of the office desk, but I didn't care. Sabrina bit me on the shoulder, then the neck, purposely leaving marks. She clawed my back, tore my skin. I grabbed her chin, slammed our lips together, and she bit me there, too, the little bitch. It was like a fistfight more than sex, all aggression and frustration.

"You'll never touch this again, boy," Sabrina moaned into my mouth. "You'll never fuck nothin' this good again."

I ripped her shirt up over her head because I *needed* Sabrina's tits in my mouth one more time. She shoved them up high for me. "*Suck on 'em, baby!*" So I sucked on 'em as long as she let me. When I couldn't contain myself one more second, I exploded inside her, but Sabrina refused to stop. "*You ain't done yet!*" She rode me and fucked me and fucked me and rode me until, finally, she planted her palms flat behind her on the desk for leverage, threw her head back, and *howled* out a final orgasm. It was the hottest, angriest, most meaningful orgasm I'd ever watched pour out of a woman.

When it was over, Sabrina threw herself forward, wrapped her arms around my back, and hugged me as if we were dying or the world was ending, as a beautiful part of it surely was. I gave it right back to her, held her as tight as I could. Ten seconds later, she released me, placed both my cheeks between her palms, and kissed me soulfully one final time.

"Don't you ever forget our time together, Pablo."

"I won't."

I haven't.

Sabrina guided me gently out of her, and then we retrieved our clothes and dressed slowly.

"We good?" I asked as I flipped on the office light and opened the door.

"We good. We can be friends again. The rest is over. Time for both of us to get on gettin' on."

"Cool."

"Go unlock the front door and get going on those dough trays in back.

I'm going to need another bucket of black olives, too."

I unlocked the front door and propped it open to clear the smell of sex from the store. I washed a stack of dough trays and prepped some veggies, feeling great. It was sad that our time had come to an end, but it was a necessary and wonderful end to a necessary and wonderful experience. Ending that way was so much better than crawling away with my tail between my legs, Sabrina glaring at me in furious judgment. I didn't want her to spend the rest of her life believing I'd been intentionally or thoughtlessly cruel. It wasn't cruelty, it was genuine ignorance. It was ignorance of life, of women, of love and lust and wants and needs and the varying levels of each ingredient that exists within all relationships. Ignorantly believing my life had no bearing on anyone else, I plowed through my days with a boner in one hand and a beer in the other, running from laugh to laugh, incapable of understanding that my life actually had some impact on those closest to me, especially the women on the other end of my penis.

Sabrina and I immediately resumed our friendship. It was good to have her back. It was good to tell dirty jokes and swap heavy metal cassettes and listen to her insult the entire Pizza Place softball team from the bleachers. It was good to hear all the store gossip – Sabrina always had the best dirt – and it was good that we could again complain about our military fathers and their endless and ridiculous rules. It was good to listen to Sabrina laugh while I ogled her body, and just like the old days, it was good to fantasize about holding her perfect ass in my grubby little paws. But my access to that perfect ass had been revoked, and I never touched Sabrina again.

* * *

"Oh my god, you're really wasted," Allie said, glaring at me.

"I've been wasteder."

"Wasteder's not even a word."

"Wrong!" I said loudly, pointing my finger in the air. "*Wasteders*, plural, isn't a word. Wasteder is. Wasted, wasteder, wastedest. Drunk, drunker, drunkest. Same shit, same shitter, same shittest, Allie."

She didn't laugh, not even a little. Damn girl wouldn't get drunkard humor if it unleashed a sour belch right in her face.

"I cannot believe you showed up for this drunk." She shook her head irritably. "You're about to make one of the biggest decisions of your life, and you show up drunk? Are you not taking this seriously?"

"Jesus, Allie, you showed up with a fucking ferret. What could be less serious than a ferret?"

We sat in the park on the bench where she first kissed me. Like that night almost two months before, Roger the Ferret was leashed to the bench, sniffing the air contemplatively, reaching rat-ish conclusions about the world from a rodent perspective. Lonnie would be back in two days, and Allie justifiably called this meeting to demand my decision. So I got good and drunk beforehand to dodge reality, or at least blur it substantially. The end with Sabrina had been hard enough – at least until the *end* of the end – and Sabrina was a stable woman with a strong emotional foundation. Allie was unstable and ungrounded. Her emotional foundation was anger magma, bubbling dangerously, always a mild tremor away from full eruption.

Allie sighed. "Then I guess I already know your answer. You wouldn't show up here drunk if you were going to stay with me. And you wouldn't be making a bunch of stupid jokes, either. I know you better than you think, Paul. You've got a romantic streak in you. If you were going to stay with me, you'd show up with flowers."

I looked over at her, held her clear hazel eyes in my bleary browns. My eyes were heartless and dry, I imagined, whereas Allie's were warm and wet, close to crying. Good lord, Allie was worth the gamble, whatever her faults, but I was so chaotically and disjointedly in love with Lonnie that I couldn't switch teams, not for the best odds. I couldn't leave Lonnie until we'd reached our proper, bitter, grueling conclusion, hearts ripped out and stomped upon. Large loves have to implode spectacularly, decimate the participants, and brand both with permanent, jagged scars.

I held Allie's eyes, shook my head very slowly and lightly, and then I shrugged a little. It was the only answer I could give.

"Say it," Allie instructed softly. "You aren't getting off that easy, Paul. You need to say it out loud." A single tear slipped over her right eyelid. I knew I better say something before more tears fell. Once a woman started crying in front of me, I'd do almost anything to make it stop.

"Allie, I'm not the right guy for you."

"Say it," she repeated, this time more forcefully. "It's not about me or what I need or what I want. It's not about what's right for me. Don't you dare try to pawn this off like you're doing me some kind of favor. You need to tell me, right now, that you're staying with Lonnie."

I blew out a long breath. "I'm staying with Lonnie, Allie."

Her hand flashed out and slapped me across the face. I absorbed it. I deserved it. Everyone needs a slap in the face once in a while.

"You are so *stupid!*" Now her tears flowed freely, all the rage and sorrow, rage and sorrow. "Stupid, stupid, stupid little boy! There is no good end for you and Lonnie! You're only delaying the inevitable, you idiot, making everything worse!"

She put her head in her hands and balled. I let her cry. I tried to reach out and stroke her shoulder, but she shoved my hand away. So I leaned my head back and listened to Allie's tears while staring drunkenly at the stars, trying to imagine what she was feeling. As beautiful as she was, I was the closest she'd had to a real boyfriend. I somehow managed to worm past her defenses, only to ruthlessly stomp on her freshly exposed emotions. Damn, how must that feel? I didn't know. The stars didn't know. Not even Roger the Ferret knew. Only Allie could understand Allie's particular pain, because only Allie was Allie, and it requires all of one's past to fully comprehend one's present. Allie brought the entire *History of Allie* to the bench that night, and that history likely confirmed that all the locks she'd previously affixed to her emotions were completely warranted. It was brutal to watch, human sorrow that I would not relieve when it was well within my power to do so. So much of life was sorrow, I realized, just beige, goddam sorrow. There was sorrow everywhere, sorrow on the micro level, the macro level, a dead turtle on the road, the end of glorious autumn, a faraway war that never seems to end.

Her sobs slowly subsided, as sobs always do, thank god. "I'm sorry I slapped you." She used her white jacket sleeve to wipe away her tears while keeping her eyes on her lap.

"Hey, somebody had to do it, and my dad and brother Dane are a thousand miles away."

"I wanted to meet them, you know, wanted to meet your whole family. Would have helped me understand you."

"Probably not, Allie. No big answers there, just a lot of apathy."

She raised her head and looked over at me. "So this is it? We just go our separate ways as if nothing happened and nothing mattered?"

"Something like that, yeah."

A new tear wrestled itself onto her cheek. "That's how people do this? They just get together, have beautiful sex, beautiful experiences, and then they just…just…*move on?*"

"Nah, we take it all with us, I think, everything we experience. We don't exactly move on so much as we keep going, I'd say. You're part of my story now. I'm part of yours. We keep going with each other somewhere in our head and heart. What that amounts to over the course of our lives, I have no idea. I guess time will tell."

She gave me a helpless smile. That smile was *almost* enough to take it all back, end my relationship with Lonnie, go back to school, get an 8:00 to 5:00 job, whatever it took to keep Allie's beautiful smile forever in place. Almost.

"That actually helps," she said. "I never told you this because I didn't want to encourage your drinking, but sometimes you come up with an interesting thought or two when you're drunk. Maybe you need booze to share your most profound ideas."

"Baby, there's a lot more drunken profundity where that came from." I reached into my jacket, pulled out my Marbs, and shook one loose. "Did I ever tell you my theory about the singularity of existence? Takes a few hours to explain, but trust me, it's worth the wait."

She smiled again, this time patiently and politely. Standing up, Allie bent over and kissed me warmly on my forehead. "I'm going to go now, Paul."

"Understood," I said. "Everything gets easier, Allie, I promise."

She smiled softly again and nodded. Stepping past me, she untied Roger the Ferret from the bench. Then, with a wave of her fingers, she turned and walked away. Her long brown curls bounced on her back, her rodent tugged at his leash, and Allie's white jacket glowed in the night as she walked out of my life.

I fired up my ciggie and watched the darkness engulf her. Few things are more profound than watching deeply wounded women dissolve into the distance. I stared after her until I couldn't see her shape anymore, and then I imagined her sad sad silhouette drifting through the east Boulder suburban streets. I think I loved her a little at that moment. There was something to love in every person on the planet – even Stalin was widely loved for his hilarious and raucous drinking games. But I couldn't love them all; I had to pick just one. Allie, Sabrina, Lonnie, Stalin; I wanted to love each of them in some capacity or another, but I had to choose. So I chose as best I could, then marched onward arrogantly, feigning confidence in my selection.

12.

Reunion

E L D O R A ,   C O L O R A D O

1 9 9 1

And then she was home.

I shielded myself behind an airport pillar at the gate, wanting to spy on her a little. She came out the jetway excitedly, her head swiveling from side to side, eyes peering around her mother, scanning for me. Lonnie's summer tan was deep and brown, her flowing blonde hair almost white, all those long afternoons on Italian piazzas and Spanish plazas baking her warmly. Her stepfather made his presence obvious right up front at the gate – no romance or mystery in that guy's soul – and Lonnie's mom stepped directly over to him for a perfunctory hug and halfhearted peck. I hid a little longer, grinning. Lonnie's excited face slowly fell as she unsuccessfully scanned the waiting area for her absent man. Once I felt the tension hit its peak, expectation and disappointment almost on equal footing, I stepped out of the shadows and spread my arms wide.

Lonnie's face exploded. Tears leapt out as she abandoned her suitcase next to her mother and bounded past all the travelers and their loved ones. She slammed into my open arms like a crazed dog who'd forgotten her way home one day, only to run across her owner on a chance meeting a month later. I held Lonnie tight with everything I had, and she squeezed my soul so hard I worried it might not be intact for eternal damnation. Satan was gonna be *pissed*. Good lord, nothing felt like Lonnie, nothing. Something radiated off her and through me, then wrapped around us like unseen tentacles, cinching us together. Other women felt mysterious or exotic or enticing; Lonnie felt like I'd found my proper place in the universe.

"I think you missed me," I said, pushing us apart a little.

She looked at me, laughed, tried to speak. She couldn't. A fresh wave of tears burst forth and she cried into my chest. I stood and held her, laughing with happiness.

Her mother and stepfather came over, and everyone pretended to like each other. The four of us kept up the charade all the way to the baggage carousel. Unfortunately, I learned that her stepfather parked within two hundred feet of me, so Lonnie and I had to walk them to their car before performing the ridiculous ritual of hugs and handshakes. We waved them off, everyone fake smiling at everyone else.

"Did you bring the van?" Lonnie asked, her eyebrows raised.

"Of course."

"Then what are we waiting for!"

And then she was naked on the bed in the back of my van, right there in the parking lot, her hand gently guiding my dick deep inside her. We muttered all kinds of things that felt true at the time — *I need you, I need you, I want you, I want you, I love you, I missed you, I need you, I love you.* It was almost a mantra, a timing mechanism, and when the chant hit its crescendo, we both came on cue. Every last thing in the universe felt right again, perfect. At that moment, it was impossible to believe that Lonnie and I would soon make so many brutal, heart wrenching mistakes.

Rolling onto our backs, staring at the van's ceiling, we lay silently immersed in our reunion. I lit a ciggie and smoked it almost all the way to the nub before Lonnie spoke. Ah, how nice to suck down a post-sex ciggie without any scolding.

"So what did you do while I was in Europe?"

A vision of Sabrina popped into my head, her legs spread wide on the desk at Pizza Place, demanding some odd form of sexual retribution. In my mind, I looked across the roof of my speeding car and saw White screaming at the stars, the wind roaring past us, the full moon drowning the Eldora valley in eerie, illuminated moonlight. Allie's tears fell into her lap, and I could not console her on the lonely sad bench of her lonely sad life. There were acid sunsets and long moments of loud laughter, beautiful women and intense sexual gratification. I'd spent countless ephedrine marathons where my hands shook deep into the night, binge-writing truly bizarre stories in my isolated mountain cabin and feeling like I was doing something very important in the world, like I *was* something very important in the world. And I knew I could not tell Lonnie most of those things, if any. I could only share a fraction of my life with the only person in the world I loved, because our expectations of each other often sentenced us to silence.

I turned my head and smiled at the beautiful young blonde lying naked next to me in an airport parking lot. She smiled back and lovingly stroked my face with her fingers. Damn, if only I were a better man, I'd…and then I'd…and then I'd…but I was not a better man. I was just me. I loved Lonnie as best I could, but I had to lie to her to preserve our drama.

"Not too much, Lon," I lied. "Honestly, I didn't do much of anything while you were away."

About the Author

P.H. Mountain was partially educated at the University of Minnesota before earning his undergraduate degree from the Boulder Public Library and his masters from The Sundown Saloon. At twenty-nine, he started a legal transcript editing company that morphed into the software company he continues to operate. He has lived in three different vehicles, fifteen different states, and five different countries, but he generally considers Colorado home. In a moment of clarity, Paul married his wife Stella in 2001. To this day, he still considers her the luckiest woman alive.

www.ingramcontent.com/pod-product-compliance
Lightning Source LLC
Chambersburg PA
CBHW071458140726
47997CB00005B/1774